Transgressive Spatial Imagination
in the 20th-Century American Novel

TRANSGRESSIVE SPATIAL IMAGINATION IN THE 20TH-CENTURY AMERICAN NOVEL

SEONGHO YOON

—

—

—

Published by HANYANG UNIVERSITY PRESS
Tel. +82.2.2220.1431
Web. http://press.hanyang.ac.kr
Email. presshy@hanyang.ac.kr

—

ISBN 978.89.7218.576.5 [93840]

Transgressive Spatial Imagination
in the 20th-Century American Novel

Seongho Yoon

HY COLLECTION 018

HANYANG UNIVERSITY PRESS

Acknowledgments

I cannot here thank each and every one among the many people who have helped propel my study in the past years. However, there are a few who do deserve special mention. First of all, this book project was supported by the National Research Foundation of Korea funded by the Korean government (NRF-2013S1A6A4017827). Without such support, this book would not exist. This book originally began life at the University of Massachusetts, Amherst, where I was fortunate enough to receive guidance encouragement, and keen insights from Margo Culley, Joseph Skerrett, R. Radhakrishnan, James Smethurst, and Jules Chametzky. As mentors and friends, they always knew what guidance I needed and they spurred and sometimes coaxed me on with grace and generosity.

My warmest thanks go to Cathy Schlund-Vials and Chris Vials who have been always kind enough to read and copiously comment on my various works with their unflagging enthusiasm since we were all graduate students. Their encouragement and suggestions has been invaluable at every stage of this project.

They sometimes changed the whole direction of my research and ultimately set me on the path to writing this book. Their enduring influence is stamped on every page.

This book has also been shaped over the course of delivering papers at conferences and making friends with a number of scholars from all over the world. Lianggong Luo, Bennett Fu, Jerry Weng have been attentive to my work for a long time. It is always a pleasant and rewarding experience to meet people whose interests I can reciprocate.

Some friends read bits of this book, some listened indulgently, some might not even know I have been writing it. I am thankful for all of them, especially all of my beloved colleagues at Hanyang University. I know very well how much they help solidify all of my research ideas in different ways. I also owe my gratitude to my graduate students, Hyoseol Ha and Yoonjeong Kim who have been along the way in every stage of proofreading and editing. Their cheer, care, and patient reading have been all together in this book. Hanyang University Press is my final benefactor. Whatever the strengths and weaknesses of this book, it is because of the institutional commitment of organizations like the press at Hanyang that books like this have any chance at all of being published and circulated. I am thus genuinely grateful to Professor Ik-sang Eom, director of Hanyang University Press, department manager Joo Sung Yang, and editor Kwang-il Ahn.

TABLE OF CONTENTS

Chapter 1

Rethinking Space, Representing Space

"The present epoch will perhaps
be above all the epoch of space."

Michel Foucault

"Geography was fate."

Ralph Ellison

Why Space?

Why space? It is a question I cannot choose but face up to before venturing a step forward to proceed on my way in this book. It may be answered by conjuring up the already fully circulated idea of the so-called "spatial turn" that has become something of a clarion call from the 1980s in the humanities and social sciences, but it immediately turns on a set of questions that have been relatively left out in the discussion of space. The very question, in actuality, not so much asks for a definition as requires an argument about why we concern ourselves with such a "turn" at all and what the engagement with it as an ongoing process entails for us in a field of perpetual renegotiation. A glance at various disciplines such as philosophy, anthropology, sociology, political science, and cultural studies as well as literary studies would help one understand how those fields in their own way have been generating new vocabularies to reframe the questions of identity, location, positionality, liminality, in-betweenness, deterritorialization, reterritorialization, and diaspora from spatial perspectives. The spatial turn in this "epoch of space" (Foucault, "Of Other Spaces" 22) leads theorists to agree that it is not time but space that is central to understanding human affairs and social relations. Fredric Jameson's "cognitive mapping," David Harvey's "time-space compression," Edward Soja's "socio-spatial dialectic," Neil Smith's "uneven development," Homi Bhabha's "third space," Gloria Anzaldúa's "borderlands," to name a few among many others, enter into an array of domains of knowledge and require us to acknowledge how much our own fields of scholarship have become *spatial* in their orientation.[1]

Indeed, space is believed to have the capacity to reshape the

---

1 I have additionally in mind Michel Foucault's through examination of the intersection of discipline, ordering, and architecture particularly in *Discipline and Punish: The Birth of the Prison* (1975), Fredric Jameson develops his notion of "cognitive mapping" in "Postmodernism, or the Cultural Logic of Late Capitalism" (1984) and in *Postmodernism, or, the Cultural Logic of Late Capitalism* (1991), and Gilles Deleuze and Felix Guattari's thesis on "the body without organs" in *Anti-Oedipus: Capitalism and Schizophrenia* (1972) and *A Thousand Plateaus: Capitalism and Schizophrenia* (1980). The current lines of thought have also combined social theory, aesthetics, and cultural critique. The productive examples of interdisciplinary research revolving around cultural geography include: Sharon Zukin, *Landscapes of Power: From Detroit to Disney World* (1991); Derek Gregory, Ron Martin and Graham Smith (eds), *Human Geography: Society, Space, and Social Science* (1994); Doreen Massey; David Sibley, *Geographies of Exclusion* (1995); Patricia Yaeger (ed), *The Geography of Identity* (Ann Arbor, MI: U of Michigan P, 1996); Linda McDowell (ed). *Undoing Place? A Geographical Reader* (1998).

perspectives from which to map out a number of aspects of human affairs and social relations that have been generally examined through the lens of class, gender, and race. Furthermore, space is used to measure interconnection and separation, similarity and difference, all of which can serve as a means of marking social divisions that both allow mobility and force impediment on others. Is space then really a master key with which to unlock the door to every kind of theory? To be sure, space does matter but a question attendant upon such recognition should be to what extent the present moment can be defined as something that calls for the spatial turn as such. As long as such a shift of emphasis is considered to be, if any, a "turn," it should be a kind of tectonic shift that breaks away from fetishizing the role of space without dissipating into premature utopianism that space can explain everything. It is, therefore, of the utmost importance to ask what it takes to theorize space at all.

It is in the 1980s that a "new" cultural geography emerged and provided a sustained critique of the Sauerian or Berkeley School that had emphasized the landscape as a result of culture's act on the medium of nature as well articulated in Carl Sauer's "The Morphology of Landscape" originally published in 1925. "The Morphology" is a Sauerian gesture to overcome a determinist inclination then dominant in geography, but, ironically, culture becomes a reified concept in the Sauerian practice of landscape interpretation. Culture, gaining an ontological status in

"Morphology," is regarded as an "agent" acting upon a medium called "nature," and then landscape becomes a "result" of such action of culture (Sauer 343). Henceforth, culture becomes a deterministic force that is entitled to transforming nature, with critical questions about the contingent nature of culture precluded. This Sauerian semi-determinism or reification of culture is the very foil for the "new" cultural geography that came to take the center stage of debate and invigorated an interest in a more sociological and political approach from the 1980s. It is at this point that historical materialism meets up with cultural geography, thereby bringing into sharp relief "the relationship between humans and nature as *historical*" (Cosgrove 1, my emphasis).

A recent direction of cultural geography has been toward the recognition of the spatiality of social life—a conceptual leap from the overused or abused idea that everything happens in space to the realization that "*where* things happen is critical to knowing *how* and *why* they happen" (Warf and Arias 1). This "socio-spatial dialectic" stands in stark contrast to the geography's traditional accounts of "things" in space or inventories of what exists in space, which may ultimately end up framing space as being simply out there and already given. Following the lead of Lefebvre, Harvey and Soja consider space as a social product and pave the way for a fresh view on space as a register of not only built forms but also embedded social dynamics. In this explanatory context, space, for example, is understood as intrinsically integrated into the organization of power and control; "new spatiality implicit in the postmodern" (Jameson, *Postmodernism* 418) is emphasized to counter a modernist aesthetics that enshrines time and the spatialization of the temporal is used as a hallmark of a new paradigm as replacing the hegemony of time with that of space; uneven development helps to unearth the ever-expanding mechanism of capitalism; the cultural phenomenon called postmodernism is discussed as a response to the time-space compression associated with the transition from Fordist capitalism to the regime of flexible accumulation. In short, all of those explanatory practices go some way to looking into the space-and-society dialectic, which suggests that space is not passively formed waiting to be filled with social relations, but plays a very active role in the formation of society itself.

Apposite would be here to discuss Lefebvre's radical conceptualization of space in his fifty-seventh book, *The Production of Space*, which is dubbed by Soja "arguably the most important book ever written about the social and historical significance of human spatiality and the particular powers of the spatial imagination" (*Thirdspace* 8).

> It would be more accurate to say that it [space] is at once a precondition and a result of social superstructure. The state and each of its constituent institutions call for spaces—but

> spaces which they can then organize according to their specific requirements; so there is no sense in which space can be treated solely as an a *priori* condition of these institutions and the state which presides over them. Is space a social relationship? Certainly—but one which is inherent to property relationships (especially the ownership of the earth, of land) and also closely bound up with the forces of production (which impose a form on that earth or land); here we see the polyvalence of social space, its 'reality' at once formal and material. Though a *product* to be used, to be consumed, it is also a *means of production*; networks of exchange and flows of raw materials and energy fashion space and are determined by it. Thus this means of production, produced as such, cannot be separated either from the productive forces, including technology and knowledge, or from the social division of labour which shapes it, or from the state and the superstructure. (Lefebvre 85)

Lefebvre earlier in the book suggests that "(social) space is (social) product" (27). It may be tautological at first sight, but the relationship of space and society is here fundamentally redefined as space as *both* a "precondition" and a "result" of society: society produces space and, more importantly, space produces society as well. The meaning of "production" in the title of Lefebvre's book, which is very Marxist in its premise, thus takes on the nature of a verb, both passive and active—space is produced and, at the same time, has a producing force in itself as an agent. This renewed interest in engaging the complex relationship of space and society can help avoid reiterating the binary understanding of the space-society relationship, which is likely to lapse into another kind of geographical reductionism. It is precisely within this context that Lefebvre's concept of space differs significantly from the Sauerian geography and its reified concept of culture.[2] Revisiting and working through the problems in traditional geography, the "new" cultural geography in a Lefebvrian vein has reconsidered space as reconciliation between the physical and social spaces, and critiques the "illusion of transparency" (Lefebvre 27)—the

---

2 Stuart Elden compares Lefebvre's attention to spatiality with the Kantian emphasis on temporality: "Lefebvre not only corrected the modernist imbalance of time over space, but also *contra* Kant, emphasized the historicality of their experience. No longer the Kantian empty formal containers, no longer *categories* of experience, time and space could be experienced *as such*, and their experience was directly related to the historical conditions they were experienced within. For Lefebvre, of course, these historical conditions are directly linked to the mode of production: hence the *production* of space. Lefebvre therefore wished to make two main moves in his work. First, to put space up with and alongside time in considerations of social theory, and in doing so correct the vacuity of the Kantian experiential containers. Spatiality is as important as, but must not obscure considerations of, temporality and history: 'space and time appear and manifest themselves as different yet inseparable'. Secondly, he wished to use new critical understanding to examine the (modern) world in which he was writing. This is accomplished through an analysis of how space is produced, and how it is experienced. Space is produced in two ways, as a social formation (mode of production), and as a mental construction (conception)" (185).

tendency to articulate space as a neutral and self-evident geometry. The "new" geographical perspectives on space bring together the material and the abstract by enumerating the ways in which space is produced and reproduced, and thereby represent the sites and the outcomes of social, political, and cultural struggle.

Given such lines of thought that converge on space, this book, under the title of *Transgressive Spatial Imagination in the Twentieth-Century American Novel*, is designed to explore some areas that are central to and yet relatively under-charted in literary studies. First, it aims to examine how spatiality meets up with literary studies in such a way that literary texts are brought to bear upon the understanding of space that is simultaneously real *and* imaginary. Second, it intends to offer in-depth critique of how some of spatial narratives gain a normative status by leveling out social and cultural differences that are actually *always already* open to other representations and meanings. Theoretically informed by the "spatial turn," this book thus proffers to mediate abstract and material lineaments of social emplacement by putting the material geography of the United States and its literary representation in historical contexts. Faced with the challenge of the spatial turn, literary studies has long been striving to overcome in its interpretative practice "empty" geography that is impervious to social content and, as a result, requires only minimal material grounding. One of the primary goals of this study is to help overcome those epistemological and methodological limitations, if not outright shortcomings, of such empty geography by adopting "transgressive spatial imagination" as the constituents of an axis of literary analysis and showing how a new form of literary analysis informed by the spatialization of transgressiveness can actually work. A reinvigorated interest in the mutually constitutive nature of the spatial and the transgressive can indeed serve as a springboard for turning the tables on traditional American studies and literary studies by bringing to the critical use a long-standing tension between literary representation and the empirical that can be mutually productive and constitutive, and can thus be brought to intervene in certain sites of critical contention and impasse.

To that end, Chapter I examines the main issues in current writing on space and attempts to produce a nuanced account of the instrumentality of space as a register of not only built forms but also of embedded ideologies and cultural investments. Chapter II addresses a more pluralistic notion of "southerness" envisioned in William Faulkner's novels by reading him as a different kind of "regionalist" who crosses regional and national boundaries while seemingly staying within his own fictional counties. Chapter III delves into what it means for displaced people to reclaim a secured placed called "home" in Toni Morrison's novels, and examines how to work through the geography of exclusion by reconceptualizing the notion of "home." Chapter IV scrutinizes through the discussion of Asian American texts how transnational migration and the flow of capital, labor, and cultures give American suburbs new faces and bring about tensions, opening up a national context to transnational frames of reference—"Third Worldization" of American suburbs in David Palumbo-Liu's words.

Space of Representation, Representation of Space

How is space defined, used, and configured across various theoretical terrains? What challenges and new possibilities does the "spatial turn" pose to literary studies? The process called "the production of space" is enacted through "spatial practice," which, Lefebvre argues, does execution in the material experience of social relations in everyday life. One can find in any given space an assembly of materiality, practice, and meaning. As long as Lefebvre's voluminous meditation on "the production of space" defines space not merely as parameters of social relations and actions but as operative in the assembly of all these, it can be understood as a theoretical gesture to overcome the duality of physical space and mental space—what Lefebvre calls a "straitjacket" (39) of binary thinking. Lefebvre explains the interrelations of these elements through his signature notion of a spatial triad: "spatial practice," "representations of space," and "representational space," each of which corresponds to three different ways to view space: "the perceived," "the conceived," and "lived" (*l'espace perçu, conçu*, and *vécu*). The first category, "spatial practices," has to do with the physical and material aspects of space—*real* space that is generated, experienced, and used. The second category, "representations of space," relates to the concepts developed by those who regards space as a mental construct—*imagined* space. The final category, "representational spaces," views space as "directly *lived*"—space as both *real-and-imagined* since it is invested with symbolism and meaning and lived "through its associated images and symbols" (39).

The distinctly Lefebvrian approach to space is one of his efforts to go well beyond the division between the mental and the physical, idealism and materialism, and theory and praxis. His triad is a kind of indeterminate and fluid typology that rarely ossifies into a mechanical thinking. Lefebvre delineates his own typology of space throughout his book in such a way that each type of space is so imbued with each other's resonance that they sometimes blur into each other's realm. In a sense, Lefebvre's highly abstruse socio-spatial theory seems to urge his readers into fleshing out his ideas with their own imagination and critical intervention. One of the difficulties of explicating the Lefebvrian spatial triad lies in his conflicting, if not necessarily incompatible, goals "to expose the actual production of space by bringing the various kinds of space and the modalities of their genesis together within a *single theory*" (16, my emphasis) while emphasizing the "dialectical character" (18) of those various kinds of space. This conflict, in turn, opens out into a deep-seated divide between material grounding of space and the figural nature of space:

> Both Thirdspace and Lefebvre's most encompassing notion of social space are comprised of all three spatialities—perceived, conceived, and lived—with no one inherently privileged a *priori*. And yet, there is an implied preference in all of Lefebvre's (and my) spatial trialectics and thirdings that derives not from ontological privilege or priority but from that a political choice that is central to Lefebvre's spatial imagination. It is political choice, the impetus of an explicit project, that gives special attention and particular contemporary relevance to the spaces of representation, to *lived space as a strategic location* from which to encompass, understand, and potentially transform all spaces simultaneously. Lived social space, more than any other, is Lefebvre's limitless Aleph, the space of all inclusive simultaneities, perils as well as possibilities: the space of radical openness, the space of social struggle. [⋯]
>
> Spaces of representation contain all other real and imagined spaces simultaneously. In different ways, appropriately understood, so too do spatial practices and representations of space, but only in so far as one can escape from the double illusions of objectivism and subjectivism that weakens their insights into the working of power. Lefebvre never made explicit his strategic "preference" for the spaces of representation, in part, I believe, because he either assumed

> it would be implicitly understood; or avoided an explicit recognition of it for fear that it would be constructed as unchallengeably fixed, a complete answer, a permanent construction that would divert too much attention away from other modes of spatial thinking (the more likely explanation). (Soja, Thirdspace 68-69)

Soja in Thirdspace (1996) engages Lefebvre by redefining the Lefebvrian triad by his own notions of First, Second, and Thirdspace, which are respectively equivalent to the three spatialities of the perceived, conceived, and lived. Soja claims that Lefebvre's seemingly typological triad is not counterintuitive to his own conceptualization of space as a complex interweaving of the material world and our conception of it. Rather, Lefebvre's interest lies, Soja continues to argue, in the dialectics between and among the material, mental, and social: Lefebvrian dialectics works through contradiction and counterpoint to shows how they are mutually constitutive and in dialectical relation with one another.

It is this "trialectics" of spatiality that allows for a possibility of "turning the tables" on traditional American Studies and literary studies of space. Is space an effect or a cause of representation? The question stems from the difficulty of deciding whether American sites of space-formation belong to the material geography of the United States or to the discourse or interpretative practices of spatiality. Space, which is "always already out there," offers itself as an object available to representation. However, the validity of space is dependent upon interpretative practices and space is mediated by representation as well. Space, therefore, is both subject to representation and suggestive of negation of representation. When the "trialectics" of spatiality is brought into focus, "imaginative" texts could open up a new possibility by mediating the simultaneously abstract and material lineaments of our social emplacement, a locatedness and relationality at once lived and socially constitutive. The spatial turn, therefore, should be an understanding of our lives as situated in an array of social and spatial relations that need to be mapped.

As such, representation does powerful cultural work not so much to produce and maintain as to challenge and question the commonly accepted notions of space. In doing so, it reshapes the narratives and syntax, which are widely used to describe the spatial experience. Analysis of textual representations of space in this book is not merely a study of images of spaces or narratives of spatial consciousness. Rather, it responds to the cultural work of representations of space, which offers us specific readings and practices for approaching the spatiality. Therefore, if one thinks of space, as Massey suggests, "in terms of the articulation of social relations which necessarily have a spatial form in their articulations with one another" (*Space* 120), any understanding of the spatial itself can be much enlarged by attention to representation and the role of the narrative in the production of space as well as to the various grammars that structure spatial articulation. It is precisely within this context that I intend to work out the meaning of place as very close to that of "*emplacement*," which has a sense of both space and place—*l'ensemble des relations* within and between spaces in a Foucauldian sense.[3] In fact, the line between space and place is always shifting as John Agnew explains:

> The question of space and place in geographical knowledge is ultimately not just about whether the question of "where" matters in the way that "when" does in explaining "how" and even "why" something happens. It is also about how it matters.

---

3 It is always highly complex and difficult to differentiate, in English as well as in French, space (*espace*) and place (*lieu*) and a number of commentators have provided a variety of succinct and sometimes very subtle distinctions. For instance, Marc Augé maintains that space is more "abstract" than place. The former refers to an area and a distance while the latter as a more tangible term is concerned with identity and related to an event or history, whether mythical or real (81-84). John Agnew in a similar vein argues that space is traditionally seen as a general and objective notion, linked to some form of location whereas places refers to the particular, related to the "occupation" of a location (142). In *Space and Place: The Perspective of Experience*, Yi-Fu Tuan defines space as an area of freedom and mobility, while place would be an enclosed and humanized space: "Compared to space, place is a calm center of established values" (54). For Tuan, space turns into place when it gains definition and becomes meaningful: "All people undertake to transform amorphous space into articulated geography" (83). Place is a landmark upon which the eye pauses when it surveys a general scene, "a point of rest" (161).

> Given that both space and place are about the "where" of things and their relative invocation has usually signaled different understandings of what "where" means, it is best to examine them together rather than separately". ("Space and Place" 316)

To one's surprise, the deep-seated divide between the material and discursive of space comes from an oversimplified, if not outright misleading, view that the world exists *out there* as a given ontological fact. As long as literature as fundamentally a mimetic art is believed to be confined to the fictional world, nobody can resolve *aporia* between representation and reality. The representation of space does not merely reproduce a referent. Rather, it has a discursive power that produce space. The unique mediating dialectic capacity of representation is at the heart of the Lefebvrian spatial triad that refutes the accusation of the literary as a potentially unreliable representation of space. The Lefebvrian understanding of the relationships between meanings, interpretative and signifying practices, and the material world brings to the fore the nature of space in representation as figurative yet grounded and indeterminate yet contextual. Representation actualizes new virtualities that interact with the real world in its own textual logic. Moreover, such virtualities are not necessarily compatible with the real world since it is also actualized in and through representation in literary texts: spatiality as both real and imaginary is integral to the social construction of the term itself. The real and the imaginary are in tension rather than in opposition; they are mutually defining.

Viewed in this light, one may ask how discourses on American places in the form of analysis of image and myth accurately reflect empirical fact[4]; do Americans, who have been preoccupied with the relation of national experience to the geographical conditions of the New Worlds ("the spirit of place" in D.H. Lawrence's words), conceive and thus shape their world, or does the world influences the ways in which they think their world?[5] It is not far-fetched to suggest here that in the so called "myth-and-symbol school" scholars can one note their negligence of the facts of the past, and their sheer confidence that the varied experiences of the past can be captured by a single unifying myth. For example, Henry Nash

---

4 D. H. Lawrence sets out on his studies in classic American literature by locating "a new feeling" or "the shifting over from the old psyche to something new" in classic American literature (1). To Lawrence, the freedom in America relates to finding "something you really positively want to be" (3) and it is deeply rooted in "the spirit of place," which is the title of the first chapter of his *Studies in Classic American Literature*, originally published in 1923.

5 The notable works concerned with those issues range from Frederick Jackson Turner's *The Significance of the Frontier in American History* (1883) to Henry Nash Smith' *Virgin Land* (1950), from Annette Kolodny's *The Lay of the Land* (1975) through Richard Slotkin's trilogy, *Regeneration Through Violence* (1973), *The Fatal Environment* (1985), and *Gunfighter Nation* (1992). Recent growing interest in borderland studies and ecocriticism share some of those research interests.

Smith's *Virgin Land* (1950), written by a professor of English and received the John H. Dunning Prize from the American Historical Association, clearly bypasses the following questions: whose ends were served in *imaginary* encounters in the West[6]; how and why have different groups interpreted depictions of the West to their own ends? As Smith puts it, a central epistemological assumption behind *Virgin Land* is that "history cannot happen—that is, men cannot engage in purposive group behavior—without images which simultaneously express collective desires and impose coherence on the infinitely numerous and infinitely varied date of experience" (ix). As Barry Marks, former student of Smith, astutely points out, a kind of the *disciplinary unconscious* of the myth-and-symbol school is "to shift primary attention away from what 'actually happened' in time past to what people thought was happening" (71). It is also the case with Leo Marx's insistence on reading in American literature various *patterns* of a pastoral ideal freed from a particular regional history.[7] As the depreciated academic currency *of Virgin Land* demonstrates, what the

6 I use the word, "imaginary" here to refer not to a unified construct but to rather a confusing and conflicting ideological terrain of values, assumptions, and desires.

7 Acutely aware of the critique of his book, Smith, in preface to the twentieth anniversary printing, admits that "there is a continuous dialectic interplay between the mind and its environment, and that our perception of objects and events are no less a part of consciousness that are our fantasies" (viii).

foundational logic of the "myth and symbol" leads to is the irony that the "facts" of Western settlement may have been ignored to serve a particular group's interests. This methodological problem of the myth-and-symbol school is not separable from a longstanding tension between literary representation and the empirical in literary studies. In order to bear upon this tension, this book's theoretical framework draws attention to "the spatial turn" that binds a set of different disciplines' shared theoretical and methodological concerns.

One of the ongoing Herculean efforts to deal with the knotty interlocking relationship between the social and the spatial is to overcome "a false epistemological precedence" over the realities of lived social space (Soja, *Postmodern* 125). Deeply concerned with the problems arising from indifference to the workings of representation in the production of space as simultaneously real, symbolic, and imaginary, theorists seem to attempt to induce a sense of spatiality as opposed to textual space and to bridge a gap between textualism and grounded literary materialism. They share a concern that the representation space may congeal into *fetishized space* wherein material practices, and that relations of space are likely to be masked by various linguistic and cognitive "acting-outs" of space. Douglass Pocock calls this a "paradox of literature" in defining "the truth of fiction" as "a truth beyond mere facts": "Fictive reality may transcend or contain more truth than physical or everyday reality. And herein lies the paradox of literature.

Although different in essence, and therefore a poor documentary source for material on places, people or organizations, literature yet possesses a peculiar superiority over the reporting of the social scientist" (11). This differentiation between "the truth of fiction" and "mere facts" may appear to reiterate the lasting debate in literary studies even originating from Plato and Aristotle, but it certainly draws on the very *condition* of literary text—incongruity between representation and reality as a condition of being. In this regard, theorists can either call for the unearthing of a neglected material space from underneath its figurative and symbolic weight, or cast an eye toward the inevitability of figuration in the representation of space to argue that the production of spatial knowledge depends on the representability of space.[8]

Given the varied disciplinary backgrounds and political orientations of theorists of space, their relative indifference to representation is justifiable. However, it is no questionable why the workings of representation in the production of space as simultaneously real, symbolic and imaginary deserve such little

---

8 For example, Miles Ogborn makes a distinction between "textual geographies" and "geographies of texts" (149). If textual geographies is focused on the examination of the conjunction of text and space, the geographies of texts is dedicated to studying the geographies of literary production, reception, and circulation. On the other hand, Patricia Yaeger's *Geography of Identity* exemplifies a twofold epistemology of cultural geography and literary studies that spawns "a new poetics of geography."

attention. One of my goals in this book is thus to reconsider the emergent field of "literary geography" with a focus on its some of indiscriminate uses of spatial theories, methodological tools, and concepts collected from various strands of geographical and spatial research. It requires a reformulation that does need to take into account competing, contesting, and alternative theories within the field. However, such interdisciplinary *tentativeness* should not end up overlooking significant socio-spatial issues that the literary representation of space addresses and delimiting the role of literary social construction as geographical. If the spatial turn in literary studies ought to interrogate the correlations between the materiality of space and its figurativity as a means of giving due historical dimension to and the essential material grounding for spatial figurations, one of the potentials of the "turn" itself is to locate the relations of power that underlie the seemingly the *taken-for-grantedness* of spatiality in texts. In other words, the very nature of space represented in a literary text can never be divorced from the strategies of representation whereby the literary constructs that space. One of the lessons one can learn from Lefebvre is that just as the social is historically shaped, so is it spatially shaped; equally, the spatial is historically and socially configured: "Social relations, which are concrete abstractions, have no real existence save in and through space. *Their underpinning is spatial*" (404). Proclaiming "the anxiety of our era has to do fundamentally with space, no doubt a great deal more than with time," Michel Foucault in this regard draws attention to the notion of "heterotopia":

> We do not live in a homogeneous and empty space, but on the contrary in a space thoroughly imbued with quantities and perhaps thoroughly fantastic as well. The space of our primary perception, the space of our dream and that of our passion hold within themselves qualities that seem intrinsic: there is a light, ethereal, transparent space, or again a dark, rough, encumbered space; a space from above, of summits, or on the contrary a space from below, of mud; like stone or crystal. Yet these analyses, while fundamental for reflection in our time, primarily concern internal space. I should like to speak now of external space.
>
> The space in which we live, which draws us out of ourselves, in which the erosion of our lives, our time and our history occurs, the space that claws and knaws at us, is also, in itself, a heterogeneous space. In other words, we do not live in kind of void, inside of which we could place individuals and things. We do not live inside a void that could be colored with diverse shades of light, we live inside a set of relations that delineates sites which are irreducible to one another and absolutely not superimposable on one another.
>
> Of course one might attempt to describe these different sites by looking for the set of relations by which a given site can

> be defined. For example, describing the set of relations that defines the sites of transportation, streets, trains (a train is an extraordinary bundle of relations because it is something through which one goes, it is also something by means of which one can go from one point to another, and then it is also something that goes by). One could describe, via the cluster of relations that allows them to be defined, the sites of temporary relaxation—cafes, cinemas, beaches. Likewise one could describe, via its network of relations, the closed or semi-closed sites of rest—the house, the bedroom, the bed, et cetra. But among all these sites, I am interested in certain ones that have the curious property of being in relation with all the other sites, but in such a way as to suspect, neutralize, or invert the set of relations that they happened to designate, mirror, or reflect. These spaces, as it were, which are linked with all the others, which however contradict all other sites, are of two main types. ("Of Other Spaces," 23-24)

Foucault's "heterotopia" clearly references both the real and unreal spaces that shape social relations.[9] In addition, serving as

---

9 Foucault first articulated the notion of heterotopia based on a 1967 lecture, but it was not published until 1984. Foucault describes heterotopia in his famous citation of Borges' heterotopic Chinese encyclopedia in the preface of *The Order of Things*. The conceptions of heterotopia that these texts provide do not reduce to one succinct definition of the term,

a mirror to the very society that has produced it, "heterotopia" becomes "a space that is other, another real space, as perfect, as meticulous, as well arranged as ours is messy, ill constructed, and jumbled" (26). Building upon and extending Foucault's notion of heterotopia, I suggest that heterotopia can act out a kind of "heterotopic mirror" to the traditional literary studies both in its invocation of the representation of space and in its constant reminder of the social realities offsetting such a sheer belief in the power of representation.[10] Heterotopia is both separate from

---

making our conception of it extremely difficult. More often than not, heterotopia has been viewed as a site of resistance. However, such an understanding is likely to obscure its primary function of making a dominant order legible. Heterotopia should be understood as an arena in which different epistemes both overlap and collide with each other, thereby creating an intensification of knowledge.

10 Foucault explains the mirror as follows: it a "sort of shadow that gives my own visibility to myself that enables me to see myself where I am absent" (24). The reflection in the mirror may be isolated from other spaces, but it is simultaneously related to other spaces: the reflection in the "glass [⋯] is absolutely real, connected with all the space that surrounds it, and absolutely unreal, since in order to be perceived it has to pass through this virtual point which is over there" (24). The reflection reconstitutes our own visibility, presenting us an alternative view of who we are. Heterotopias reconstitute knowledge, presenting a view of its structural formation that might not otherwise be visible. Therefore, Foucault suggests via the image of heterotopic mirror that "I come back toward myself" (24). This movement offers a way of seeing that image in a new way from a new site and the mirror puts into question our own perception of ourselves by describing that image as produced the paradoxically real and unreal space of the mirror. As Foucault explains in the preface to *The Order of Things*, heterotopia makes legible the ground on which knowledge

and yet connected to all other spaces, and this connectedness is precisely what inscribes contestation into heterotopia. While an imaginary space such as utopia exists outside of order and thus does not challenge it, heterotopia provides an alternative order to the governing principles of order rather than remains separate from other spaces, creating new means of making sense of the ways one makes sense of the world and opening up a new possibility of mediating the simultaneously abstract and material lineaments of our social emplacement at once lived and socially constitutive. Of course, such a heterotopic conception of space does not mean jettisoning the materiality of space by shifting focus to representation alone, nor does it merely appropriate spatial concepts to revitalize symbolic analysis as well exemplified by the myth-and-symbol school. The concept of spatial articulation instead highlights the sociality of space and the spatiality of language. For this alone, a literary critique of space and a spatial reading of literature may prove useful.[11]

---

is built by complicating that ground.

11 It is in this context that James Hillis Miller observes that "the notion that landscape provides grounding for novels has hardly given rise to a distinct mode of the criticism of fiction, as has the criticism of character or of interpersonal relations, or of narrators and narrative sequence" (9). Regardless of Miller's questionable distinction between novel and ground, I would contend that until recently a literary critique of space and place has rarely received serious consideration except some occasions such as Joseph Frank's widely

Being Spatial, Being Transgressive

If the world can never be known in a manner that is not somehow socially mediated and spatial relations are constituted in such ways in chosen narratives, representation signifies spatiality and spatiality is actualized in and through representation. The very claim to the nature of space as being "produced" and "producing" then challenges the assumption that space is simply the manifestation of the natural terrain. Viewing space as produced, productive, and producing means viewing it dependent, at least in part, on narrative for its productive effects—as active and generative rather than as inert and transparent. It involves the processes that reconfigure the ways in which space is understood, envisioned, defined, and variously experienced.

This recognition gains an added meaning as it touches upon paradoxical aspects of American history. When European settlers moved into a new continent that several million native people had already inhabited, the very act of calling it "empty" was predicated upon the imposition of cultural power such as Manifest Destiny over the claims of indigenous peoples, the symbolic merger of reality and fiction that becomes the mythos of the taming of the frontier, the reality of violence followed by the symbolic violence

---

claimed 1945 essay on the role of space in modernism in *The Idea of Spatial Form* (1991).

of historiography, and a willed amnesia that allowed America to fulfill its promise of forging a nationhood. Such imposition of cultural power served as a backdrop against which the traditional categories of American space such as nature, region, the pastoral, and the frontier have been constituted. In the course of using the lens of the epistemology of history making in terms of "geography," I would like to keep paying attention to how the space of the imaginary, which characterizes literary representation, is transformed into a representation of space that is bound up with the relations of production and the order those relations impose. Understanding such a transformation can offer a critical inquiry into an hegemonic space wherein a Universal Subject is constructed, from which marginalized and displaced subjects are systematically separated, and provide an antidote for accusing literary studies of precariously straddling the material grounding of space and imaginary cloak of space.

For example, New Americanist projects such as *Cultures of United States Imperialism* (1996) co-edited by Amy Kaplan and Donald Pease give an eye to intriguing spatial binaries—inside/outside, domestic/foreign, center/periphery—that have historically sustained hegemonic narratives of the nation. Kaplan in her introduction "Left Alone with America" argues that the founding ideas of the nation such as the *one* Nation, its origin myths, it unitary political entity have long been replaced by the realities of the United States as an imperial power with shifting boundaries and hegemonic effects.[12] Of particular interest in this appreciation of the multi-faceted nature of American culture by New Americanists is the idea that the excluded, who are presumed to be outside of nation's universal norms and its coherence, figure as a split that calls into question the construction of an *imagined* national community by becoming "a duality as a force permanently external to the nation, yet, *simultaneously*, immanent to the national integrity" in Pease's words:

> [T]he contradictory relation between difference and sameness out of which national narratives and national identities were

---

12 In her introduction, Kaplan heavily draws on Perry Miller's 1959 preface to *Errand into the Wilderness*. Kaplan begins to attribute the beginning of American Studies to Miller. Miller's preface seems to at a glance to be structured to suggest that to understand a nation one must look at multiple aspects of that nation—an epiphany Miller realizes when moving oil in Africa. However, Kaplan provides a critique of Miller's myopia, contending that it is reconsidering what America is and where America is among all the nations of the world that the real challenge for American Studies lies in. America is not necessarily regarded as an empire, but it has an international power. Therefore, it becomes more important to understand that America is culturally and historically diverse and it is not an empire since it does not have one cultural identity. This understanding is not a mere reiteration of the ideal rhetoric, "*e pluribus unum*": while American may turn out to be an empire on an international level, it is ironically its cultural differences (gender, race, nationality of origin) that makes America *not* an empire, which should be an essential part of American Studies. This appreciation of cultural diversity and difference is the only way for America to remain truly "alone"—living in and through cultural diversity and difference while appearing to be an empire.

fashioned could only be resolved into a unity through the state's intervention. When it exercised the power to make a unity out of difference, however, the state also threatened its individual subjects' relation to this unity with disruption at the paradoxical space wherein unification was accomplished (see Bhabha, "DissemiNation"). If state power was required to constitute (and enforce) the national unity that the individual presupposed as a property intrinsic to the nation, however, that accomplished unity would always lack at least one part. Since it required the intervention of the state's power as a force external to the (not-yet-united) nation, the unified nation would always lack the part played by the state in constituting its integrity. Contrarily, insofar as an individual could only consider him or herself as a part of the nation *after* recognizing his or her apartness from it, her (or his) national identity could only be achieved through an act performed by this part lacking the whole. When either the state or the individual performed the action(s) necessary to make a whole out of these part actions, however, the national unity and the national identity accomplished out of these performatives were manifestly the effect of this paradoxical social logic—the whole nation minus this part (action or the partial national identity) in addition to the whole nation. [···]

The operations nationalism required to produce for itself the illusion of universalism take place as supplemental scenes in its

> national narratives. These supplemental scenes effect elisions of the nation's lack of universality otherwise evident at the site of the state's unification of the nation. Racism, according to Balibar's model, effects a generalized misrecognition of the sovereign power the state exercised there by displacing the state's nation-making act (making "one out of many") with representations of the national people's collective abjection of stateless (racialized) persons. These representations effect the related nation-making illusion that, rather than functioning as the precondition for the individual's act of identification with the nation-state, the condition of apartness refers only to non-nationals and results from the national people's abjection of racialized others. Racism, that is to say, effects the collective illusion of the nation as a concretized universal (of nationalism) through its occlusion of the paradoxes associated with the nation's unification (the whole nation plus or minus the part making a whole). (Pease "National Narratives," 546-47)

Benefiting from New Americanists' revisionist approaches to U.S. history and culture and postcolonial studies' consideration of narrativity as implicit in the construction of nationhood, an essential point of consideration in this book is that the "non-Americanizable" or "non-assimilable" is actually a *structural* necessity for the already narrativized order. The very way U.S. national narratives have "taken place" then poses a paradox in clearly spatial terms: the expressions of national narratives have always contained within itself "a constitutive outside" opposed to the particular articulation of them. The seemingly secured stability and boundedness of space are actually forged by establishing enclosure and by constructing others beyond boundary and counter-position with it. The insideness of space cannot be available without the specificity of its interactions with its outside, and the particular mix of relations that are thus part of what defines the uniqueness of space is by no means all included within that space. It includes relations which "stretch beyond" such as the outside as part of what constitutes the inside and the global as part of the local.[13]

---

13 As Kaplan and Pease forcibly argue in their introductions to *Cultures of United States Imperialism*, national euphoria and doctrines of American Exceptionalism need to be replaced by critical "postnational" terms, which de-link the study of American culture from reproduction of various systems of domination and exclusion. Glocalism, decentered cosmopolitanism, globalized space, and the transnational are an emergent set of geographical signifiers through which New Americanists have begun to grasp one of the more embattled terms in American political rhetoric—"imperialism." However, those terms should be understood cautiously. Despite their ambitious space-spanning thrust, globalization and transnationalization aspire to operate in a transparent medium and, in reality, they must work their way through the channels that refract it in different ways. Globalization and transnationalism are reconfiguring political agendas, but geographical scales, among them the nation, are still providing the dominant forms of political action. National identity is not always a mythical or ideological construct; rather it should be understood as existing in a balance between material and discursive processes in a given space. The material processes are at the roots of the automatism with which the discursive processes are universally assumed within national space. From this perspective, globalization and transnationalization's reconfiguration of traditional political patterns does not diminish the nation's role; it resituates the nation in relation to other form of political-geographical integration. In fact, globalization and transnationalization presume a plurality of spaces, not superseding but qualifying the former hegemony of nation-state. In other words, global and transnational forces act differently upon the space that used to be monopolized by the nation-state, contributing to the reappearance of previously hidden territorial identities or to the appearance of new ones.

Therefore, while arguing that deterritorialization has destabilized the fixity of "us" and "them" in a clearly salutary sense, we still need to theorize how space is being reterritorialized. In this regard, space of postcolonial hybridity, for example, becomes highly problematic: "the only place in the world to speak from was at a point whereby contradiction, antagonism, the hybridities of cultural influence, the boundaries of nations, were not shut into some utopian sense of liberation or return. The place to speak from was through those incommensurable contradictions within which people survive, are politically active, and change" (Bhabha, *Location* 67). The space of enunciation makes up such a space of incommensurable contradictions. It does not indicate a fixed topographical site between two other fixed locales (nations, societies, cultures) but an interstitial zone of displacement and deterritorialization that shape the identity of the hybridized subject. The interstitial zone between stable spaces definitely should not be dismissed as marginal zones, and yet I would like to point out that even the conceptualization of interstitially is likely to sidestep further questions: to which spaces do the hybrid cultures of postcoloniality belong; do not indeterminate soaces, albeit their emancipatory potentials, name the practices of regional, local articulations through which a heterogeneous or a displaced area is discursively transformed into an abstract unity? I suggest that homogenized ideas of global diaspora and transnationalism, all of which are being increasingly deployed as emancipatory paradigms, in fact are revealed to be limited when applied to the question of their specific constituency such as race. Diaspora and transnational connections are significantly marked by the issue of race. Paul Gilroy, despite his critique of cultural

I, mapping the matrix of spatiality, seek to complicate in this book the vexed matrix of inside and outside of space by advancing an argument that a master narrative such as the U.S. national narrative is itself dislocated insofar as it depends on an outside, which it both denies and requires as a necessary condition. Such a master narrative may seek to assimilate its outside into a space of ruling assumptions and yet its universality is ironically predicated upon the inapplicability of those assumptions to others constructed as of "outside."[14] Vis-à-vis the epistemology of such spatial logic, all the texts examined in this book capture the very moments when the figures excluded from the realm of the master narrative emerge at those internal splits as *unintegrated outsideness* that transgresses the boundedness prescribed by the

---

nationalism and his invocation of the transnational in *The Black Atlantic* (1993), is thus convinced of the importance of race in the construction of modernity and the critical thinking that gives rise to cultural studies. Rejecting both essentialized and depthless representations of Black identity, Gilroy's diaspora points toward the spatiality which contingently mediates Black authority in the explicit knowledge that an imagined space of diasporic identity is located within global systems that not only make such claims context specific but also make communication through the myriad forms of cultural syncretism inevitable.

14 Homi Bhabha's notion of "colonial mimicry" has much in common with this idea: "it is difficult to conceive of the process of subjectification as a placing within colonial discourse for the dominated subject without the dominant being strategically placed within it." (*Location* 72)

master narrative and exposes the seemingly universal identity as a contingent construction. Embedding my study in such critical, theoretical contexts paves the way for an intensive literary analysis of the twentieth-century American novel in subsequent chapters. I make no claim for inclusiveness in the selection of the texts; they are rather settled on primarily for the range of concerns they demonstrate about this book's theoretical assumptions. Nor do I seek to endow to the writers and their texts a false unity. Providing an entrée into the discussion of those texts through the lens of the spatial as a configuration of social relations "stretched beyond," I instead attempt to make visible the multilayered factors that prompt more nuanced approaches to study on space without lapsing into unexamined tautologies of space and identity, or overall morphology of space in literary studies. No one can live in an abstract framework of geometric spatial relationships. Comprised of materiality, meaning, and practice, spaces are duplicitous in that they cannot be reduced to the concrete or the merely ideological; they display an uneasy and fluid tension between them, always open to counter-meanings and different manners of other representations. Materiality, meaning, and practice are all linked and the materiality of space is made by people doing things according to the meanings associated with that space. Meanings may gain a measure of persistence when inscribed into the material landscape, but they are open to contestation by practices that do not conform to the expectations that come with space. Historicity underlying social relations produces different spaces, and these spaces in turn call for new forms of representation and new ways of imagining one's space in the world. All the texts under discussion in this book offer a kind of counter-geographies—spatial narratives challenging those that have gained a taken-for-granted status. These geographies become recognizable when one is attentive to minute constitutions of space—how competing impulses and strategies are enacted in and through space. Instead of reading the novels as part of a lengthy discourse on the dynamics of a dualistic realm in which center is pitted against periphery or inside against outside, I will analyze how multiple, contradictory, fluid impulses and strategies work to determine the configurations of center and periphery, and inside and outside, which in turn requires the examination of the protean shifts of configurations space resisters, enforces, and encode.

In my study, Faulkner's South, Morrison's "home" for the "outdoored," and the American suburbs in Asian American literature all refer to historically contingent and culturally charged clusters of signifiers, through which each space makes sense and becomes sensible as a place. In a fundamental sense, these are the geographical sites made up of a competing set of imperatives of interests, power, and vision of the historically produced relationships. For instance, while created by a preeminent U.S. southern white male writer who serves as a *de facto* prod for iconoclastic New World/trans-America studies, the Faulknerian world ironically brings home to us the importance of rethinking the hemispheric by way of the regional. It is not a mere coincidence that Glissant, who is not from Mississippi or the United States, provides the most profound insight into the Faulknerian world. In this sense, Glissant's *Faulkner, Mississippi* (1996) can be read as "Glissant/Mississippi, Faulkner/ Martinique." The utopian vision embodied in all-Black separatist establishments in Morrison's *Paradise* is arrived at only through its juxtaposition with both specific Black nationalist movements and the U.S. foundational myths. Moreover, the postwar suburbs in Asian American texts demonstrate that our local knowledge is framed only in tandem with a general set of wider relations since encompassing spatio-temporal references are meaningless unless they are *always already* situated in space. With in mind the pluralistic notions of the U.S. South that are both globally and intra-nationally inflected, the contradictions implicit in all-Black utopian visions, and transnational imaginaries in the American suburb, this book ultimately examines the ways in which counter-narratives are set in motion by spatial imagination that transgresses any normalizing and universalizing drives.

Chapter 2

Home for the Outdoored in Toni Morrison's *Paradise*

"I am a turtle,

wherever I go I carry 'home' on my back."

Gloria Anzaldúa

Being Put Out, Being Put Outdoors

In her first novel, *The Bluest Eye* (1970), Toni Morrison makes an interesting distinction between "being put *out* and being put *outdoors*." Morrison writes, "if you are put out, you go somewhere else; if you are outdoors, there is no place to go. The distinction was subtle but final. Outdoors was the end of something, an irrevocable, physical fact, defining and complementing our metaphysical conditioning" (18). This sense of being "put outdoors" rather than merely being "put out" captures how the American sense of possibility and mobility is sometimes imposed upon others by subjugation, coerced mobility, and forcible movement. As a parallel, an acute collective awareness of exclusion prevails as not so much a provisional regression as a historically conditioned plight. The very dissonance between the mythos of great American place and the willed amnesia about the violence

> of "taming" and appropriating place has given rise to a tragic casting of American history and allowed America to fulfill its alleged promise of "perennial rebirth" and ventures into the unbounded "virgin land."[15] It is in this context that the enduring symbology of "down home" or "back home," particularly in African American culture, serves as an empowering rhetoric to a displaced and uprooted southern rural folk through the notions of racial past and authenticity aligned with southern rural geographies.

Unraveling the realities of what it is like to be "homeless," Morrison fashions arguments for the appropriation of a place called "home" as an antidote for the angst of homelessness and uprootedness, and she theorizes community for "outdoored"

---

15 Since the publication of Frederick Jackson Turner's influential, if contested, *The Significance of the Frontier in American History* (1883), there has been a rich literature in cultural and literary studies on national experience through the lens of the geographical conditions and American rhetoric of the land. Henry Nash *Smith's Virgin Land* (1950), R.W.B. Lewis' *The American Adam* (1955), and Annette Kolodny's *The Lay of the Land* (1975), to name a few, deserve critical attention here. For a cross reading of that traditional scholarship on American place, New Americanists' insights into the divergence between founding ideas of the nation and the realities of the US as a hegemonic power could be utilized to bear upon the points enumerated here. For an introduction of the New Americanist interventions, see *Cultures of the United States Imperialism* (1993) edited by Amy Kaplan and Donald Pease.

subjects through her own concepts of "village values," "ancestors," and "neighborhood."[16] By teasing out the notion of home as a central operator, I will examine in this chapter the ways in which Toni Morrison's *Paradise* (1998) interrogates the meaning of constructing, reconstructing, and deconstructing a place called home for "outdoored" people by calling into question the utopian visions upon which all-Black towns are founded. Tracing divergences between social realities of all-Black separatist establishments and their vision of home as a place of a mythic origin of belongingness, I argue that a new vision of home, in order to be mobilized as a politically tenable and viable project, should be conceived as an ever-shifting, contested social geometry riddled with creative instabilities and existing in a state of continuous revision rather than as a mere object of nostalgia for

---

16 Morrison in her "City Limits, Village Values: Concepts of the Neighborhood in Black Fiction" defines collective values as a powerful social force that is deeply embedded in a unique African American tradition: "community values (I call them village values) are uppermost in the minds of Black writers, and it may be this feeling for village values as opposed to Gopher Prairie despair that causes so much misadventure in white criticism of Black writers: such critics tend not to trust or respect a hero who prefers the village and its tribal values to heroic loneliness and alienation. When a character defies a village law or show contempt for its values, it may be seen as a triumph to white readers, while Blacks see it as an outrage" (38). Commenting upon an "extraordinary sense of place" in her novel, Morrison, in an interview with Stepto, also maintains that she "felt a strong sense of place, not in terms of the country or the state but in terms of details, the feeling, the mood of the community, of the town" (10).

an original loss. The enduring symbolic imports of "down home" and "back home" has made "home" an integral part of compelling African American narratives as a place reflective of yearnings and memories. In line with African American mobility embodied by historical experiences such as the Middle Passage, the Underground Railroad, the Great Migration, Morrison's works are replete with trips, travels, and migrations. Many of her characters undertake journeys between the U.S. South and the North, and they engage in emotional and psychological journeys as well as in physical movement. Throughout all kinds of movement, the ultimate destination, whether geographical or not, always plays an important role in the configuration of African Americans' lives in the form of "home."

In "Going to the Territory," Ralph Ellison portrays how the geographical conditions that have shaped American narratives affects the ways in which Americans understand history—the "two basic versions of American history" in Ellison's words:

> [H]aving had no adequate model to guide us in establishing what we told ourselves was to be classless society, it has often been difficult for us to place people and events in a proper perspective of national importance. So it is well that we keep in mind the fact that not all of American history is recorded. And in some ways we are fortunate that it isn't, for if it were, we might become so chagrined by the discrepancies which

> exist between our democratic ideals and our social reality that we'd soon lose heart. Perhaps this is why we possess two basic versions of American history: one which is written and as neatly stylized as ancient myth, and the other unwritten and as chaotic and full of contradictions, changes of pace, and surprises as life itself. Perhaps this is to overstate a bit, but there's no denying the fact that Americans can be notoriously selective in the exercise of historical memory.
>
> Surely there must be some self-deceptive magic in this, for in spite of what is left out of our recorded history, our unwritten history looms as its obscure alter ego, and although repressed from our general knowledge of ourselves, it is always active in the shaping of events. It is always with us, questioning even when not accusing its acclaimed double, and with the two locked in mute argument which is likely to shock us when it becomes visible during periods of national stress. Meanwhile, yearning and thirsting for a rational social order, and being forced as human beings to live in what we like to identify as the "present," we go on struggling against the built-in-conditions which comprise the pathology of American democracy. (123-24)

Given the impetus for finding "home," claiming the secured domain of home in terms of needs and desires of the "outdoored" becomes a politically expedient project as a response to the mechanisms that bar the "outdoored" from homes by constructing relations of domination and keep the "outdoored" in the realm of "what is left out" from official history. While the political dimension of home should never be eclipsed by stabilized topoi of home as a place of belonging, nurturing, and origin, the significance of home is ironically heightened by conflicting factors that configure the very notion of home. Not only a physical location teeming with material intimacies but also an emotional place embedded in a deep register of nostalgia, home is associated with an array of meanings from an immediate, personalized setting to a larger human nexus. Amid such a wide range of multi-layered meanings of home, of particular interest here is an abiding assumption that home is a "given" space as either an actual geographical location that can be affirmed tangibly or a site located in memory. What is missing from this articulation of home only through the prism of its "given-ness" is the recognition that home is not only a place of location that is lived in but also a site of social relations that is to be *made*. The overemphasis on "given-ness" of home is likely to reduce home to a passive and neutral space by limiting it to unfolding what preexists. However, the way we come to know "home" lies not in the fact that home exists "always already there" but in having the actuality of home available to a narrative form that discloses intersecting relations, which are oriented toward, dominated by, and separated from home. It is precisely through this recognition of the wider dimensions of home that the other version of American history—"unwritten," "chaotic," "full of contractions" as Ellison argues—is brought to light. "Home" for African Americans, then, becomes a kind of "Thirdspace" in Soja's terms, existing between a physical, material space in which we live and our conceptions of it, each of which Soja respectively dubs "Firstspace" and "Secondspace," or "the perceived" as spatial practices and "the conceived" as representations of space in Lefebvre's words.

Viewed in this light, the experience of having a place of one's own called home connotes more possibilities of movement and mobility than stasis and immobility, and the meaning of belonging and the experience of having and reaching home become conditional and relational. The very moment that such conflicts and contradictions inherent in conceptualizing the notion of home as a place that is experienced and interpreted differently become visible, home no longer becomes an empty space passively waiting to be filled with social relations, but a shifting, ever-mobile location constituted by porous boundaries. Several critics have located variations of the theme of American founding mythologies such as American exceptionalism, American Jeremiad, "the city upon a hill," "American romance of displacement" in *Paradise* from an African American perspective.[17] The reconceptualized

---

17 "*Paradise* denotes the unsettling paradox of a nation born as the first modern democracy that excluded whole populations from its citizenry based upon precisely such

notion of "home," I would like to argue, comes to stand in for the African American intervention in those exceptionalist national mythologies.

The inextricable linkage between home and nation also serves as a methodological reference point upon which to examine the issues of gender, domesticity, femininity, and womanhood that can never be dispensed with in the construction of home. As Amy Kaplan demonstrates in "Manifest Domesticity" (1998), creating an American empire in antebellum America was predicated upon imaging the nation as a home, the notion of home conceived as a "feminine" space is central to the construction of communal unity and nationhood.[18] Since not only spaces appear

---

'rigid and legalistic' construction of identity" (Gauthier 395); "taking as her starting point the idea that the African American community lives its own version of the exceptionalist narrative, she [Morrison] explores its function within this community" (Dalsgard 236); "Mavis takes to the road. She steals Frank's Cadillac and heads West, her life conforming to a certain familiar romance of American displacement" (McKee 216); "*Paradise* attests to the centrality of religious symbolism, especially taken from Puritan theology and American civil religion, in the formation of ethnic identities" (Fraile-Marcos 6).

18 Amy Kaplan extricates imperial symbols and rhetoric from her discussion of domesticity, which she maintains have both a familial and a national connotation: "When we contrast the domestic sphere with the market or political realm, men and women inhabit a divided social terrain, but we opposed the domestic to the foreign, men and women become national allies against the alien, and the determining division is not gender but racial demarcations of otherness. Thus, another part of the cultural work of domesticity might be to unite men and women in a national domain and to generate notions of the

as (en)gendered but gender is also allocated certain spaces, home becomes a discursive space that invite different interpretations of a gendered positionality through spatial configurations of the domestic-public dichotomy. All-Black utopian towns in *Paradise* are founded upon the construction of external "others," and, not coincidentally, the "others" are women. This intersection of home and gender takes on added importance when weighed against Black Nationalist agendas and mythic preoccupation with the notion of authentic blackness, which are ingeniously embedded in the separatist establishments in the manner of palimpsest.

"Home" as a tactic of intervention may connote a "return"—a return to the origin characterized by unique vernacular and expressivity and indigenous culture. This desire for return in contrast to the present condition of displacement and homelessness is not be dismissed merely as nostalgic, fundamentalist, or essentialist because the return does not necessarily have to be based upon the notion of ontological purity. It is rather a matter of political choice by a people on behalf of

---

foreign against which the nation can be imagined as home. The border between the domestic and foreign, however, also deconstructs when we think of domesticity not as a static condition but as the process of domestication, which entails conquering and taming the wild, the natural, and the alien. Domestic in this sense is related to the imperial project of civilizing, and the conditions of domesticity often become markers that distinguish civilization from savagery" ("Manifest Domesticity" 582).

their own authenticity, and there is hardly anything inordinate about people revisiting the past and claiming their own home with the intention of reclaiming it. However, what is called for here in the politics of return is that the location of the present should be also interrogated critically: how does the process of reclaiming home speak for itself; as one voice or as many related voices, as monolithic identity against the backdrop of racial unity or as identity hyphenated by intersecting relations? All these questions are at the heart of the utopian desire for home in *Paradise*. bell hooks, in this light, explains why she has to leave the "space called home "to move beyond boundaries," yet she needs "also to return there":

> We sing a song in the black church tradition that says, "I'm going up the rough side of the mountain on my way home." Indeed the very meaning of "home" changes with experience of decolonization, of radicalization. At times, home is nowhere. At times, one knows only extreme estrangement and alienation. Then, home is no longer just one place. It is locations. Home is that place which enables and promotes varied and everchanging perspectives, a place where one discovers new ways of seeing reality, frontiers of difference. One confronts and accepts dispersal and fragmentation as part of the construction of a new world order that reveals more fully where we are, who we can become, an order that does not

> demand forgetting. "Our struggle is also a struggle of memory against forgetting." (148)

According to hooks, a new vision of home, in order to be mobilized as a politically tenable and viable project, should be conceived as an ever-shifting, contested social geometry riddled with creative instabilities and existing in a state of continuous revision rather than as a mere object of nostalgia for an original loss. Building upon this baseline proposition, I will discuss why the experience of having a place of one's own called home connotes more possibilities of movement and mobility than stasis and immobility. Finally, this chapter offers an examination of how geographies of exclusion are imposed upon the "outdoored" by way of constructing gendered spaces, and how *Paradise* reconceptualizes the notion of home through a postethnic vision and provides an entrée into a discussion of which character is white, posed by the provoking opening line, "[t]hey shoot the white girl first."

Place of Memory, Memory of Place

The temporal focus of each of Morrison's novels pinpoints crucial moments in African American history during which social and cultural forms underwent disruption and transformation. Both

The Bluest Eye and *Sula* pictures the period of 1940s characterized by heavy black migration from the rural South to the cities with the emergence of black "neighborhoods": Her debut interrogates psychic injuries of internalized racism by touching upon the meaning of "Black is beautiful" from a viewpoint in 1941; *Sula* portrays a "new world black and new world woman" who has grown up to be "disruptive, imaginative, modern, out-of-the-house, outlawed, unpolicing, uncontained and uncontainable" (Morrison, "Unspeakable Things Unspoken" 25) partly from the cultural soil of the 1960s. uncontainable" (Morrison, "Unspeakable Things Unspoken" 25) partly from the cultural soil of the 1960s. *Song of Solomon* (1977), mostly set in the 1960s, traces Milkman's lineage back to the time of the Freedman's Bureau and directly confronts political awareness of the era with historical events embedded within the main plot such as the murders of Emmett Till and four black girls in a Birmingham church. *Tar Baby* (1981) locates aftermaths of the Civil Rights Movement in the 1980s. As the final work in the trilogy that includes *Beloved* (1987) and *Jazz* (1992), *Paradise*, tracing back to the immediate era after the Emancipation, is narrated from the lens of the late years of the Civil Rights Movement; *Beloved*, set in Cincinnati eight years after the end of the Civil War, directly confronts historical residuals of slavery and provides an nuanced commentary on the failed utopian promise of Civil Rights by presenting the end of the Freedmen's Bureau; set in the era of the

Harlem Renaissance and the mass migration against the backdrop of a panoramic presentation of the 1919 procession of veterans of the 369 Regiment on Fifth Avenue and the East St. Louis riots, delineated in *Jazz* (1992) is the frustration of African Americans facing the falling away of a utopian impulse after World War I. *Paradise* (1997), moving back to the immediate era after the Emancipation, is narrated from the lens of the late years of the Civil Rights movement. In company with each character's journey into Bill Cosey's legacy in *Love* (2003), readers are drawn into the history of the woolly mid-twentieth century America, which references indirectly, the Civil Rights era.[19]

In those temporal arrangements are inscribed African Americans' strenuous efforts to retain cultural roots and to reclaim history. More importantly, the temporal experiences of African Americans, who were caught both in the mire of the haunting past and in the uncertainty of a future, are integrally conjoined with spatial experiences, as displaced peoples configure

---

19 In addition, it is no less noteworthy that Morrison published *Dreaming Emmett* (1981), her first play, and *Remember: The Journey to School Integration* (2004), which provides an account of experiences of the children who lived in the age of "separate but equal" schooling in a blend of fictional narrative, historiography, and archival photographs. *Remember* was published on the 50th anniversary of the historic Brown v. Board of Education Supreme Court decision ending legal school segregation, which had persisted until May 17, 1954.

their relations to space through memory overlaid with claims to space. Different forms of space, not as a static template in a specific temporal disjuncture but as an integral component of memory, succeed each other through time, and the traces of erased histories of displacement are conjured up. Memory and space thus translate into a "symbolic geography," as Robert Stepto suggests in *From Behind the Veil: A Study of Afro-American Narrative* (1979): "a landscape becomes symbolic in literature when it is a region in time and space offering spatial expression of social structures and ritual grounds on the one hand, and of *communitas* and *genius loci* [spirit of place] on the other" (67). In a widely quoted passage from *Beloved*, Sethe crisscrosses her experience of time and "rememory" in a grid of spatial configurations:

> I was talking about time. It's so hard for me to believe in it. Some things go. Pass on. Some things just stay. I used to think it was my rememory. You know. Some things you forget. Other things you never do. But it's not. Places, places are still there. If a house burns down, it's gone, but the place—the picture of it—stays, not just in rememory, but out there, in the world. What I remember is a picture floating around out there outside my head. I mean even if I don't think it, even if I die, the picture of what I did, or knew, or saw is still out there. Right in the place where it happened [···] Someday you be walking down the road and you hear something or see something going on. So

> clear. And you think it's you thinking it up. A thought picture. But no. It's when you bump into a rememory that belongs to somebody else. Where I was before I came here, that place is real. It's never going away. Even if the whole farm—every tree and grass blade of it—dies. The picture is still there and what's more, if you go there—you who never was there—if you go there and stand in the place where it was, it will happen again; it will be there for you, waiting for you. (35-36)

Morrison maps out this spatially configured (re)memory once again in "The Site of Memory," which appeared in the same year that *Beloved* was published. As noted in the very title of the essay, Morrison argues that space and memory merge into a "site of memory"—an excavation site from which the remnants of past experiences should be recovered with a particular "act of archeology" rather than merely imagined with nostalgia:

> You know, they straighten out the Mississippi River in places, to make room for houses and livable acreage. Occasionally the river floods these places. 'Flood' is the word they use, but in fact it is not flooding; it is remembering. Remembering where it used to be. All water has perfect memory and is forever trying to get back to where it was. Writers are like that: remembering where we were, what valley we ran through, what the banks were like, the light that was there and the route back to our

> original place. It is emotional memory—what the nerves and the skin remember as well as how it appeared. (119)

The archeological act of excavating "the site of memory" is, I would argue, an act of "*re*-membering" against "*dis*-remembering" by redesignating things in a given place, time, and circumstance. This archeological act, in its turn, enables displaced peoples, dispossessed of the space they once claimed for themselves, to regain control of the space through a dynamic conception of time-space relations.

The spatial and the temporal not as two divergent axes but as intersecting vectors paves the way for a new understanding of Morrison's works, particularly her migration narratives. A group of critics have placed migration at the center of the study of African American narratives: Melvine Dixon's *Ride Out the Wilderness: Geography and Identity in Afro-American Literature* (1987), Farah Jasmine Griffin's *Who Set You Flowin'?: The African-American Migration Narrative* (1995), Charles Scrugg's *Sweet Home: Invisible Cities in the Afro-American Novel* (1993), and Lawrence Rodgers' *Canaan Bound: The African-American Great Migration Novel* (1997) are all noteworthy contribution to the field. Griffin considers the genre of migration narrative to be one of the twentieth century's important forms of African American cultural production that captures the massive dislocation of black peoples. Defining migration as movement from provincial

Southern and Midwestern regions to more urban spaces, she ends up reproducing a familiar typology of migration as a journey from rural south to urban north. It is also the case with Rodger's explanation of the migration novel in terms of a symbolic journey from south to north. Rodgers argues that it is the migrant's yearning for a livable home that entails migration and that this desire is closely tied to an ontological quest for identity. Griffin and Rodgers thus delineate the trajectory of migration narratives through the divides of rural/urban, collective/individual, south/north, and agrarian/industrial—a clear indication of those studies' indebtedness to Robert Stepto's *From Behind the Veil*[20]:

> To begin with, I should mention that my working definition of symbolic geography, in all its obvious indebtedness to the

---

20 Undoubted, such typological study's formal construction also reflects influence from slave narratives and the biblical exodus motif. Dividing his book into two sections, "The Call" and "The Response," Stepto bases each section upon "a fairly discrete period in the history of Afro-American narrative as a literary form": "'The Call' begins with a discussion of four types of slave narratives"—which I term the eclectic narrative, the integrated narrative, the generic narrative, and the authenticating narrative—and complete itself by describing how Booker T. Washington's *Up from Slavery* and W. E. B. Du Bois's *The Souls of Black Folk* revise and revoice the latter two slave narrative types" (xvi). What is relatively ignored in the emphasis of this typological study on the symbology of "ascent from bondage to freedom" in geographical terms is the acknowledgement of actual movements such as reverse migration and move to more industrialized southern regions.

ideas of Professor [Victor] Turner, focuses on the idea that a landscape becomes symbolic in literature when it is a region in time and space offering spatial expressions of social structures and ritual grounds on the one hand, and of *communitas* and *genius loci* [spirit of place] on the other. The distinction between the two pairings has to do quite simply with time; social structures and ritual grounds exist in time while spatial expressions of *communitas* and *genius loci* are, as Turner says of *communitas* alone, "moments in and out time." The social structure confronting the Afro-American hero-narrator and most often providing the point of departure for his ritualized journey is, in a word, slavery, even though a contemporary phrase such as "institutionalized racism" may better describe the more subtle structures besetting the modern pilgrims. What interests me is the fact, confirmed by the narrative literature, that the confining social structure (slavery) is not a fixed geographic or symbolic space; it is not quite simply and powerfully "Georgia" or "Mississippi" (even through Mississippi has come to have a certain popular resonance in this century) but, in its various dimensions and symbolic meanings, many states and regions, including that nebulous but universally known realm referred to as "downriver." (Stepto 67-68)

Stepto's symbolic geography smacks of Northrop Frye's

formalist impulse in its theoretical assumption of "pregeneric myth" stored in African American literature.[21] While attempting to overcome formalist ahistoricity by incorporating space in time, Stepto's geographical imagination is predicated on the divide of the geographical in terms of "in" and "out of" time and it is therefore caught in the bipolar conception of time and space in which space is associated with stasis and time with historicity. It leads to a questionable differentiation between a pregeneric mythical space cut off from the torrent of historical reality and a space that bears meaning through spatial expressions of oppressing social structures such as the color line. One of the problems attendant upon this dualistic notion of geographical imagination is to reiterate a typology of black migration: the further north African Americans move, the more likely they are

---

21 Terry Eagleton finds in Frye's scientific impulse a more formalist inclination than that of New Criticism: "Frye's work emphasizes as it does the utopian root of literature because it is marked by a deep fear of the actual social world, a distaste for history itself. In literature, and in literature alone, one can shake off the sordid 'externalities' of referential language and discover a spiritual home. The *mythoi* of the theory are, significantly, pre-urban images of the natural cycles, nostalgic memories of a history before industrialism. Actual history is for Frye bondage and determinism, and literature remains the one place where we can be free. It is worth asking what kind of history we have been living through for this theory to be even remotely convincing. The beauty of the approach is that it deftly combines an extreme aestheticism with an efficiently classifying 'scientificity,' and so maintains literature as an imaginary alternative to modern society while rendering criticism respectable in that society's terms" (81)

to lose their cultural roots; the further south they move, the closer they come to spiritual rebirth.

Morrisonian "symbolic geography," however, can hardly be defined solely by such typology. While some of her characters go north in *The Bluest Eye*, *Sula*, *Beloved*, and *Jazz*, other characters in *Song of Solomon* and *Tar Baby* undertake journey home to the South. Pilate, Milkman, Therese, and Son undergo "immersion rituals" through the movement to the South, that movement is supplemented by migration in reverse. Therefore, it is not merely a geographical location that enables Morrisonian symbolic geography to have particular meaning. It is rather the combination of physical movement from one place to another, the experienced practice of movement, and the representation of movement, all of which are bound up with one another. Movement itself is presented as adventure and freedom, but sometimes as tedious and threatening within the ever-shifting context of demographical change and different attitudes towards the sense of place. It bears the traces of historical and cultural change, thereby making difficult an understanding of the experience of migration in unitary terms. In this light, all those studies of Griffin, Rodgers, and Stepto stop short of inquiry into the shift from the study of *things in space* to the actual *production of space*, à la Lefebvre. In *Paradise* particularly, "[i]t is not moving through space, but responding to what is in space in order to make a safe place for its occupants that is most crucial to freedom in *Paradise*" (McKee

221). My interest thus lies not in the typological understanding of migration in the form of moving from one place to another but in a reflection of the relations of conflicting forces—the changing geography of changing relations. In Morrison's writing, the urgency of the encounter with the past through "rememory" must be interpreted through this commitment to a continual questioning of location, movement, and position.

The Other Side of a Black Utopia

With a temporal focus aligned with a historically palimpsestic landscape of space, *Paradise* locates a utopian desire inherent in the impetus for self-governing, all-Black establishments from the post-Reconstruction era of the nineteenth century through the mid-1970s. In the aftermath of the overthrow of Reconstruction governments, the freedmen "8-rock" families of Zechariah Morgan, Drum Blackhorse, Brood Poole, Jupe Cato, Able Flood, a Beauchamp, and the two DuPres, who had skin as black as "eight rock, a deep deep level in the coal mines" (193), moved westward to Oklahoma from Louisiana and Mississippi, looking for better opportunities not available to them in the South. In explaining how the "old Indian Territory" transformed into the state of Oklahoma in the wake of Emancipation and the betrayal of the Reconstruction, Ralph Ellison writes in "Going to the Territory":

> At that time the state of Oklahoma had attracted many of the descendants of the freed slaves, who considered it a territory of hope and a place where they could create their own opportunities. It was a magnet for many individuals who had found disappointment in the older area of the country, white as well as black, but for Negroes it had a traditional association with freedom which had entered their folklore. Thus the uneducated and educated alike saw Oklahoma as a land of opportunity. [···]
> I assure you that it was wild! Yes, but wild mainly in the sense of its being a relatively unformed frontier state. I have stressed that in this country geography has performed the role of fate, but it is important to remember that it is not geography alone which determines the quality of life and culture. These depend upon the courage and personal culture of the individuals who make their homes in any given locality. (132-34)

As Ellison portrays Oklahoma as a new "home" shaped by the "fate of geography," *Paradise* is geographically presented as a compelling drama of founding a black utopia. The migration of "eight rock families" are characterized by hardships and exclusions. Particularly, those families went through a formative experience when they were "disallowed" to settle by the light-skinned people of the town of Fairly, Oklahoma. In Fairly, racism had been replaced by a revamped racial hierarchy in which dark black skin was devalued. In response to this humiliating experience dubbed "the Disallowing," the families, a "tight bond of wayfarers bound by the enormity of what had happened to them" (189), established the separatist, all-Black town of Haven, Oklahoma in 1890. A subsequent migration took place when many of Haven's men returned from World War Two. Disillusioned with still-racist America and witnessing the town collapsing, they decided to move farther into Oklahoma as their "old fathers" had done sixty years before. The newly established town, "Ruby" becomes another "site of memory" for the "new fathers" who learn the importance of giving a voice to the sense of being rooted in a safely enclosed place and to a feeling for the past of their Old Fathers' long and painful journey of repeated exclusions. As a way of ensuring the continuation of salvation from suffering, the founding narrative of what happened after the "Disallowing" ordains the 8-rocks as God's chosen people by grounding the history of migration fraught with humiliation and frustration, on a collective destiny of the original fathers.

Implicated in this process of establishing the exclusive two black towns is a call for communal unity based upon a common origin—or "imagined ties," using Benedict Anderson's terms—and a destiny addressed only to those who exclusively appropriate belonging to certain organic terrains that entitle one to admittance to the community.[22] This impetus toward solidarity, however, often leads to an authoritative closure of entrance to those deemed unworthy of membership in the community, and the problem of admittance by necessity creates a binary of inclusion and exclusion:

> Ten generations had known what lay *Out There*: space, once beckoning and free, became unmonitored and seething; became a void where random and organized evil erupted when and where it chose—behind any standing tree, behind the door of any house, humble or grand. *Out There* where your children were sport, your women quarry, and where your very person could be annulled; where congregations carried arms to church and ropes coiled in every saddle. *Out There* where every cluster of whitemen looked like a posse, being alone was being dead. But lessons had been learned and relearned in the last three generations about how to protect a town. (16, emphasis mine)

---

22 One of the problems of depending on Anderson to uncover the ways in which the all-Black towns are founded and maintained is that the towns are "primordial villages of face-to-face contact" while his concept of "imagined communities" is applied mostly to communities larger than "primordial villages." But I will continue to count on Anderson in this chapter because very way the foundational narrative of the all-Black towns takes effect meshes well with his idea that "communities are to be distinguished not by their genuineness or falsity but by the style in which they are imagined" (6).

It is at this juncture that a tension between belonging and homelessness meets up with a creation of "them" lurking "Out There" as opposed to "us," raising a number of questions centering on the all-Black utopian vision of Ruby.

One of the ironies in founding the towns of Haven and Ruby is the townspeople's complicity in replicating an overarching system of domination: they consolidate their own sense of racial superiority by constructing light skin as impure, since the experience of the Disallowing informs the town's communal identity "like a bullet in the brain" (109). As Benedict Anderson observes in *Imagined Communities* (1982), the very ideas of collectivity and the common past are what must be imagined in the sense that they are made available by constructing narratives that are supposed to be shared by community members. The original fathers' experience of suffering and humiliation is recreated through sharing of narratives, such as the conflation of the story of the Old Fathers' migration with that of baby Jesus, perpetuated through the annual school Christmas pageant. The town's founding "myth" is also nourished by the "powerful memories" of the twin brothers, Deacon and Steward Morgan. The twin brothers "remember the details of everything that ever happened—things they witnessed" and even the things "they have *not*" (13, emphasis mine). The town of Ruby as a newly found home, then, becomes an imaginative location, a space created by longing and nostalgia for an original place, complete with an affective investment by idealized notions of wholeness. As a result, it remains to be seen whether the new fathers keep a critical distance to their own founding narratives because it is "not history per se, but a history that has become official and monolithic, and hence dangerous to the well-being of the community" that "afflicts the community of Ruby"(Peterson 87-88). As Reverend Richard Misner, a young, progressive minister of the town, points out, Ruby becomes a more and more self-enclosed place because its members create "no stories to tell of themselves" and "nothing to say, pass on" beyond the founding of Haven, as if "past heroism was enough of a future to live by" (168). It is not just the repetition of the same story and history that is problematic here; what is missing from the townspeople's rigidifying conceptualization of home and subsequent myth of unitary origin is a call for the redefinition of one's sense of belonging and their perception of the "slippage" that the very process of repetition inevitably entails—a slippage that raises doubts about the original itself.[23]

---

23 As the original dissolves and is drawn away, the original itself, called into question in a Derridian sense, reemerges into a chaotic flux of aggregates. Following the lead of J. L. Austin's differentiation of the "performative" and "constative," Jacques Derrida shows why the possibility of being repeated in changing circumstance is the fundamental nature of language through the notion of "general iterability." According to Derrida, language is intrinsically "performative" since it does not merely convey information but "performs acts" by its repetition of established discursive practices. In this process of the rhetorical operations of the performative can be forged the resources from which displacement and

The rigidity with which the people of Ruby sustain the town's history is made clear in the disputes over the inscription on the Oven, a "community kitchen" (99) originally built for the residents of Haven. The Oven was a practical center of the town for meals and celebrations, and a historical monument symbolizing the past of the town. A biblical motto that the first Morgan placed on the lip of the Oven's iron in 1890 becomes gradually indecipherable during the intervening eighty years as the first word is worn away. Standing for another unchangeable "original," as a sharp warning from God to be moral and obedient to traditional order, the inscription should read "Beware the Furrow of His Brow" in the elders' view. The original message of the inscription is indelibly marked in the town's collective memories that have developed the utility into a shrine. But it is actually a product of the town's ideological investments: "It is still not clear where the words came from. Something he heard, invented, or something whispered to him while he slept curled over his tools in a wagon bed. His name was Morgan and who knew if he invented or stole the half-dozen or so words he forged. Words that seemed at first to bless them; later to confound them; finally to announce that they had lost" (7).

By the 1970s, someone paints a red fist on the Oven, intended

---

subversion can be activated. See also Butler's elucidation of sexualized and gendered body in the context of repetition and copies of the original, expounded later in this chapter.

as a symbol of Black Power, and the Oven becomes a center of dissident voices and internal divisions within the community. It begins to lose its influence as a functional, unifying part of the town as the younger generation voices radically different views about the wording of the Oven's inscription. Armed with a new political consciousness fueled by the Black Power Movement, the younger generation claims that the motto read, "Be the Furrow of His Brow": Ruby should never be immune from the political upheavals of the Civil Rights era and the townspeople should be their race's instrument beyond the confines of the insular town's restrictive morality. Lamenting over the loss of communal consensus, the men of Ruby are never able to accept the challenge of the younger generation to their authority. Steward Morgan, a self-ordained guardian of the town's tradition and his grandfather Zechariah's legacy, decides to protect the presumed original meaning of the inscription by asserting, "if you, any one of you, ignore, change, take away, or add to the words in the mouth of that Oven, I will blow your head off like you was a hood-eye-snake" (87). Ruby thus remains as it used to be—a place where "Booker T. solutions trumped Du Bois problems every time" (212), as Misner later thinks to himself. The all-Black town, seething with the dissensions, lays bare a limited utopian vision of Ruby, raising a question of "how could so clean and blessed a mission devour itself and become the world they had escaped?" (292). Just as the original fathers advocated their authentic blackness as a tactical assertion and as a counterpoint to the traumatic experience of the Disallowing, the residents of Ruby seek to reinforce their communal unity by placing boundaries and delving into the past for internalized origins. However, they ironically end up unwittingly reinscribing the very relation of domination by internalizing racial hierarchies.

If difference as a tactical oppositional position is what makes cultural and ethnic specificities, which would be muted or ignored otherwise, articulated, then, the emphasis on the category of difference, embodied in the internalized history of Ruby as a place reclaimed as "home" and the town's obsession with the idea of authentic "blackness," has the merit of making a politics of articulation possible. Particularly when the creation of difference is about the empowerment of a socially and historically disinherited people through the preservation of their distinctiveness, relinquishing the concept of difference might have negative political implications. For it strikes people, who have been historically disposed of their positions, empty of their firm footing from the outset. However, this immediate urgency to a politics of articulation is enmeshed in a tricky problem ensuing from the binary system: if no articulation can occur without relations of difference, how can one transgress the binary frame without posing it first? Even when the rhetoric of difference is utilized as a site of cultural and political critique, this perspective itself is authorized by the existing center as a confirming presence of what is *not* the Other. Consequently, the Other's oppositional position remains caught in a dyadic relationship that inadvertently reinforces existing power structures, and any attempt to transcend those binary structures is likely to result in a proliferation of margins, an ever-renewed process of differentiation. This dilemma is at the heart of the notion of home envisioned by pitting "us" against "them" in Haven and Ruby, which leads the town's residents to "become the world they had escaped."

However, I would caution against facilely casting as nostalgic or essentialist the spatial reclamation prominent in the history of the all black towns' impetus for establishing home. If the dominant culture lays claims to the category of otherness and appropriates otherness to secure a privileged position, there is nothing regressive about people reclaiming the past for a struggle against forgetting, which is means of constructing cultural knowledge and survival. It is rather a political choice by the people on behalf of their authenticity when confronted with loss and dispossession. Haven's exclusive gesture can be viewed as a reaction to the repeated exclusions. For example, in the very name of the town Ruby, which is name after the Morgan twins' sister, is inscribed the tragic story of the girl who died on a hospital bench while a nurse was trying to find a veterinarian to treat her instead of providing any proper medical care which the nurse believed the girl rarely deserved because of her race. What is at issue here is how the claims to memory, the past, and a place of their own should not duplicate the structures of domination, should not be based on a notion of ontological, epistemological purity, and should not reinscribe communities within the confines of an internalized, timeless history ever renewed in a present instance. This idea is not without its implications for the need to redefine the boundaries of what constitutes home as a more mobile and less stabilizing place rather than as an anchor and source of origin—a need for a reconceptualized notion of home dangerously poised between rootedness and flexibility.[24] A methodological problem to be resolved in conceiving of the notion of home is how Morrison deploys a desire for home without reproducing the rigidity with which the very structure of domination is maintained, and, simultaneously, without losing "home" as a site of oppositional possibility.

---

24 In regard to this dilemma, Spivak, arguing that to merely reverse binary hierarchies is likely to keep us caught within a structure conditioned by the presence of the opponent, suggests that while the reversal is mobilized, it, *simultaneously*, must be succeeded by the displacement of the terms in opposition: "Without this supplementary distancing, a position and its counter-position [···] will keep legitimizing each other" (*In Other Words* 345).

Home of Theory, Theory of Home

In parallel fashion, the conflicting desires revolving around building a black utopia can be productively examined in tandem with the strained circumstances of theorizing an African American literary theory. The ideas of racial purity and authentic blackness are constitutive of the theoretical and critical positions and practices of African American literary theory. To identify the vital context for such discussion can thus profitably unpack a certain perspective on *Paradise* to locate the novel in a larger context of the tradition of African American literary studies. To that end, I will first enter the debate that took place in a 1987 *New Literary History* issue among Joyce, Gates, and Houston Baker Jr.

"What's Love Got to Do with It?"—it is the title of an article by Henry Louis Gates Jr., which is pitted against Joyce A. Joyce's concerns over the loss of an abiding respect for blackness as a communicative tool with liberating potential as a result of black literary critics' embracing "extraneous" and "alien" perspectives of poststructuralism and postmodernism. When he names his article after the title of Tina Turner's well-known song, Gates intends to deride Joyce's simplistic understanding of "black people" and "black experience" as stable and pre-given categories and her ensuing claim for black critics' responsibilities for their own race. Contesting the appropriateness of adopting "white" theories to read African American texts, Joyce in her article,

"The Black Canon: Reconstructing Black American Literary Criticism," defines a "black literary tradition" by summarizing its characteristics: its antagonistic relationship to "the oppressive economic, social, political, and psychological strictures imposed on the Black man by white America" (338); the traditional role assigned to the Black American critic "to serve as an intermediary in explaining the relationship between Black people and those forces that attempt to subdue them" (339). Joyce views as execrable the "exogamic, elitist, epistemological adaptations" of the "new" African American critics and the self-alienating "merger of Negro expression with Euro-American expression" in contemporary African American literary criticism (337, 339). Such adaptations, she argues, entail a denial of "a direct relationship between Black lives, Black realities, and Black literature" (338). In an opening anecdote concerning a student's inability to understand an essay by James Baldwin, she emphasizes the responsibility of black writers and critics to makes their ideas reach a broader audience. To Joyce, the proponents of "Black poststructuralist criticism" should be condemned for having dissociated themselves from their audiences with a detached and alienating perspective: "Black poststructural critics have adopted a linguistic system and an accompanying world view that communicates to a small, isolated audience [···] 'dulling' themselves to the realities of the sensual, communicative function of language" (339-40).

Interestingly, Joyce's argument is fraught with filial overtones presupposing a direct relationship between black lives, black realities, and black literature. She argues that the black critic ought to be an "intermediary," repudiated by black poststructuralists who try to cater to the white critical establishment: "Black creative art is an act of love which attempts to destroy estrangement and elitism by demonstrating a strong fondness or enthusiasm for freedom and an affectionate concern for the lives of people, especially Black people" (343). Acting as a mediator between the utilitarian political interests of the black community and the aesthetic aspects of literary analysis, the critic, according to Joyce, should facilitate the creation of a black counter-hegemony based on the overarching principle of familial love and loyalty. As such, the thrust of Joyce's argument, based upon the definite categories of "Black people" and "Black lives" in contrast to "extraneous" and "alien" elements, is vulnerable to the charge of essentialism and reductiveness. But there is a legitimate claim underlying her contention that the poststructuralist "sin" lies in its attempt to disassociate the literary text from the social and historical contexts in which it is produced.

A claim for cultural authenticity as an operational term and a collective unity through preservation of ethnic and cultural specificities shared in the popular experience of suffering can serve as a site of oppositional possibility. It is in this context that the Black Aesthetic movement emerged in the 1960s along with the radicalization of the word, "black." Many writers involved in the movement such as Amiri Baraka, Hoyt Fuller, Haki R. Madhubuti, Maulana Karenga among others discern in previous movements of black American culture, particularly the Harlem Renaissance, an uneasy tendency to imitate Western art. They argue that the urgent task for true black artists is "snapping off the shackles of imitation" (Fuller 8) and serving as "a means of helping black people out of the polluted mainstream of Americanism" (Gayle Jr. xxiii). For these writers, authentic black art should be a social tool that speaks directly to the concerns of the black people.

Likewise, when Stephen Henderson conceives of the notion of "saturation" as black poetry's horizon of signification in an immutable "meteorology" of what black people "simply know," saturation, then, becomes the authenticity of "the Black Experience" and "Blackness" of poetry (Henderson 104). What underlies Henderson's argument is the idea that an enabling condition for African American art should be the possession of blackness by expressive cultural practices. From a different angle, Barbara Smith in her seminal essay "Toward a Black Feminist Criticism" seeks to comprehend the "creative function of difference" in black women's literature to both restructure and supplement the ideological program of black cultural nationalism. On the one hand, she attempts to displace the prescriptive model of black identity that is unified around the sign of race prompted by Black Aesthetic critics. On the other hand, she contends that black women authors constitute an identifiable literary tradition based upon at once the common lived experiences of the black women writers and a distinct black female language in a no less similar vein of authentic blackness.

Despite their liberatory potentials, it should be noted that both the Black Aesthetic movement's separatist stance and Smith's black feminist consciousness are haunted by essentialist and exclusionary logic. As Deborah McDowell suggests, the Black Aesthetic emphasis on a "'positive' black self, always already unified, coherent, stable, known" later operates as a dogmatic agenda with race constructed as "the sole determinant of being and identity, subsuming sexual difference" while such a black self is remarkably disruptive of the structure of domination when first articulated (57-58).[25] In this sense, utilizing radical difference as a

---

25 Historically, the complexities of gender issues are also bound up with local and national ramifications of the civil rights movement. One needs to remember that as a wide spectrum of local and grassroots level civil rights struggles developed into a nationwide-scale movement, the movement leaders were confronted with an increasing need to cope with conflicting demands. Attention to localized activities necessarily brings to the fore issues of gender, because the tension between local and national priorities is inextricably linked to the conflicting agendas of male-dominated organizations and female-centered grassroots organizations. When the local-national *dichotomy* is reconfigured into a local-national *hierarchy*, the hierarchy serves as a fundamental condition for female oppression and gender erasure. For example, when whites were voted out of the SNCC (Student Nonviolent Coordinating Committee) in 1966, the decision to expel whites was a reassertion by blacks that the movement was "a black movement for the purpose of empowering black people" (Evans 96). "We shall have our manhood," pledged Black

site of cultural critique is ironically dependent on the continuing existence of what blackness is *not* or what black femininity is *not*. Engineered by almost the same internal logic, the terms such as "black women," "black people," and "black experience" ultimately tend to congeal into stable and given categories. More importantly, the notions of "blackness" and "authenticity" as well as the correctness of criticism are predicated on the premise that one must be *within* a cultural and racial reality—in other words, authentic, black, or (black) feminine enough to define or interpret that reality. It is precisely at this point that Gates and Baker begin to land hard blows on Joyce.

Against Joyce's exclusivist proposition that the role of black critics and black creative art should be "an act of love" for black people, Gates argues for a "truly pluralistic notion of the institution of literature," receptive not only to "any tool that enables the critic to explain the complex workings of the language of a text" but also to the specificity of different literary traditions (351-52):

Panther Minister of Information, Eldridge Cleaver in his 1968 *Soul on Ice*, promoting the new priorities of the black struggle for self-proclaimed liberation warriors (61). Cleaver indicts black women for being the cause for the problems of all blacks and accuses them of disloyalty almost in the same vein as the Moynihan Report (1965), which diagnosed the inordinate strength of black women as "the principal source of most of the aberrant, inadequate, or antisocial behavior that did not establish, but now serves to perpetuate the cycle of poverty and deprivation" of black families" (qtd. in Rainwater 29).

> We critics in the 1980s have the especial privilege of explicating the black tradition in ever closer detail. We shall not meet this challenge by remaining afraid of, or naïve about literary theory; rather, we will only inflict upon our literary tradition the violation of the uniformed reading. We are the keepers of the black literary tradition. No matter what theories we seem to embrace, we have more in common with each other than we do with any other critic of any other literature. We write for each other, and for our own contemporary writers. This relation is a sacred trust. (352-53)

Throughout his career, Gates's theory of black literature has aimed at critiquing the precepts of the Black Aesthetic Movement and its lack of methodological rigorousness as he terms it as "race-superstructure" criticism: "The race and superstructure critics would have us believe that the function of the critics is to achieve an intimate knowledge of a literary text by recreating it *from the inside* [⋯] Only a black man, therefore, can think (hence, rethink) black thought" (*Figures* 39, emphasis mine). Where Joyce unabashedly constructs a univocal voice for African American culture as the unchallengeable measure of authenticity against any threat of internal pluralism, Gates considers it unfruitful to make a choice between absolute autonomy and complete subservience: "We commit intellectual suicide by binding ourselves too tightly to nonblack theory; but we drown just as surely [⋯] if we pretend that theory is 'white,' or worse—that it is 'antiblack'" ("What's Love" 353).

Houston Baker Jr.'s article, "In Dubious Battle," targets the same adversary. He contends that it is nothing but a "new black conservatism" that blames the contemporary "desirable expansiveness, diversity, originality, and yes, complexity in the Afro-American critical and theoretical arsenal" (363). He particularly derides Joyce's "mythical" understanding of intellectual relations in a multicultural society and suggests that "the myth of an exclusively white mainstream into which Afro-Americans can 'merge' by choice is utter and patent nonsense—a fiction perpetrated by rich Anglo-American males and rejected out of hand by most Afro-Americans from 1619 to our multiethnic, multidimensional, and complex present" (365). His critique of Joyce's exclusive standpoint should come as no surprise, given that Baker has attempted to incorporate cultural materialism and deconstruction into what he calls "the liberating vision of poststructuralism" (365). When he defines the blues as the locus of the authentic rural black southern culture and as a "matrix" in his *Blues, Ideology, and Afro-American Literature* (1984), Baker thus maintains that "[t]he matrix is a point of ceaseless input and output, a web of intersecting, crisscrossing impulses always in productive transit" (3).

The poststructuralist theory would appear to some minority scholars to undermine the very ground of cultural mobilization that needs to deploy the notion of self-identity, experience, and representation as the base of an effective and collective political resistance. In addition, the poststructuralist critique of the human subject and traditional notions of presence, voice, experience, and representation would seem to (re)banish minorities to silence and invisibility at the very moment they are seeking to constitute themselves as legitimate subjects in history. The poststructuralist perspective, however, can be deployed as an empowering critique of white western regimes of knowledge and dominance. When contending that he appropriates contemporary theories "not to 'apply' them to black text, but rather to transform by transgressing them into a new rhetorical realm" ("What's Love" 351), Gates is certainly aware of this double-edged nature of adopting "alien" tools. In "Introduction: Criticism in De Jungle," he argues that "to think oneself free simply because one can claim—can utter—the negation of an assertion is not to think deeply enough," since basing a theory on opposition is "to take the terms of one's assertion from a discourse by an Other" (125). He asserts that the black literary tradition should not be marginalized by its own critical practices. If a black aesthetic exists only in terms of its opposition to external critiques, black writers then allow the dominant culture to determine the terms of the debate and, therefore, they renounce the authority to tell their own narratives: "To attempt to appropriate our own discourses by using Western cultural theory uncritically is to substitute one mode of neocolonialism for another [⋯] We must redefine 'theory' itself from within our own black cultures, refusing to grant the racist premise that theory is something that white people do" ("Canon Formation" 174-75).

In *Signifying Monkey* (1988), Gates certainly tries to depart from both the entire denial of difference and the isolationist stance of the Black Aestheticians: "whereas black writers most certainly revise texts in the Western tradition, they often seek to do so 'authentically,' with a black difference, a compelling sense of difference based on the black vernacular" (xxii). To fail to grasp this "mulatonic" constitution or "two-toned heritage" (xxiii) is to fall into what Gates defines as an *unstrategic* exclusivist "enclosure of negation," or an equally unacceptable inclusivism, "fated to obey the suggestion of an external milieu, for lack of auto-suggestion from within" (54).[26]

Given the overlapping and conflicting assumptions underlying the debate, it is futile to assess the debate merely in

---

26 Gates's call for being "strategic" here brings up Gayatri Spivak's idea of "strategic essentialism," or "affirmative deconstruction." Spivak suggests that it is possible to utilize specific signifiers of ethnic, cultural identity for the purpose of contesting the discourses that exclude the specificities, while simultaneously revealing internal contradictions and slippages of the identity to ascertain that such essentialisms will not be reproduced and proliferated by the very apparatuses one seeks to disempower. See Spivak ("Subaltern Studies" 205-07).

terms of its oppositional nature such as a polarity between the essentialist and the pluralist standpoint. As Tejumola Olaniyan suggests, one may address the nature of the debate mainly as the clash of the "two essentialisms"—an essentialism of "I am who I am" and an essentialism of "I am not what I am" (537), but this viewpoint is still vitiated by missing the legitimate claims arising from each position. What is called for here is not just to specify contestations between the two positions but also to find illuminating ways of explicating what is at stake and what is gained in maintaining or critiquing each position. To put it another way, it is necessary to bring into legibility how they are forged in and through interactions, engagements, and conflicts.

Let me ask the following question to vindicate Joyce first: if a minority group were not coerced into an antagonistic relationship with the dominant order, would the group still feel a need to authenticate itself? One would rather ask why and for what purpose it has to authenticate itself in the first place. These are the questions Gates and Baker fail to pose in criticizing Joyce. In contrast, Joyce rarely taps into what it takes to claim authority to theorize an authentic African American literary theory. She instead appears to be securely within the dichotomy between "indigenous" values that serve "our" own best interests and "alien" ones that do not. She asks "how can the extraneous, alien poststructuralist practices serve as the 'prelude to the definition of principles of literary criticism peculiar to the

Black literary traditions'?" ("Who the Cap Fit" 382). Within the confines and constraints of this logic, she can never grope for the ways to reconsider how "alien" ideas can ever serve "our best interests"—only left with a recurrent vapid question of "is it ours?" Gates's idea that "naming the black tradition's own theory of itself is to echo and rename other theories of literary criticism" may be a clear sign of his awareness of the limitation of essentialism: "to name out tradition is to rename each of its antecedents, no matter how pale they might seem. To rename is to revise and to revise is to signify" (*Signifying* xxiii). Gates gropes his own way toward a theoretical debate of African American theory that is capable of developing its themes and problems autonomously. This is where I locate the political importance of his theoretical endeavors. Nevertheless, his attitudes toward the political implications of his own theory still remain ambivalent.

For instance, Gates frames race as a postmodern construct of language: "Race has become a trope of ultimate, irreducible difference between cultures [⋯] because it is very arbitrary in its application" ("Editor's Introduction" 5). In *Signifying Monkey*, Gates develops his project of investigating rhetorical structures of African American literature by privileging the mechanics of signification and foregrounding the "materiality" and "willful play" of signifiers (59). For Gates, "blackness is produced in the text through a complex process of signification" and "there can be no transcendent blackness, for it cannot and does not exist beyond manifestations in specific figures" (*Signifying* 237). Just as Gates's theory of "signifying" is deeply embedded within the rhetorical traditions of black vernacular folk speech, Baker's blues aesthetic is grounded in the black text's internal logic of signs as a juncture where codified meanings and historical experience intersect. The blues derives its "veritable playful festival of meaning" from the rural folk culture of the black South to serve as a locus of cultural authenticity for "interpretations of the experiencing of experience" (*Blues* 5, 7).

What has been overlooked in black literary studies, Gates and Houston vehemently argue, is the importance of close reading from which a specifically black critical theory can emerge as a means of refusing to imitate white theory. Gates believes that a distinct black literary tradition must be identifiable in language to the extent that the blues transforms into another kind of text in Baker's theory. The blues and the signifying figures then become a product of the text for Gates and Baker. Their theories cannot exist outside of the texts because they are the very product of the text. This is a notable progress of a new black literary scholarship as a more defined critical framework than the combative stance of the 1960s' Black Aestheticians. That said, such progress simultaneously illustrates an emergence of what one critic calls "the New Black Formalism" (Harris 8) with its increasing emphasis on close textual analysis. In this light, Ann DuCille contends that "however attractive and culturally affirming, the valorization of the vernacular has yielded what I would argue is an inherently exclusionary literary practice that filters a wide range of complex and often contradictory impulses and energies into a single modality consisting of the blues and the folk" (69).

Unlike vulgar anti-postmodernist and anti-poststructuralist views, Gates and Baker never suppose that it is impossible to assume the existence of subject, history, and truth since theories call into question the very process of signification, in which one is believed to have the truth—the "truth" that functions as a conduit for the monopoly of the dominant episteme and turns histories of domination into textual amnesia. Nonetheless, it is not yet clear how Gates's denial of the "transcendent blackness" differs from the logic of indeterminacy of postmodernists, which brackets the sociopolitical economy of race based on the notion of the constructedness of race and the notion of text as a limit of intelligibility. How and why has race acquired its oppressive meanings across various social fields? Does Gates really make a distinction between the textual inscription of race and its extra-textual effects in history? How can Baker differentiate the blues as the existence of the black southern vernacular expressivity from the blues as a textual matrix? Are those critics at best acrobats agile in changing their positions between the denial of transcendental signifiers and desire for original differences?[27] All of these questions are open-ended in the debate and, as a result, brings into focus my argument that theory is precisely what different theories themselves contest.

All things considered, the theoretical problems the debate has posed are as follows: on the one hand, while racial consciousness and cultural specificities can be a site of oppositional resistance in that the creation of counter discourse is at least in part about the empowerment of the formerly marginalized and underrepresented, it is likely to lead to the paradox that any confrontational modes of decentering the center can

---

27 Harold Fromm, a white male scholar, makes a biting remark that Gates masquerades "white" and he is "a virtuoso at exploiting white liberal guilt": "His most salient characteristics are his two well-worn metaphysical jumpsuits—one white, the other black—which he is able to zip on and off, sometimes in mid sentence, with dizzying bravado as rhetorical needs urge him on. [···] Gates can play everyone against everyone else while presuming to emerge with virtue unscathed [···] by alchemizing the primal metal of black writings into 'texts' of gold, subjecting them to the currently fashionable 'white' critical methodologies, and living off the academic capital produced there from" (52). Gates, for Fromm, is dexterous in moving from a black subject position to a white one by making use of discursive traits of racial difference to his advantage. Despite his insightful analysis of what lies beneath the veneer of Gates's intellectual and academic gestures, it is noteworthy that Fromm's attack is also based upon his static, simplistic notions of black and white differences. In my view, it should be admitted that it is a rare achievement for Gates to deftly navigate between black vernacular expressivity and (white) high theory by illustrating a transgression of firmly established racial and discursive boundaries.

simultaneously recenter it in a Derridian sense. On the other hand, while it should be admitted that opponents have to be fought on their ground with their own methods being used against them, it is apt to be either absorbed into the center of a larger, official multiculturalism, or dissipated into premature utopianism through a postmodern relationality.

We have thus arrived at a crossroads in theorizing African American literary theory—the stalemate in the debate arising from the difficulty of reconciling a lingering power of essentialism with poststructuralist and postmodern theories. Can we ever claim originality in theorizing African American literary theory with "improved" methods that may render obsolete all prior theories? What comes after (dis)placing the ground of African American literary theory? Jonathan Culler exquisitely put into a context of these questions the idea that "the nature of theory is to undo, through a contesting of premises and postulates, what you thought you knew, so the effects of theory are not predictable" (17). Each critic in the debate presents his or her position as inclusive—to be deeply *within* the black tradition or versatile *enough* to define what it takes to own legitimacy of theorizing African American literary theory. Yet such claim for inclusiveness is ironically contradicted by the very presence of its constitutive outside that is informed and placed by their opponent(s) in opposition to the particular articulation of the claim itself. They neither radically tackle the perspective from the outside looking in nor demand that the insider should look outward and then inward. They do not problematize the insider's insidedness and the outsider's outsidedness, either. What emerges here is a very strange reflection distorted concavely or convexly by what dictates a distinction between the inside and outside of African American literary theory without utilizing the "unpredictable" effects of theory in a productive way.

bell hook's argument serves as a case in point here:

> The unwillingness to critique essentialism on the part of many African-Americans is rooted in the fear that it will cause folks to lose sight of the specific history and experience of African-Americans and the unique sensibilities and culture that arise from that experience. An adequate response to this concern is to critique essentialism while emphasizing the significance of "the authority of experience." There is a radical difference between a repudiation of the idea that there is black "essence" and the recognition or the idea that the black identity has been specifically constituted in the experience of exile and struggle. (29)

hook's strategy of awaking from a delusion of essentialism and simultaneously recognizing "the authority of experience." If one wishes to opt out of any of the terms and conditions of the debate, there is not much to be gained from it. What should be learned from the debate is the way to read one position against the grain of the other and consider them to be mutually constitutive rather than polarize them with the divide between being inside but regressive and being outside but more refined. Viewed in this light, what we have been looking for is not so much *the* theory but a theory in the sense that theory is ironically what different theories themselves contest. The question of what African American literary theory is never asks for a definition but for an argument about why we always concern ourselves with such theory at all. Likewise, we can now understand why it is actually meaningless to ask who is "the last man standing" in the debate. What becomes decisive in revisiting the debate are then how to take into account all the various intersecting lines within and between the positions and how they are given articulation. Can the revisitation of the debate bring about a new "home" African American critics build for themselves or another "ghetto" they inhabit to satisfy the dominant world? Interestingly, the question of how to build a home of theory carries over into the quest for "a real earthly home" (213) in *Paradise*—a home not as a mere object of nostalgia for an original loss but as a site riddled with creative instabilities and existing in a state of continuous revision. If the act of building a home of theory should hinge on "a persistent critique of what one cannot *not* want" in Spivak's words ("Bonding in Difference" 28, emphasis mine), it is necessary to redefine the points, lines, and planes that build a home in Paradise—an act of (dis)placing the ground of the desire for home.

"The Mutiny of Mares": Black Utopia as a Gendered Space

Paradise opens and ends with the story of a murderous attack made on the Convent by the men of Ruby, which was never an actual convent but a former Catholic school for "Indian girls" and originally an embezzler's pleasure dome. This puzzling reaction of the men of Ruby to the Convent women is one of the key stories in the novel. To the men of Ruby, the Convent, as a "place of all places" not twenty miles from their "orderly community," stands in marked contrast to Ruby, where there is not "a slack or sloven woman" (8). The Ruby men's animosity toward the Convent women requires an understanding of how the town's gesture to police goes beyond the category of race and includes the regulation of gender. In Ruby, where authentic blackness plays an important role in determining how each citizen and family is ranked, women hold the key to a racial purity that can be *imagined* and maintained only through legitimate heterosexual reproductive relationships. Women, framed by normalized patterns of domestic and gender relationships, should live up to the standards of their reproductive role in this ideal gender role. Women, functioning as guardians of a community's continuity that denotes something to which one is naturally tied, are represented as an authentic repository of tradition and positioned in limited sexuality. As Reverend Misner suggests, most of the youth have "not yet recovered from the blow to their esteem upon learning that adults would not regard them as humans until they mated" (145). Thus, one of the growing divisions within the community is "not about infant life or a bride's reputation but about who controlled the mares and their foals" (150). Tracing the town's genealogies, Patricia Best Cato, an unofficial community historian, arrives at an understanding of the meaning of gender regulation in Ruby for maintaining its communal identity:

> The generation had to be not only racially untampered with but free of adultery too. "God bless the pure and holy" indeed. That was their purity. That was their holiness. That was the deal Zechariah had made during his humming prayer. It wasn't God's brow to be feared. It was his own, their own." Is that why "Be the Furrow of His Brow" drove them crazy? But the bargain must have been broken or changed, because there were only seven now. By whom? The Morgans, probably. They ran everything, controlled everything. What new bargain had the twins struck? Did they really believe that no one died in Ruby. Suddenly Pat thought she knew all of it. Unadulterated and unadulterated 8-rock blood held its magic as long as it resided in Ruby. That was their recipe. That was their deal. For Immortality. (217)

Given the desire of Ruby men for racial purity, everything that troubles the New Fathers must come from women. Because the men see the women as "[b]itches. More like witches" and the "sluts *out there* by themselves" who never step foot in church" and who "don't need men and they don't need God" (276, emphasis mine), the Convent women, to the Ruby men, represent a threat to the community. Consequently, the Ruby men think that "the mess is seeping back into *our* homes, *our* families" (276). As the Ruby men realize the internal frictions within their community—such as the generational conflict over the meaning of the inscription on the Oven and the Fleetwood's children dying of a congenital disease, which results from the inbred bloodlines of the insular town obsessed with the idea of racial purity—they seek to find something "out there" for a reason behind the impending collapse of their town. Posing an absolute Other "out there" to define a collective identity and consensus in opposition secures a notion of community as a space of belonging. Not coincidentally, the Other existing out of their boundaries is imagined as a wholly female space "permeated with a blessed malelessness" (177) in contrast to their patriarchal order characterized by normative, regulated gender relationships. When the men enter the Convent and begin to murder its inhabitants, the place "permeated with a blessed malelessness" is inexplicably linked to a "female malice that hides here" (4)—the dangerous female sexuality getting out of the clutches of the town's sexual norms. Thus, this feminine space, which was once an embezzler's gaudy pleasure dome flaunting sensual ornaments and fixtures, is "ravished" once again by the men who project their restrictive gender norms onto that place.

A significant tension between the group of "unbridled" women who reside at the Convent and the repressed, insular town of Ruby also stems from colliding visions of "home" and the "Out There" that threatens it. When the wayward women end up in the Convent, it becomes a place they can return to whenever they want, a haven that protects them from the painful past that still haunts them. The Convent is defined by Consolata, resident of the Convent, as a place they "could not leave," but, simultaneously, "they were free to leave" (262). As a place for the "outdoored" women to find both shelter and a freedom to leave, the Convent becomes "a home away from home" (Rubenstein 144). The Convent as a more flexible home for the women stands in stark contrast to the "backward noplace ruled by men" who have "the nerve to say who could live and who not and where." The men are witnessing in the "lively, free, unarmed females the mutiny of mares," and the mutineers should be "got rid of" (308).

The ways in which the Ruby men conceive of home are fleshed out with the images of door and window. When attacking the Convent women, the Ruby men are obsessed with feelings that "there are no windows" in the kitchen, and that doors are "locked" or "closed." Doors and windows are presented to the men only as objects that should be "blown open" and "smashed" with the butts of their rifles to chase their "preys." Given the fact that doors and windows physically and figuratively exist on the border-line surface where outside and inside are both intimate and ready to intermingle, the very way in which the men picture the Convent as a windowless and impenetrable space provides a clue as to understanding why they have to murder the women: "That is why they are here in this Convent. To make sure it never happens again. That nothing *inside* or *out* rots the one all-black town worth the pain" (5, emphasis mine). The Convent women bring about a sudden doubt as to the certainty of inside and the distinctness of outside, which is the core value that buttresses the town of Ruby.[28]

In this light, they embody a radical geography of women, and yet "a paradoxical geography" as Gillian Rose, a feminist geographer, argues:

> The subject of feminism, then, depends on a paradoxical geography in order to acknowledge both the power of

---

28 Megan Sweeny captures "prison imagery" to focus on "black men's profound vulnerability to the disciplinary power of the state" (48). She argues, "the constant threat of lynching and dispossession that blacks faced in the Reconstruction South, and moving through the race riots of the late teens, the 1921 bombing of Tulsa, the continuing hostility that black soldiers encountered after returning from World War II, the assassinations and racial uprisings of the 1960s, the violent retaliations against Civil Rights activists, the 1971 Attica rebellion, and the state sacrifice of black soldiers in the Vietnam War" are detectable as subtexts in *Paradise*.

> hegemonic discourse and to insist on the possibility of resistance. The geography describes that subjectivity as that of both prisoner and exile; it allows the subject of feminism to occupy both the center and the margin, the inside and the outside. It is a geography structured by the dynamic tension between such poles, and it is also a multidimensional geography structured by the simultaneous contradictory diversity of social relations. It is a geography which is as multiple and contradictory and different as the subjectivity imagining it. I have already suggested how some of the founding antinomies of Western geographical thought are negated by this feminist subjectivity: its embodiment which overcomes the distinction between mind and body; its refusal to distinguish between real from the interpretation of places. All these threaten the polarities which structure the dominant geographical imagination. They fragment the dead weight of masculine space and rupture its exclusions. Above all, they allow for the possibility of a different kind of space through which difference is tolerated rather than erased. (155)

The Convent as a discursive space of women's geography and an ensuing sense of an "elsewhere" encourages us to ask if the difference of the Convent as a wholly female space is reducible, could an insistence on such reducibility eventually lead to practices of an inverted sexism, as is the case with Ruby's internalized racial hierarchy? How might one build a relational and conditional difference without resorting to the totalizing and preconceived notion of what it is to be a "woman"? These questions take on added meanings when aligned with the black nationalist agendas in the 1960s and 1970s. For instance, it can hardly require an explanation that the Black Arts Movement of the 1960s was by and large culturally nationalist in the face of such strong resistance, on the part of mainstream American society, to the emergence of Black America into something like citizenship. Blackness, a key concept advocated by the movement, in operational terms, has more to do with an essentialized tactical assertion as a counterpoint to overwhelming white supremacy, which tries to pose itself as an unmarked category. When the representation of race, however, stresses a shared history of suffering, unique artistic expressiveness, and (biological) kinship ties as its semiotic strategies, it is likely to put too much emphasis on opposition, gravitating toward totality and threatening to erase all nuances. In actuality, the Black Aesthetic Movement "discouraged any literary exploration of gender and other differences that might complicate a unitary conception of the black experiences" (Dubey 1).[29] In

29 Dubey uses the term "Black Aesthetic," borrowing it from Addison Gayle, Jr., "in a specific sense to refer to the aesthetic program advocated by black cultural nationalists of the 1960s and 1970s" (163). Butler-Evans also defines some objectives of the Black Aesthetic as follows: "1. Through elaborate self-representation, architects of the Black

the claim to their own specificities which possess *essentially* black discursive properties is a hidden assumption that we can have unmediated access to what the blackness is. That assumption makes us overlook the fact the notion of the blackness itself is laden with historical, social implications and is value-laden, leading to an epistemological impasse: the Black Aesthetic unwittingly repeats the logic by acknowledging racial determinism utilized by white supremacy to maintain the hierarchical binary of superior/ inferior. Suffice it here to say that the very problem is most clearly evidenced by the limitations of the utopian visions of Haven and Ruby.

What is at issue is then how to develop a specific (Black) feminist model without reproducing a monolithic conception of identity—a "double gesture" enabling both "a continuing appreciation of the cultural model of a whole, cohesive self" and "a vigilant attention to the differences within the black experiences that confound any totalized, unitary definition of black identity" (Dubey 4). In her seminal essay, "Toward a Black Feminist Criticism" (1977), Barbara Smith suggests that Black

---

Aesthetic Movement attempted to produce a counter-discourse, generally identified as Black consciousness, to displace the dominant Western mode of representing Black 'reality.' 2. Through semiotic mediation, particularly the appropriation of the experiences that undergirded ordinary Black life, they attempted to construct narratives of a mythical Black nation" (20).

feminist criticism, which emerged in the wake of the Black Aesthetic movement, realized that "the politics of sex as well as the politics of race and class are crucially interlocking factors in the works of Black women writers" (27-28). Smith, however, reinscribes an essential black femininity by asserting that "Black women writers constitute an identifiable literary tradition" due to both the common lived experiences of the writers and what she saw as a distinct black female language (32). One may find the same dilemma in Morrison's ambivalent attitudes toward (Black) feminism. Morrison in "Rootedness: The Ancestor as Foundation" casts doubt on exclusive feminism:

> I don't have much to say about that [···] except that I think there is more danger in it than fruit because any model of criticism or evaluation that excludes males from it is as hampered as any model of criticism of Black literature that excludes women from it. For critics, models have some function. They like to talk in terms of models and developments and so on, so maybe it's of some use to them, but I suggest that even for them there is some danger in it. (344)

On the other hand, in an interview with Claudia Tate, Morrison argues that "black men don't write very differently from white men" but that there is "the most marked difference" in the narratives of black and white women (161), and thereby subtly claims black women's discursive specificities. Are there any fundamentally disparate black feminine experience and consciousness that are different from those of black men as well as white women? Can black women's writing be "blacker" than that of black men? Can nationalist agendas and feminist concerns be deployed without excluding each other while they are kept theoretically tenable? Can one come up with a counter-discourse that can be deployed as a multi-accentual sign without silencing divergent voices within? In order to answer these questions, the feminine space embodied in the Convent should overcome geographies of exclusion while simultaneously claiming a kind of separatism that helps mobilize the category of "woman" and gain political leverage.

Paradise encourages us to ask, if the difference of the Convent as a wholly female space is reducible, might an insistence on the reducibility eventually lead to practices of an inverted sexism, as is the case with Ruby's internalized racial hierarchy? How might one build a relational and conditional difference without resorting to the totalizing and preconceived notion of what it is to be a "woman"? In her 1990 *Gender Trouble*, Judith Butler outlines her account of gender as "performance" and demonstrates how gender becomes "performative" by being constituted contingently through sustained social performances in a cultural matrix of regulatory conventions and norms. One of Butler's central arguments is that gender is not established by a universal order but constituted through "a stylized repetition of acts" (140), which becomes celebrated and reinforced as constituting the ideal.

> The point here is not to seek recourse to the exceptions, the bizarre, in order merely to relativize the claims in behalf of normal sexual life. As Freud suggests in *Three Essays on the Theory of Sexuality*, however, it is the exception, the strange, that gives us the clue to how the mundane and taken-for-granted world of sexual meanings is constituted. Only from a self-consciously denaturalized position can we see how the appearance of naturalness is itself constituted. The presuppositions that we make about sexed bodies, about them being one or the other, about the meanings that are said to inhere in them or to follow from being sexed in such a way are suddenly and significantly upset by those examples that fail to comply with the categories that naturalize and stabilize that field of bodies for us within the terms of cultural conventions. Hence, the strange, the incoherent, that which falls "outside," gives us a way of understanding the taken-for-granted world of sexual categorization as a constructed one, indeed, as one that might well be constructed differently. (140)

One of the effects of these repeated performances is a collective understanding of an ideal that relates an appearance of gender with a natural expression of a particular gendered body. It is this repetition that institutionalizes gender by making sexual practices correspond to culturally constituted sites of "body" in the name of the ideal of gender behavior. While marking what is circumscribed as "proper" and making visible the ways in which the discursive circumstance serves as the basis for generating relations with an exterior distinct from what is proper, the act of copying also displaces the ideal itself. What is telling in Butler's argument is that the very activity of the repetition of regulatory norms ironically opens up the possibility that those norms can be subverted, with the ideal itself called out as a construction. What emerges from the subversion of the norms is "possibilities of 'subjects' that do not merely exceed the bounds of cultural intelligibility, but effectively expand the boundaries of what is, in fact, culturally intelligible" (39).

It is when Consolata draws templates around the Convent women's bodies in a process of healing their trauma that the Convent women's "gendered bodies" swerve from regulatory gender norms. Painting the body outlines on the floor and piecing together their stories of the past little by little, these fugitive women begin to come to terms with their festering wounds by learning how to relate to the "copies" of their bodies: at first, they are "reluctant to move outside the mold they had chosen" (263), but they soon locate their abused, neglected, and exploited bodies that were pegged as culturally "unintelligible" through the practice of stepping *in* and stepping *out*. Along tortuous paths of disavowal, recognition, and repossession, they learn to relate the drawings to their bodies that they "perform" as "accusations directed to the dead and long gone are undone by murmurs of love" (264). Mavis overcomes her guilt over the death of her twins; Seneca, who was sexually assaulted by men, chooses to "mark the open body lying on the cellar floor" (265) instead of cutting herself as she repeatedly did; Gigi exorcises the haunting image of a boy killed in the Oakland riots and discloses a desire for reunion with her parents; Pallas accepts a life growing in her body by painting a fetus in her figure on the floor and coping with, though not completely, her painful memories of the rape. These healing ceremonies culminate in their rain dance right before the attack—a mnemonic ritual that enables the dislodging of trauma and the creation of a revised feminine space through its parallel meaning of "home away from home," combining gender with the sense of belonging. It is at this point that the *ourdoored* women are fully *housed* and "no more haunted" (266).

"A Real Earthly Home"

In discussing with Patricia the meaning of Africa for African Americans, Reverend Misner raises a need for redefining home as "a real earthly home":

> "This is their home; mine too. Home is not a little thing."
>
> "I'm not saying it is. But can't you even imagine what it must feel like to have a true home? I don't mean heaven. I mean a real earthly home. Not some fortress you bought and built up and have to keep everybody locked in or out. A real home. Not some place you sent to and invade and slaughtered people to get. Not some place you claimed, snatched because you got the guns. Not some place you stole from the people living there, but your own home, where if you go back past your great-great-grandparents, past theirs, and theirs, past the whole of Western history, past the beginning of organized knowledge, past pyramids, and poison bow, on back to when rain was new, before plants forgot they could sing and birds thought they were fish, back when God said Good! Good!—there, right there where you know your own people were born, and lived and died. Imagine that, Pat. That place. Who was God talking to if not to my people living in my home?" (213)

What Misner means by his idea of "a real earthly home" is a quest for "home" not as a place embedded in nostalgia where we originate but as a place firmly grounded in the people's shared experience of displacement, exclusion, and oppression. Subsequently, Misner's emphasis on rootedness—"if you cut yourself off from the roots, you'll wither"—is complemented by Patricia's different perception that "[r]oots that ignore the branches turn into termite dust" (209). But the people of Ruby, as Misner reflects, have created a "hard-won heaven defined only by the absence of the unsaved, the unworthy and the strange," and they end up self-destructively reproducing what they want to leave behind: "They think they have outfoxed the whiteman when in fact they imitate him. They think they are protecting their wives and children, when in fact they are maiming them" (306). In marked contrast to this exclusive and, ultimately, self-destructive logic of the Ruby men, Consolata tells the women in the Convent to "[n]ever break them in two. Never put on one over the other. Eve is Mary's mother. Mary is the daughter of Eve" (263). The drama of being homeless and finding homes in *Paradise* calls to mind the importance of exploring the alternative ways in which one can negotiate the meaning of home between rootedness and flexibility through the critique of the traditionally stabilized topos of home—a home that posits no terminal utopia no matter how tenacious a deep-rooted desire to secure a place called "home" where one is safely tied may be.

Coming full circle, the reconceptualized notion of home is immediately related to the knottiest issue in this novel—the racial puzzle of which character is white, as posed by the opening line, "[t]hey shoot the white girl first." Morrison seems to deliberately withhold tangible proof that would enable readers to arrive at a definite conclusion concerning the issue. Instead, she carefully articulates a critique of racial essentialism as a key to the solution of the puzzle as she does in *Playing in the Dark* (1992) to explain how she did "an experiment in the removal of all racial codes from a narrative about two characters of different races for whom racial identity is crucial" in her short story, "Recitatif": Morrison places stress on learning "how to maneuver ways to free up the language from its sometimes sinister, frequently lazy, almost always predictable employment of racially informed and determined chains" (xi)[30]. In her essay, "Home," Morrison provides more substantial clues to the puzzle by bringing up a notion of home as "a place where race both matters and is rendered impotent" and where she can assess "whether or not race-specific, race-free language is both possible and meaningful in narration" (9):

---

30 See also Morrison's "Unspeakable Things Unspoken," in which she articulates both her concerns about the critical risks involved in essentialist moves and a need for an essentialized tactical assertion as a counterpoint to white supremacy: "Now that Afro-American artistic presence has been 'discovered' actually to exist, now that serious scholarship has moved from silencing the witnesses and erasing their meaningful place in and contribution to American culture, it is no longer acceptable merely to imagine us and imagine for us. We have always been imagining ourselves. We are not Isak Dinesen's 'aspects of nature,' nor Conrad's unspeaking. We are the subjects of our own narrative, witnesses to and participants in our own experience, and, in no way coincidentally, in the experience of those with whom we have come in contact. We are not, in fact, 'other.' We are choices. And to read imaginative literature by and about us is to choose to examine centers of the self and to have the opportunity to compare these centers with the 'raceless' one with which we are, all of us, most familiar" (8-9).

> Could I decorate, redesign, even reconceive the racial house without forfeiting a home of my own? Would life in this renovated house mean eternal homelessness? Would it condemn me to intense bouts of nostalgia for the race-free home I have never had and would never know? Or would it require intolerable circumspection, a self-censoring bond to the locus of racial architecture? In short, wasn't I (wouldn't I always be) tethered to a death-dealing ideology even (and especially) when I honed all my intelligence toward subverting it?
> These questions, which have engaged so many, have troubled all of my work. How to be both free and situated; how to convert a racist house into a race-specific yet non racist home. How to enunciate race while depriving it of its lethal cling? (4-5)

By deliberately counter-balancing each possible interpretation of the female characters' racial markers with another of equal credibility, Morrison clearly evokes a "*post*ethnic" moment in her "racial house:" she urges us as readers to recognize a need for a new politics of ethnicity that "effectively draw[s] the political boundary lines without which political contestation is impossible, without fixing those boundaries for eternity" (Hall, "New Ethnicity" 28)[31]. The graffiti inscribed on the Oven reads in

---

31 Hollinger phrases his definition of "postethnicity" as a "rooted cosmopolitanism":

the final chapter, "We Are the Furrow of His Brow" (298), serving as an *illocutionary* act predicated on drawing in the "We" that includes not only the Convent women and the people of Ruby but also the novel's readers. It embodies a more inclusive solidarity than the exclusive collectivity of Ruby which never conceives of the way to fix its problems "by extending a hand in fellowship or love" (275). It is in this context that the slaughtered women's bodies disappear, leaving competing versions of the raid among the people of Ruby. Depicting the Convent women as "characters-on-the-move" by making the presumably murdered women appear and disappear again, Morrison renders the Convent not an

---

"A *post*ethnic perspective develops and applies cosmopolitan ideals in a specific historical context: that of the past quarter-century's greater appreciation for a variety of kinds of *ethnic* connectedness. In contrast to the liberal critique of ethnocentrism prominent during the middle decades of the century, recent thinking about 'community' has attributed to local, regional, religious, and ethno-racial units a capacity for the formation of human character said to be lacking in the national and global affiliations favored by universalists. [⋯] The term *postethnic* marks an effort to articulate and develop cosmopolitan instincts within this new appreciation for the ethnos. Cosmopolitanism itself is more generic. It is an impulse toward worldly breadth associated especially with the Enlightenment of the eighteenth century but found also in antiprovincial intellectuals in a host of times and places. As 'citizens of the world,' many of the great cosmopolitans of history have been proudly rootless. But postethnicity is the critical renewal of cosmopolitanism in the context of today's greater sensitivity to roots. 'Rooted cosmopolitanism' is indeed a label recently adopted by several theorists of diversity whom I take to be moving in the direction I call postethnic" (4-5). See also Werner Sollors' *Beyond Ethnicity* (1986), which Hollinger regards as the principal source of his notion of "postethnicity."

endpoint but a place of departure since the Convent itself becomes a part of migration and the women depart from that departure. Ending *Paradise* with an image of the "voyage home," Morrison implies in the image that "the unambivalent bliss of going home, to be home" involves "shouldering the endless work" we are all "created to do down here in Paradise" (318), and demanding a continual rewriting of boundaries of what constitutes home, which is "both free and situated" through an affirmation of otherness constructed as of "outdoored"—an otherness not imposed but recreated.

Chapter 3

Taking Geographical Detours in William Faulkner's *Light in August*

"To hide everything while revealing it:
the deferral of the south's damnation"

Édouard Glissant, *Faulkner/Mississippi*

"This is where I was when I moved again"

William Faulkner, *The Town*

"New" Faulkner, New "Faulkner"

Can anything new be said by and about Faulkner's works? Can Faulkner studies ever be updated with "new" readings that outmode prior ones? No Faulkner scholars could evade these probing questions as long as they grapple with, if any, foibles of the field. Confronted with such questions, scholars seem to share a belief that twenty-first century readings of Faulkner will coalesce into the emphasis on the relationship between and among the regional, the national, and the transnational. For example, the essays collected in *Faulkner in the Twenty-First Century*, originally presented at the 27th annual Faulkner and Yoknapatawpha Conference, July 2000, are united by their strongly held belief that the seemingly closed world of Faulkner scholarship grounded in one's ideological orientation has given room to a new array of approaches to examine the inextricable linkage of the local and the global and of the national and the transnational. Undoubtedly, this is still earning its keep throughout the twenty-first century. The 2006 Faulkner and Yoknapatawpha Conference under the title the "Global Faulkner" set as its goal putting into question "a narrative of human universality" on which Faulkner's fame was largely based and thus brought into focus the impact of transnationalism and globalization on Faulkner studies and the "question of Faulkner's international reception, translation, and influence" as a means of studying "mutual influence or confluence" (Trefzer ix). The current Faulkner criticism may be said to rearticulate his novels' representation of vexing problems such as race, gender, and class practices in the South, and yet such re-articulation is being extended into new multicultural, postcolonial, postnational, and transnational contexts. Viewed in this light, it should not come as no surprise that one of the most radical transformations of our understanding of Faulkner has been made by those who are not actually from the US south or the United States. Those pathfinders such as Édouard Glissant and Gabriel García Márquez find the Faulknerian world inspirational and they believe that it can open the door to the new worlds Faulkner ironically never saw himself.

Such a change in Faulkner studies requires that it break away from the 80 years of agrarian cultural traditionalism and take into account not only the southern but also the American and inter-American perspectives. What this shift of focus entails is the reconsideration of how the country's wholeness itself has long been dependent upon constructing a regional other called the South: "To have a nation of 'good,' liberal and innocent white Americans, there must be an outland where 'we' know they live: all the guilty, white yahoos who just don't like people of color" (Baker and Nelson 233).[32] My interest, however, lies not in the abjection of the region itself but in how to perceive through the lens of the regional abjection the crucial locus of the country's transition from colonies to confederation to nation against the backdrop of a regional other. As C. Vann Woodward maintains in *The Burden of the Southern History* (1960), the US South's unique historical experiences such as "military defeat, occupation, and reconstruction" (190) can never be jettisoned as the exceptional experiences limited to a particular region but ironically redefined as "contributions that balance and complement the experience of the rest of the nation" (16). In addition, the US South, particularly the coastal states of Texas, Louisiana, Mississippi, Alabama, and Florida, should be understood as northern rim of the Caribbean—a space densely fraught with the historical legacy of slavery, colonial plantation, creole nativism, and miscegenation that call for a multivalent and far extended perspective beyond the

---

32 In a discussion of southern literature within the context of nation building, Greeson argues that "the consistent and pervasive relocation of colonial attributes onto the figure of the South in early national literature suggests that the nationalization of the United States was built in part upon an intra-national, regionally-inflected symbolic geography, in which the term 'South' and 'U.S.' formed an ideological juxtaposition" (210).

regional and national borders.

What is at issue is then to understand how the residual coloniality was furtively and ingeniously projected onto the South for the peculiarization of the slaveholding South by the rest of the United States in its nation-building process while the interconnectedness of the South with the postplantation culture throughout the New World was neglected in that process. The peculiarization of the South was intrinsic to the formation of an "imagined" community of nationhood and it was a kind of invented nationalist ritual conducted to justify the emerging US exceptionalism and to mask imperial indifference to the country's colonial origins. As such, the abjection of the South largely differentiated from the United States was constitutive of a coherent narrative of a nationalist identity, reminding one of what the country contrived to forget was no less important than what it remembered. This ordering of nationalist remembrance and forgetfulness put together the country's constituent memories into a single narrative for the emergence of a genealogy of a people with a common origin. Such a narrative subsequently carried over into reactionary self-absorbed insularity within the South.[33] My focus

---

33 This self-absorbed insularity is reminiscent of the notion of "nativism," which has been widely used by postcolonial critics and became prominent in the 1950s. It basically means a belief in or desire for reclaiming indigenous values and cultural forms that exist prior to colonization. This desire to return to the authentic, if any, rootedness that

thus turns to the extent to which the meaning of the U.S. South for Faulkner can be revealed through *geographical detours*—the regionally, intra-nationally, transnationally inflected symbolic geography of the U.S. South well beyond the divide of nation and South as an imaginative construct. What I mean by "geographical detours" is that we need to rethink a "place" called the US South in a wider sense across changing temporal and spatial axes that are ultimately opened out to its multiple definitions.

Methodologically, the "geographical detours" should be taken to establish the theoretical perimeters of Faulkner studies in new ways that lead to examining how Southern, American, postcolonial, transnational studies can work both in a concerted way and in different registers. If the marginalization of the South precludes any possibility of engaging American exceptionalism, it has had a no less detrimental effect on Southern studies wherein forging a distinct regional self solely defined as stable, coherent, unified as a means of snapping off the shackles of the

---

is believed to be more culturally nourishing and more politically effective can be put into question due to its problematic desirability of doing so. It is precisely what Fanon means by "pitfalls of national consciousness" in *The Wretched of the Earth* (1961)—a nationalist failure in achieving liberation across class boundaries as long as nationalism is locked up in racial and cultural determinism. This problem can be also found in the Agrarian critique of U.S. nationalism, articulated by the Fugitive literary movement in the 1920s and the conservative Agrarian politics in the 1930s.

marginalization is ironically self-defeating in its effect. Such a cultural critique by defining a unified, essential native self is itself authorized by the existing hegemonic colonizing other that is equally essentialized: southern nativism is dependent on the continuing existence of a unified, colonized native self that is valorized against an equally essentialized colonizing other. For example, Allen Tate in his 1945 essay "The New Provincialism" articulated the Agrarian critique of US literary nationalism by contending that "not even literary nationalism could abort a genuine national literature when it is ready to appear, when, in fact, we become a nation" (536). It is a kind of regional nationalism grounded on the mythical understanding of the South as an "imagined community" that can be *imagined* with the belief that the role of the critics is to inform an intimate knowledge and assessing indigenous values of a literary text *from the inside*. Such a critique is vitiated from the outset by its own cultural insiderism as it is inevitably achieved by constructing a univocal voice as the unchallengeable measure of authenticity against any threat of marginalizing center and internal pluralism such as the internal voices of white women and of African Americans.[34] As a

---

34 Here I have in mind Toni Morrison's revisionist approach to American literary history, particularly her notion of "Africanist presence" in *Playing in the Dark* as a means of unveiling of "the parasitical nature of white freedom" (57), which bears some relevance to the Faulknerian understanding of the US South: "As for the culture, the imaginative

result, it allows the dominant center to determine the terms of its own cultural identity since basing its articulation on opposition amounts to taking the terms of its assertion from a discourse by an Other. In this regard, the binary of Northern center and Southern margin always overdetermines the debates revolving around American and Southern studies and requires a major intervention in the narcissistic nativism of the South that is ultimately exceptionalist as much as the marginalizing Northern center is. It is precisely within this context that I call for a need for "geographical detours" as a means of throwing light on southern hybridity or plural notion of southernness—the U.S. South that is indelibly both "Yankee" and "hemispheric."

"Geographical detours" poses the following questions: is there any other alternative way to view the U.S. South *not* through the prism of the narcissistic nativism from the inside and the marginalizing imperial gaze from the outside; how can one

---

and historical terrain upon which early American writers journeyed is in large measure shaped by the presence of the racial other. Statements to the contrary, insisting on the meaninglessness of race to the American identity, are themselves full of meaning. The world does not become raceless or will not become unracialized by assertion. The act of enforcing racelessness in literary discourse is itself a racial act. Pouring rhetorical acid on the fingers of a black hand may indeed destroy the prints, but not the hand. Besides, what happens in that violent, self-serving act of erasure to the hands, the fingers, the finger-prints of the one who does the pouring? Do they remain acid-free? The literature itself suggests otherwise" (46). See also Ralph Ellison's "What America Would be like without Blacks?"

articulate the connections between the colonial, postcolonial, postnational, and the New World perspectives? The utmost caution should be executed when one considers what may lurk behind all the revisionary impulses to rethink the boundaries of the South in reading Faulkner. In other words, while extending the very notion of Southernness nationally, postnationally, and transnationally, we may unwittingly redraw another boundary no matter how much we try to cross it, eventually allowing room for new forms of redemptive marginality and triumphant nationalism. Consequently, as I see all those revisionary accounts of various forms of southernness, I am brought back to the fact that the very way we read Faulkner is overdetermined by what southernness signifies. Despite a plethora of efforts to lay down a definition of its identity, the South has never been reducible to a geographical criterion. The south is actually made up of *many* Souths such as geographical, temporal, and illusory rather than merely set in the South itself.

Given the boundaries of different constituencies that shape a fundamental compulsion of the U.S. South's ongoing regional—albeit far more stretched than that as expounded so far—identity, this chapter is devoted to reading Faulkner's *Light in August* (1932) to overcome the idea of a monolithic South. The selection of *Light in August* as a main source of discussion in this chapter is intentional. It has been relatively ignored for a long time in recent Faulkner studies, which is remarkable when compared with scholars' abiding interest in *Absalom, Absalom!* (1936).[35] It is not only because *Absalom, Absalom!*'s engagement with the legacy of racialized chattel slavery in the Afro-Caribbean and Euro-American colonial web enables critics to read Faulkner as a different kind of regionalist beyond the confines of regional and national boundaries, but also because consideration of race in *Light in August* predictably has occupied center stage in the criticism of the novel.[36] I would put forth an argument here that *Light in August* is the text that articulates a pluralistic notion of southernness receptive not only to racial and cultural entanglements but also to intrusive and hybridizing forces of history and ideology that unpredictably makes the insular town of Jefferson a disruptive site of intersecting impulses always in tension. Faulkner's South is subject to and implicated in

---

35 For a comprehensive study of creole connections in the text, see Kutzinsky's "Borders and Bodies: The United States, America, and the Caribbean" and Matthews' "Recalling the West Indies: From Yoknapatawpha to Haiti and Back" among many others.

36 Patricia McKee examines in a chapter titled "Playing White Men in *Light in August*" in her *Producing American Races* (1999) the southern tragedy as the fatal inextricability of white and black lives and the discussion of Joe Christmas as "blackness" that is "transformed into a formless fluid" (145); Weinstein analyzes the effect of interpellation on Joe as a racial subject in his comparative study of Faulkner and Toni Morrison; Thadious Davis looks into the disfiguration of black lives through the lens of racial stereotypes during Jim Crow. James Snead considers Joe Christmas to be a semiotic embodiment of transgressing the binary cultural codes of the segregated South.

distinctive forms of representation. As a matrix of ceaseless input and output of unpredictable forces of history, southernness in *Light in August* comes to entertain a set of representations that never stop at an "empty" geography of pure textuality but continue to recuperate material grounding and historical content. In order to bring into legibility how southernness in *Light in August* as a marker of an ongoing compulsion of the Southern identity is forged in and through interactions and engagements of conflicting forces of history, I begin my discussion with a critical dialogue with traditional and current Faulkner studies—taking "methodological detours" before proceeding to "geographical detours."

Critical Detours: Locating Faulkner in Southern Studies

It is always of genuine interest to remember that Faulkner was first dismissed by early journalistic reviews usually as either a naturalistic, sensational Southern regionalist or a southern gothic writer. It was only in the 1950s that Faulkner was inducted into the hall of fame of the great American writers gifted with the power to articulate the American national imagination. For instance, R.W.B. Lewis includes Faulkner in this "great" tradition together with Nathaniel Hawthorne, Herman Melville, and Henry James who, Lewis observes, created the quintessential prototype of the "American Adam" through "a genuinely myth-making imagination" (127). The praise of Faulkner as a great "American" writer is founded on the old verities of Faulkner criticism represented by the Southern Agrarians and New Critics such as Cleanth Brooks, Hyatt Waggoner, and Robert Penn Warren to name a few who constructed a narrative of human universality with which Faulkner's early fame was credited. This critical attention to the "universal" Faulkner had remained central in Faulkner studies for a long time before it was under attack by a new generation of scholars who began to examine how Faulkner transcends local values. It is not a mere coincidence that both Waggoner's *William Faulkner: From Jefferson to the World* (1959) and Brooks' *William Faulkner: The Yoknapatawpha Country* (1963) emphasize Faulkner's art of fictional geographical construction not only in their titles—Jefferson and Yoknapatawpha rather than Oxford, Mississippi and Lafayette in contrast to Glissant's *Faulkner, Mississippi*—but also in their discussion of archetype, mythical pattern, and ritual. What is problematic here is that these critics' prolonged silence on the local and provincial subjects is not accidental but structural: what such silence entails are a move from the empirical to textual creation and a discursive locus that endorses a particular ideology.

Beneath the portrayal of the universal Faulkner transcending the ephemera of his provincial materials lies New Criticism's intense but masked desire for restoring a lost organic unity of the old South stripped of its particularity as Terry Eagleton points out: "New Criticism was the ideology of an uprooted, defensive intelligentsia who reinvented in literature what they could not locate in reality" (47). Based upon the Fugitive literary movement in the 1920s and the conservative Agrarian politics in the 1930s, New Criticism's critical apparatus deflects attention away from the real world in which Faulkner himself was so much immersed and instead creates a self-enclosed object substantially intact to the extent that the torrent of historical realities can never enter into a crystallized imaginary world. It is heavily colored by nostalgia for a lost world and the very necessity of the *return* to that world is predicated on the premise that indigenous values existed prior to the historical experiences of defeat and domination. And then the present conditions of literary and cultural production that are unmoored in any authenticity are meaningful only as long as they exist for the return to an organic unity—the integration with what it *was*.

It was in the 1980s that a group of scholars such as Eric Sundquist, Lee Jenkins, Thadious M. Davis, and Walter Taylor among many others began to challenge the New Criticism's several decades' stranglehold on Faulkner studies. Their critical interest lies not in finding the formal unity and universal resonance of his work but in creating a "new" Faulkner by drawing attention to the unresolved tensions, contradictions, and inconsistencies lingering around the Faulknerian world. They may show different critical sensibilities, but they all share a belief that it is Faulkner's immersion in his own provincial materials—"my own little postage stamp of native soil" as the he said in *The Paris Review* interview in 1956—that should shape the essential premises of Faulkner criticism. To those scholars, New Criticism's call for close reading is to do more than insist on due attentiveness to the text. As they think that it always goes hand in hand with disentangling the text from social and historical contexts, they seek to rescue Faulkner from the aesthetic complacency of New Criticism. The very newness of their approaches arises from the ways in which they absorb contextual insights and reconfigure the Southern experience within particular contexts. Sundquist's *Faulkner: The House Divided* is a case in point here, in which he defines the novels that truly deserve critical attention as "the ones in which the nation's most tragic and defining *historical experience* found its appropriately convulsive forms of expression" (xi, my emphasis). Subsequently, postcolonial, transnational, and regional studies have found rich lodes in an entangling web of conflicting forces that deny a transparent agenda in Faulkner studies and instead call for an objective of overcoming the notion of "a monolithic South." In what follows, I shall discuss such efforts in Faulkner criticism by categorizing into what I call an "inward" path and an "outward" path respectively.

When one takes a first step inwardly, Richard Gray's idea of "southern self-fashioning" in his 2000 *Southern Aberrations:*

Writers of the American South and the Problems of Regionalism catches the eye of any scholar whose interest consists in how southern writers have constructed the idea of the South through the lens of the interplay between aesthetics and culture. Michael Kreyling's *Inventing Southern Literature*, Patricia Yaeger's *Dirt and Desire: Reconstituting Southern Women's Writing, 1930-1990*, Scott Romine's *The Narrative Forms of Southern Community*, and McKay Jenkins' *The South in Black and White: Race, Sex, and Literature in the 1940s* (1999) are also in line with Gray's revisionary impulse to reconsider all the critical assumptions underlying the traditional notions of southern literature and regional identity and thereby recreate a more pluralistic notion of southernness.

Gray's major argument in his *Southern Aberration* is that the notion of southernness can be located by gauging the extent to which the South is distanced from a national cultural capital and southernness itself is being perpetuated by constructing South as an alternative center—"aberrance" from both a national norm and its own literary-historical traditionalism. What he is truly interested in is not so much the distance between margin and center as the risks the South has to take when it reacts to its cultural alienation by redefining itself as an *insider*, from whose insideness is ironically constructed an alternative center complete with its own master narrative. For instance, Gray reexamines Edgar Allan Poe in this light by exploring Poe's ambivalence—to "compensate or revel in his 'deviance'" (34) from both the center of the American nation and the putative Southern mainstream. As Gray shows through the discussion of how the Agrarian critics of the 1930s to 1950s made their own institutionalized canon through a reconfiguration of "norm" and "aberrance" within both national and regional contexts, a group of southern writers whose writings did not fit in with the prevailing Southern literary tradition were defined as "aberrant" and eventually ignored. Gray thus makes visible the "intrinsic plurality" *inwardly* by reconsidering the dominant literary traditions and our own understanding of the regional and national cultures. In accordance with Gray, Romine finds it necessary to reconfigure regional identity with an eye toward overcoming the idea of "a monolithic South." He looks into the ways in which the southern compulsion is expressed in a southern narrative form to construct close-knit communities and protect them from both within and without. As such, when faced with the exclusive forces that work to keep the marginalized marginalized in the name of reconstructing an authentic cultural tradition, one cannot help finding the generally accepted notion of southern community itself actually fraught with tension and divide and the myth of homogeneous South itself quite questionable. And some of the mainstays of cultural beliefs by which southern culture has shaped its own identity are thus called into question.

An "outward" way of problematizing the notion of

southernness can be called a "post-regional" approach that draws new borderlines between the US South and the rest of the postplantation New World. It leads us into a new vista of the US South and the New World as mutually constitutive rather than as divided into "wilderness" and "jungle" as in an exceptionalist model.[37] For instance, *Look Away! The U.S. South in New World Studies* (2004) edited by Jon Smith and Deborah Cohn looks into the plantation complex as a means of taking a detour from

---

37 In the preface to his 1956 *Errand into Wilderness*, a foundational text in American studies, Perry Miller recounts the so-called "jungle epiphany" on the banks of the Congo: "I came there seeking 'adventure,' jealous of older contemporaries to whom that boon had been offered by the First World War. (Nobody had the prescience to teach me patience, to assure me that I too should have my War.) The adventure that Africa afforded were tawdry enough, but it became the setting for a sudden epiphany (if the word be not too strong) of the pressing necessity for expounding my America to the twentieth century. [⋯] It was given to me, equally disconsolate on the edge of a jungle of central Africa, to have thrust upon me the mission of expounding what I took to be the innermost propulsion of the United States, while supervising, in that barbaric tropic, the unloading of drums of case oil flowering out of the inexhaustible wilderness of America" (vii-viii). The epiphany is used throughout the book to trace the Puritan origins of the American self as unique and exceptional. However, it can be also read against the exceptionalist vision of America—America as part of the interconnected spaces of African, Europe, and the New World in which underlying fear of miscegenation is deeply embedded. Amy Kaplan in her introduction to *Cultures of United States Imperialism* constructs an alternative genealogy of American studies by identifying the ways in which Miller tells the early American frontier and the "blank" jungle that should be kept "blank" to evade the responsibility for the US imperial practices and desires. The bipolar of a "blank" jungle and a noble frontier serves as a condition of possibility of the narrative of American exceptionalism.

the US South to the southern hemisphere and back.[38] Such a detour is carried to hitherto relatively underexplored areas that inspire recognition of the entangled web of regional, national, and transnational relations in the Americas. *Look Away!* critiques the parochial boundaries of the traditional American scholarship by rethinking those boundaries through the prism of the problematic figuration of the South in the New World contexts.[39]

Given that not a few Southern writers have been compelled to transgress the bounds of region and nation to reach out to

---

38 It should be noted that to consider the plantation as a mythical southern archetype always runs a risk of reifying it and ultimately reinforcing some entrenched stereotypes about the South and its culture.

39 See also Deborah Cohn's *History and Memory in the Two Souths: Recent Southern and Spanish American Fiction* (1999) and George Handley's *Postslavery Literatures in the Americas: Family Portraits in Black and White* (2000). In a stimulating manner, the New World context in rethinking the South can signify on a variety of geographical scales and thus bring into relief new connections among Anglophone, Hispanaphone, and Francophone writers. It is not far-fetched to think within the context of Handley's discussion that the abjection of the South by the rest of the nation can lead to the consideration of the South as the first colony of US imperial drive. It is necessary to remember here that the integration of the New South after the Civil War by the Union was ironically carried out by consolidating the plantation complex on a hemispheric scale, which the North actually had disparaged for a long time: "despite its domestic attempt to move beyond the legacies of slavery after the Civil War, the United States manifested the symptoms of the plantation discourse by exploiting land and slave labor beyond U.S. boundaries while attempting to keep at bay the Africanized Creole cultures that it had helped to forge" (Handley 45).

the New World, the "outward" path can be immediately aligned with the "postnationalist" agenda the New Americanists such as Donald Pease and Amy Kaplan articulated in 1992, which is characterized by its insight into how the "fiction" of a coherent and homogeneous national space in its imperial design necessarily excludes raced and gendered others. That insight paves the way for an exploration of how the postplantation Americas are forged by constituting their centers and rims and, as a result, how "imagined communities" are formed. A counter-narrative of the nation can be thus weaved as a means of questioning the ways in which the very constructed identity of nation works as a totalizing force. It is truly a counter-narrative in the sense that it has a considerable discursive power to remind one of how the nation is "imagined" and how the constructedness of its identity is disguised as it has always been as such.[40] In this light, I would argue that Faulkner's work always can serve as a conduit for offering a new plane of intelligibility that stretches one's imagination well beyond the bounds of a geographical South and inspires recognition of its multiple connections with other peoples and territories outside its borders.

---

40 Homi Bhabha conceptualizes the counter-narratives of the nation as those "that continually evoke and erase its totalizing boundaries—both actual and conceptual—disturb the ideological maneuvers through which 'imagined communities' are given essentialist identities" (*Location* 149).

While the "inward/outward" paths' potentials for problematizing the notion of a monolithic South have been demonstrated, it remains to be seen if each path can really overcome both a narcissistic insiderism of the South and a marginalizing imperial gaze of the nation on the U.S. South. A defiant border-crossing desire is at the heart of a hemispheric and inter-American reading of Faulkner, but its Achilles heel is a seducing impulse to dismiss all the conventional conceptions of the regional and the national. Such a tendency is quite understandable as the very notion of southernness is being continually explored in accordance with the diminishing of the master narrative derived from the conflict between and among a plethora of classes, sub-regions, smaller communities, cultures, histories. However, it is still of utmost importance to make an effort to understand, if not necessarily pin down, the ever-changing nature of southernness. In this regard, it is interesting to find Sau-ling C. Wong's "Denationalization Reconsidered: Asian American Cultural Criticism at a Theoretical Crossroads" in *Postcolonial Theory and the United States: Race, Ethnicity, and Literature* (2000) edited by Amritjit Singh and Peter Schmidt. Originally published in 1992, Wong's article examines how an excessive preoccupation with the "diasporic" and "transnational" runs the risk of losing the focus on "domestic" issues in Asian American culture and history. Wong suggests that Asian American studies should have an eye for the experience of the national exclusion of Asian immigrants as a result of the U.S. imperialist design in the Pacific Rim areas. To her, the roots of Asian American culture lie in that experience and the ensuing formation of the identity of Asian Americans as a minority population of the United States.[41]

The inclusion of Wong's article in the volume serves as a case in point here to demonstrate what is gained and what is lost in celebrating the impulse to transgress all the geographical boundaries that are not infrequently likely to form a certain geographical fiction, illustrating the merits of inter-American approaches and the demerits of jettisoning the national altogether. There has been a vigorous debate since the early 1990s about how to apply postcolonial theory to the analysis of the U.S. history and culture. It may have contributed to disturbing the

---

41 For an incisive critique of Wong's "domestic" concerns, see Susan Koshy, who argues that "the term 'denationalized' is widely used in neoimperialist theory where it refers to the indigenous elites who collaborate with transnational corporate interests, setting them in an exploitative relationship to, and severed from the interests of, the people at large. Is Wong implying a parallel between transnational cultural critics and such elites? Since she does not indicate the source of here terminology, the prior association of the term makes her usage highly problematic. I would also argue that, in the politically contentious nineties, where the rhetoric against immigrants is so highly charged, a term like 'denationalization' can be easily appropriated into right-wing arguments about the difficulty of incorporating Asians into American nationhood" (340). I also bring up the complex linkage between the national and the transnational alongside the ongoing national frames and the academic turn towards transnationalism in the context of Asian American studies when reading Chang-Rae Lee's novels in the last chapter.

U.S. centrism, but it has also turned on other problems such as viewing the U.S. culture through the lens of internal colonialism and relating postcolonialism to ethnic studies in general. Obviously, U.S. culture has some complexities that should be explored through postcolonial perspectives, but this does not necessarily mean that the current progressive narratives of the postcolonial and hemispheric are always at odds with regional and national concerns. Those complexities should be discussed by reconsidering the following questions: can all racial and regional minorities particularly in the United States be considered to be postcolonial; what constitutes the postcolonial aspects of US culture in general and US southern culture in particular; how can the prefix "post" in postcolonial be periodized and differentiated from the "post" in postnational and the "trans" in transnational?[42] Accordingly, it becomes much more challenging to ask how one can avoid redeeming the validity of each perspective—regional, national, transnational—in the name of broadening the field of

---

42 For a consideration of the temporality of the "post," see Anthony Appiah, 58; Robert Young, 4; Radhakrishnan, *Diasporic*, 157-59. Radhakrishnan suggests: "My point is that the chronotope of the 'post' can be studied with reference to the 'time-space' after colonialism without necessarily privileging the 'post' as a free-floating signifier. For, in a real sense, aren't 'we' all looking for a genuine 'time-place'—that is, *after* colonialism, a chronotope that has made a break from the *longue durée* of colonialism? The challenging and complex question is how to enable a mutually accountable dialogue among the many locations that have something important to say about 'the after' of postcoloniality" (158).

southern studies beyond region and nation.

Interestingly, Faulkner appears as a major component of the debate in *Look Away!*—a preeminent white-male-southern-modernist Faulkner whom most contributors to the volume consider to be a transnational touchstone in American literature.[43] The contributors use Faulkner's oeuvre as a springboard not only for jumping out of the bounds of the regional and national but also for returning to the roots of U.S. southern culture. Straddling the borders precariously, Faulkner reminds us that any attempt to reach the hemispheric can be made possible only by taking a detour around the regional and the other way around. It is precisely at this point that "regional" and "post-regional"—inward and outward paths in my words—converge and bring forth a set of tensions in reading Faulkner. Geographical and methodological detours I have taken so far can open up a space in which the shift of focus from *the* South to a South or South*s* becomes possible.[44]

---

43 As Wendy B. Faris, Ilan Stavans, and other contributors to *Look Away!* observe, Hispanophone and Francophone writers have read Faulkner in hemispheric terms for quite some time. Jorge Luis Borges reviewed several Faulkner novels in the late 1930s and translated *The Wild Palms* in 1941. Carlos Fuentes commented on his connection to Faulkner in "La novella como tragedia" (1970). Glissant linked the Mississippi writer to Carpentier, Garcia Marquez, and other novelists of the Americas in *Caribbean Discourse*, first published in French in 1981.

44 I would like to build upon Doreen Massey's "A Global Sense of Place" here as a useful guidance for a redefinition of place as an "inclusive" but "progressive" site of social

---

life. The search for an authentically rooted sense of place is understandable in a deeply ambiguous postmodern life as long as the political use of the particularity of place can be acknowledged as a form of resistance against the encroachment of global capitalism. One of the problems attendant upon this kind of thinking is that the investment in place often lapses into an exclusionary force by which people try to build their own communities and define themselves against threatening others who are not included in the particular vision of place being enacted. Such a tension is textualized into Massey's essay: "Many of those who write about time-space compression emphasize the insecurity and unsettling impact of its effects, the feelings of vulnerability which it can produce. Some, therefore, go on from this to argue that, in the middle of all this flux, people desperately need a bit of peace and quiet—and that a strong sense of place, of locality, can form one kind of refuge from the hubbub. So the search after the 'real' meanings of place, the unearthing of heritages and so forth, is interpreted as being, in part, a response to the desire for fixity and for the security of identity in the middle of all the movement and change. A 'sense of place,' of rootedness, can provide—in this form and on this interpretation—stability and a source of unproblematic identity. [⋯] There are some serious inadequacies in this argument. There is the question of why it is assumed that time-space compression will produce insecurity. There is the need to face up to—rather than simply deny—people's need for attachment of some sort, whether through place or anything else. Nonetheless, it is certainly the case that there is indeed at the moment a recrudescence of some very problematic sense of place, from reactionary nationalism, to competitive localism, to introverted obsessions with 'heritage.' We need, therefore, to think through what might be an adequately progressive sense of place, one which would fit in with the current global-local times and the feelings and relations they give rise to, *and*, which would be useful in what are, after all, political struggles often inevitably based on place. The question is how to hold on to that notion of geographical difference, of uniqueness, even of rootedness if people want that, without it being reactionary" (*Space* 151-52). She suggests that any place exists not as separating itself from the world outside but as defining itself through its interactions with a wider world outside.

As Doreen Massey argues, the "progressive" sense of place is here predicated on the idea that a sense of place comes into being when a particular "constellation of social relations" comes together in a place that is always open to an alternative interpretation of it: "what gives a place its specificity is not some long internalized history but the fact that it is constructed out of a particular constellation of social relations, meeting and weaving together at a particular locus" (*Space* 154). Massey does not necessarily repudiate a sense of rootedness, a singular form of place-bound identity, and a clear sense of boundaries all together. Rather, she views the notion of place as a *process* made up of multiple identities and histories. When brought to bear upon critical debates in Faulkner studies, Massey's "progressive sense of place" is suggestive of the new ways of thinking that echo Glissant's "relational space." Glissant's conception of Martinique/Caribbean space does not completely resist comprehension, but it is suggested as something that can be perceived within the context of a larger plane of intelligibility. While influenced by Fanonian nationalism and Césairean negritude that seek to stabilize postcolonial space by operating on the ideological planes of intelligibility, Glissant takes a step further by cultivating the fertile historical ground of which the materiality is articulated by global awareness. In doing so, he conceives of a Caribbean space within a New World archipelago that has no redemptive origin. His literary project is thus characterized by lodging itself in a collective hemispheric consciousness through a critical *detour* around the Americas—the poetics of relation that can be made possible by moving outward to understand better the point of departure and moving back inward to have a keen insight into the repeated crossings the detour makes rather than searching for an origin and stabilizing the center.

> Faulkner's work, somehow theological. This writing is about digging up roots in the South—an obvious place to do so in the United States. But the root begins to act like a rhizome; there is no basis for certainty; the relation is tragic. Because of this dispute over source, the sacred—but henceforth unspeakable—enigma of the root's location. Faulkner's world represents one of the thrilling moments in the modern poetics of Relation. At one time I regretted that such a world had not gone farther, spreading its vision into the Caribbean and Latin America. But, perhaps, this was a reaction of unconscious frustration on the part of one who felt excluded. (*Poetics* 21-22)

If Faulkner's South is not the site of lost origin but a place that can be arrived at only by taking "detours," the tortuous path to it can lead to envisioning new relations and connections that allow for a new representation. Such a potential is precisely what Glissant calls "one of the thrilling moments in the modern poetics of Relation," which can be put to creative use to challenge the notion of a monolithic South without lapsing into the tautology of benign hybridity or another redemptive myth of relationality. Thus far I have examined a set of critical questions embedded in different registers of various perspectives in an effort to provide an interpretive frame for the analysis of *Light in August*. In the next part, I will bring into focus what can be revealed through such geographical and critical detours around, through, and to the South.

"Doomed with Movement"

What I pursue first is to break away from a formalist approach to a more nuanced discussion of how Faulkner both creates and negotiates a place called the South and how that place speaks in and from the space of narrative within a framework of spatial imagination. A group of earlier critics called attention to the geographical parallels between Faulkner's fictional Yoknapatawpha County and Oxford, and Lafayette County and Oxford, Mississippi.[45] While skeptical of such parallels, Faulkner

---

45 See Ward L. Miner's *The World of William Faulkner* (1952), Calvin S. Brown's A *Glossary of Faulkner's South* (1967) and "Faulkner's Geography and Topography" (1962). Charles S. Aiken also calls attention to the issues from a geographer's perspective in his articles: "Faulkner's Yoknapatawpha County: A Place in the American South" (1979);

scholars are still preoccupied with the verities of the Faulknerian cosmos in relation to the world he lived in.[46] It is hard to deny that Faulkner's representation is deeply rooted in the southern sense of place, culture, and history. As Charles Aiken argues in *William Faulkner and the Southern Landscape* (2009), "Faulkner leaves no doubt as to the exact location of Yoknapatawpha" and "[t]he setting of Yoknapatawpha is accurate even to perception of location" (21). However, Faulkner's portrayal of reality is not necessarily limited to reality itself.[47] Unlike the approaches of

---

"Faulkner's Yoknapatawpha County: Geographical Fact into Fiction" (1977).

46 For example, Calvin Brown raise the question of "what we mean when we say that Faulkner's Jefferson 'is' Oxford—or, more emphatically, 'is really' Oxford": "Jefferson is a fictitious town inhabited by people of Faulkner's creation, no matter how much raw material local scenes and characters may have supplied to his imagination. Nor can it be maintained that everything stated about the history of Jefferson is true about the past of Oxford" (652). His idea is more finely developed than the approaches of earlier critics, but it still depends on the sharp divide between reality and fiction, and thus lacks scrupulous attention to the complex interrelation between them.

47 Malcolm Cowley in his *The Portable Faulkner* explains this "intertextuality" by identifying "a double labor" in Faulkner's novels: "The pattern was based on what he saw in Oxford or remembered from his childhood; on scraps of family tradition (the Falkners, as they spelled the name, and had played their part in the history of the state); on kitchen dialogues between the black cook and her amiable husband; on Saturday-afternoon gossip in Courthouse Square; on stories told by men in overalls squatting on their heels while they passed around a fruit jar full of white corn liquor; on all the sources familiar to a small-town Mississippi boy—But the whole of it was elaborated, transformed, given convulsive life by his emotions; until by simple intensity of feeling the figures in it became a little more

those critics whose interest lies in creating more mimetic or accurate maps by finding similarities between the "real" world and the "fictional" world, foremost attention here rests on the intertextuality in *Light in August* between the world he lived in and his own created cosmos. What I mean by the "intertextual" is that Faulkner's narratives operate between the geography of the real and the geography of the imaginary—as the "real-and-imagined" space as discussed in the first chapter—and thereby establish new forms of representation and new ways of imaging place.

It is noteworthy that Joe Christmas is presented from the beginning in terms of rootlessness and homelessness: "there was something definitely rootless about him, as though no town nor city was his, no street, no walls, no square of earth his home" (27). His rootlessness and homelessness are closely associated with the ambiguity of his racial identity, from which arises an intriguing question—is he neither black nor white or both black and white? Joe is not a black man who passes for white. If the underlying

---

than human, became heroic or diabolical, became symbols of the old South, of war and reconstruction, of commerce and machinery destroying the standards of the past. There in Oxford, Faulkner performed a labor of imagination that has not been equaled in our time, and a double labor: first, to invent a Mississippi county that was like a mythical kingdom, but was complete and living in all its details; second, to make his story of Yoknapatawpha County stand as a parable or legend of the Deep South" (viii).

assumption of racial passing is that one can know the secret of his or her own racial identity and the closure of a narrative of racial passing is related to the subject's self-recognition within the binary of black and white, *Light in August* presents Joe's racial dilemma not through the disclosure of a secret about his racial identity but through the *creation* of a secret.[48] Those who surround Joe see the white-skinned protagonist as black the moment they learn that Joe's biological father may be of black or mixed race ancestry. Joe Christmas in turn sees himself through the eyes of those who alternately see him as white and as black. The thirty-year span of the troubled relations he has born to blacks and whites teaches him that when people do learn of the *possibility* of his "black blood," he will be immediately considered black. As Joe's identity is left as a secret to himself, he is disempowered by the secret itself and becomes a stranger to himself. At times he would trick "white men into calling him a negro in order to fight them." At other times, "he fought the negro who called him white" (225). Joe would sleep with white and black women in the North and the South. When low on money, Joe would sleep with white

---

48 For the discussion of various aspects of racial passing and its cultural representation in US literature and culture, see Gayle Wald's *Crossing the Line: Racial Passing in Twentieth-Century U.S. Literature and Culture* (2000); Stephen Belluscio's *To Be Suddenly White: Literary realism and Racial Passing* (2006); Marcia Alesan's *Racial Passing and the Color of Cultural Identity* (2012).

prostitutes and then tell them he was a negro. Horrified by this knowledge, the white women would not accept payment as if to deny that the sexual encounter had ever occurred. As such, his whole identity has been put at risk by the very gesture by which he seeks to secure his racial identity: denying his whiteness and affirming his blackness bring him no closer to realizing his identity as a black man than affirming his whiteness and denying his blackness bring him to securing his identity as a white man. Joe is neither a person of mixed race seeking to find his true identity as black or white nor a black person attempting to pass for white. He is not a white person either who has discovered he is black. Rather, he happens to suspect that his whiteness is not pure or original: "I think I got some nigger blood in me [⋯] I don't know" (196-97). As a result, it hardly matters to decide if Joe is black or white, weighed against the traumatic burden placed upon his shoulder by the very *possibility* of ever being black.

In a frequently quoted passage in *The Souls of Black Folk*, W. E. B. Du Bois speaks of an African American "double consciousness," a "two-ness" of being "an American, a Negro" (9). At the heart of this "sense of always looking at one's self through the eye of others" (9) is an internal conflict in the African American individual between what is "African" and what is "American." Whereas Du Bois's discussion of double consciousness concerns an internal split of African Americans, Joe's racial dilemma becomes more complicated in the sense that his racial identity is not so much "two-ness" but "nothingness." Faulkner once made an account of Joe's tragedy of being "nothing":

> He didn't know what he was, and so he was *nothing*. He deliberately evicted himself from the human race because he didn't know which he was. That was his tragedy [···] that he didn't know what he was, and there was no way possible in life for him to find out, which to me is the most tragic condition a man could find himself in—not to know what he is and to know that he will never know. (qtd. in Gwynn 72, emphasis mine)

An irony arising from Joe's unstable perception of himself is that he becomes a threatening presence to racial classification in the post-Emancipation South that seek to flatten him into a presence of one or the other color. Racial categorization itself actually has nothing to do with color *per se*, since his presence calls into question all the claims to a fixed and stable racial identity and highlights the constructedness of race, both black and white.[49] If "blackness has no meaning outside of a system of race-

---

49 James Baldwin maintains in a similar vein that "You can only be destroyed by believing that you really are what the white world calls a nigger" (4) at the beginning of 1963 *The Fire Next Time* and that "color is not a personal reality; it is a political reality" (104) by the end of it. He pushes forward this idea further by arguing that white supremacism is ironically trapped in a history which white people themselves do not know: "they [white

conscious people and practices" (West 38-39), so does whiteness in *Light in August*. It is precisely in this context that Toni Morrison demonstrates in *Playing in the Dark* why and how whiteness has no meaning but in relation to blackness in American literature and culture. If Du Boisian double consciousness signifies a self-conscious manner in which African Americans experience divided racial identity, Morrison's notion of "Africanist presence" (6) within the obsessive white imagination renders dramatically visible the desperate manner in which the *invention* of whiteness seeks to repress or erase such historical legacies as slavery and discrimination, depending, at the same time, upon the *invention* of blackness. Morrison argues that whiteness is, in fact, nothing without blackness or "Africanist presence" as she terms it. Put otherwise, the constitution of the quintessential identity of America—based upon the American promise of equality, freedom, and democracy—depends integrally on the four-hundred-year-old presence of blacks in America. This "Africanist" presence becomes "something the Unites States cannot do without" (47), thereby revealing the "parasitical nature of the white freedom" (57).

---

people] have had to believe for many years, and for innumerable reasons, the black men are inferior to white men. Many of them, indeed, know better, but [···] people find it difficult to act on what they know" (8-9).

As shown in the District Attorney Gavin Stevens' theory that "it was the black blood which snatched up the pistol and the white blood which would not let him fire it" (449), the metaphor of blood comes to replace the physical signs of race.[50] Joe Christmas, then, as "an American double-being who breaks all the semiotic codes of society" (Snead 81), lays bare both the black self-conscious experience of irreducible psychological, cultural division and the white's delusion of psychological, cultural autonomy. As such, Joe Christmas paradoxically becomes a kind of *nothing* that dramatizes the parasitical nature of white identity formation and the devastating effect that such racial identity-defining process imposes on the person who unmasks the white supremacism's fabrication of blackness. His presence as a particular reference to the possibility of miscegenation reminds one that identities of those who appear untouched by race are *always already* deeply inflected by race. The doubleness/nothingness of Joe's racial identity offers sufficient evidence that

---

50 One may find an interesting parallel of Stevens' theory in Mark Twain's *Pudd'nhead Wilson* (1894), in which Roxy, a "white negro," connects blood to behavior: "It de nigger in you dat's what it is. Thirty-one parts o' you is white en only one part nigger, en dat po little one part is yo soul" (157). In parallel fashion, if Joe is framed into being a "Negro" by the oppressive racial discourse, "Negro becomes a superficial delineation which is not a matter of blood but a matter of life style, adherence to preconceived behavioral norms" (Davis 131-32).

whiteness is constructed not merely as white but as *not* black as much as blackness not merely as black but as *not* white. Such recognition both extends and broadens the critical scope of racial identity formation as "a social construct" (Davis 130) that is highly unstable, indeterminate, and even fictive, thereby making visible all the specious claims to whiteness and blackness through Joe's presence as both "doubleness" and "nothingness."[51] Throughout the novel, Joe Christmas figures as "the carrier of an originless blackness that clandestinely inserts its way into the presumably pure [southern] genealogies" (Snead 113) while falling a victim to the South's refusal to admit its own racial and cultural hybridity.

---

51 Here I have in mind Etienne Balibar's understanding of a "fictive" aspect of race in his discussion of the relationship between racism and nationalism: "No nation, that is, no national state, has an ethnic basis, which means that nationalism cannot be defined as an ethnocentrism except precisely in the sense of the product of a *fictive* ethnicity. To reason any other way would be to forget that 'peoples' do not exist naturally any more than 'races' do, either by virtue of their ancestry, a community of culture or pre-existing interests. But they do have to institute in real (and therefore in historical) time their imaginary unity *against* other possible unities" (49). In addition, Balibar invokes a paradoxical moment when universalism and racism are not so much opposed as intertwined features of the nation-state by identifying a "fluctuating gap" between "the representations and practices of racism and nationalism" (54). This gap effects an externalized action of excluding national others, which Balibar describes as necessary to effect the nation's internality. Racism constitutes "a supplement of nationalism or more precisely a supplement internal to nationalism, as always in excess of it, but always indispensable to its constitution and yet always still insufficient to achieve its project, just as nationalism is both indispensable to and always insufficient to achieve the formation of the nation" (54).

The way Faulkner presents Joe's "originless" racial identity is to move him around circles that he "has never broken out of" and "cannot ever undo" (339). This circular form utilizing spatial elements stands in stark contrast to Lena Grove's slow but consistent movement along a straight line. The contrast of the circle and the straight line begins to take on more complicated symbolic meaning through a series of spatial reconfigurations from the barren, ruined fields, the broken gate to the vignettes of "dark" houses of Joanna Burden and Hightower that are suggestive of the residents' lives cut off from the outside world. Joe's fifteen years of wandering through streets accentuates the stasis underlying his movements—the streets which "ran into Oklahoma and Missouri and as far south as Mexico and then back north to Chicago and Detroit and then back south again and at last to Mississippi" (234). As such, he is "doomed with movement," which portends his returning to the same point—his "originless" racial identity and, ultimately, willed death:

> He thought that it was loneliness which he was trying to escape and not himself. But the street ran on: catlike, one place was the same as another to him. But in none of them could he be quiet. But the street ran in its moods and phases, always empty: he might have seen himself as in numberless avatars, in silence, *doomed with motion*, driven by the courage of flagged and spurred despair; by the despair of courage whose opportunities

> had to be flagged and spurred. He was thirtythree years old. One afternoon the street had become a Mississippi country road. He had been put off a southbound freight train near a small town. He did not know the name of the town; he didn't care what word it used for name. He didn't even see it, anyway. He skirted it, following the woods, and came to the road and looked in both directions. It was not a graveled road, though it looked to be fairly well used. He saw several negro cabins scattered here and there along it; then he saw, about a half mile away, a larger house. It was a big house set in a grove of trees; obviously a place of some pretensions at one time. But now the trees needed pruning and the house had not been painted in years. But he could tell that it was inhabited, and he had not eaten in twentyfour hours. 'That one might do,' he thought. (226, emphasis mine)

The deceptive mobility of Joe who is "doomed with motion" is textualized into the Faulknerian space-time foundation of Yoknapatawpha. Basically, it has its roots in the Southern sense of pace, but it is also what should be stretched out with Joe wandering "a thousand savage and lone streets" (220), going as far south as Mexico, then as far north as Chicago and Detroit, then back south again, finally ending up in an abandoned slave cabin behind Joanna Burden's mansion. Glissant defines wandering as a person's destiny characterized by "the capacity to maintain oneself in living suspension, far from foundational and systematic certainties" (*Faulkner* 117). To Glissant, the capacity to wander is tied to the difficulty of criticizing one's community and yet remaining part of it, which runs through all of Faulkner's major novels, fraught as they are with contradictions and inconsistencies. It is precisely at this point that the fictional and regional settings of Jefferson lead to a larger discussion of the South that is to be stretched out far beyond region and nation, and *Light in August* serves as a text that offers one of the most profound insights into the cultural and historical heritage of slavery as well as racial hysteria in the post-Emancipation South. The very anxiety that plagues him thus reflects a foundational uncertainty as to what constitutes the boundaries of the South, and it should come as no surprise that Joe ends up in a deserted "negro cabin" behind Joanna's old colonial mansion still overshadowed by the heritage of the past such as plantation life and slavery "loud with the treble shouts of generations" (385). Joanna's house is a place haunted by the somber forces of the past and functions as a setting for the owner's nightmarish struggle with the heritage of white man's sin and burden colored by her own anachronic attachment to a stern Calvinism.

The Burdens Burdened by History

If Joe Christmas is interpellated by Miss Atkins, a dietician at the orphanage, as "nigger bastard" (122) in a primal scene, another bizarre scene that foreshadows Joanna Burden's strained and troubled relationship unfolds when her father, Nathaniel, shows his four-year-old daughter the hidden gravesites of her grandfather and brother.[52] He tells her that "[t]he curse of the black race is God's curse. But the curse of the white race is the black man who will be forever God's chosen own because He once cursed him":

> Remember this. Your grandfather and brother are lying there, murdered not by one white man but by the curse which God put on a whole race before your grandfather or your brother or me or you were even thought of. A race doomed and cursed to be forever and ever a part of the white race's doom and curse for its sins. Remember that. His doom and his curse. Forever and ever. Mine. Your mother's. Yours, even though you are a

---

52 I am here indebted to the Althusserian concept of "ideological interpellation of subject," which means that individuals are always-already subjects who, ignorant of how they have thus been subjectified, accept their roles within the system of production relations. He defines ideology as a representation of the *imaginary* relationship of individuals to their real conditions of existence. See Althusser, especially 127-86.

> child. The curse of every white child that ever was born and that ever will be born. None can escape it. [···] I saw all the little babies that would ever be in the world, the ones not yet even born—a long line of them with their arm spread, on the black crosses. I couldn't tell then whether I saw it or dreamed it. But it was terrible to me. I cried at night. At last I told father, tried to tell him. What I wanted to tell him was that I must escape, get away from under the shadow, or I would die. "You cannot," he said. "You must struggle, rise. But in order to rise, you must raise the shadow with you. But you can never lift it to your level. I see that now, which I did not see until I came down here. But escape it you cannot. The curse of the black race is God's curse. But the curse of the white race is the black man who will be forever God's chosen own because He once cursed him." (252-53)

What Nathaniel is trying to pass down to his young daughter—the message that the black man's curse is the problem of white people— poses a set of questions due to its ambivalence. Nathaniel suggests that if the curse of the black man is put by God, the white man in turn should accept responsibility for the black man's curse since the curse of the white man is that the black man is cursed. This sense of responsibility leads to the Burdens' "burden" of uplifting blacks. In the undercurrent of Nathaniel's logic is the reiteration of the "white man's burden" in so far as he believes that the white man is cursed by the very presence of the black man and by the responsibility of caring for the cursed black man.

However, Nathaniel, to one's surprise, never forgets to send a compelling message to his daughter. It is a message of what he has picked up while living a troubled life as a "nigger lover" in the South: she will not be able to "lift it (the black race) to [her] level" (253) no matter how much she endeavors. What does he mean by exhorting his daughter to help raise blacks without explaining why he considers that they cannot be elevated to an equal level of whites? Is he implying that the Burdens can never break away from the value of white supremacy and thus can never accept the full equality of blacks? Or, is he insisting that certain inherent differences between blacks and whites exist and that these differences will make impossible such efforts toward equalization? Nathaniel's warning here reveals the extent to which the Burdens' perception of blackness is not completely dissociated from the southern understanding of blackness despite the family's antislavery inclination. In actuality, establishing herself as a Burden ostensibly demands that Joanna should adopt the role of white philanthropist, and, in turn, adopting that role inevitably depends on the presence of blacks upon whom the philanthropist can bestow altruistic care. In other words, Joanna's identity as a Burden necessitates her identification of herself as a white philanthropist who stands in opposition to blacks whom she perceives to be in need of charitable assistance—the ironical and almost parasitical dependence of the Burdens' familial identity on blacks.

Viewed in this light, the Burdens can be said to harbor a conflicting desire for a recognizable other that can be reformed without posing any threat. This difference should not only sustain the distinction between whites and blacks on whom the Burdens' philanthropic guidance depends but also acknowledge blacks' potential for reformation and gradual approximation to the elevated condition of whites through the redeeming experience of white benevolent lead. At the same time, the Burdens' view on blacks demands that blacks be similar but different to the extent that the difference itself cannot threaten the white race's superiority. Accordingly, there is an ironic ambivalence in the Burdens' attitudes toward blacks as both comforting similarity and threatening difference "*as a subject of a difference that is almost the same, but not quite*."[53] This ambivalence explains

---

53 I have borrowed this phrase of "*as a subject of a difference that is almost the same, but not quite*" from Homi Bhabha. He interprets the regime of stereotype as evidence not of the stability of the disciplinary gaze of the colonizer, but of the *degree* to which the colonizer's identity is in fact fractured by contradictory psychic response to the colonized other—both desirous and afraid of the other: "Within that conflictual economy of colonial discourse which Edward Said describes as the tension between the synchronic panoptical vision of domination—the demand for identity, stasis—and the counterpressure of the diachrony of history—change, difference—mimicry represents an *ironic* compromise. If I may adapt Samuel Weber's formulation of the marginalizing vision of castration, then colonial

why Nathaniel has arrived at the realization that blacks cannot be raised to a level of whites while teaching his daughter to help uplift blacks. It is in this context that Joe Christmas provides Joanna Burden a perfect opportunity to secure her white identity while her abolitionist heritage and uplift work for blacks lead the Jefferson community to view her as a "nigger lover."

When Joe Christmas ends up sneaking into her house in desperate need of food and a place to live after many years of wandering around the country, Joanna Burden attempts to bolster her identity as a white patron in the tradition of her philanthropic family by molding a man of "unknown" race into a black man in spite of his white skin color. Such an attempt is made in their sexual relationship in the "honeymoon" (258) phase. She manipulates Joe by programming him into playing a variety of games she

---

mimicry is the desire for a reformed, recognizable Other, *as a subject of a difference that is almost the same, but not quite*. Which is to say, that the discourse of mimicry is constructed around an ambivalence; in order to be effective, mimicry must continually produce its slippage, its excess, its difference. The authority of that mode of colonial discourse that I have called mimicry is therefore stricken by an indeterminacy: mimicry emerges as the representation of a difference that is itself a process of disavowal. Mimicry is, thus the sign of a double articulation; a complex strategy of reform, regulation and discipline, which 'appropriates' the Other as it visualizes power. Mimicry is also the sign of the inappropriate, however, a difference or recalcitrance which coheres the dominant strategic function of colonial power, intensifies surveillance, and poses an immanent threat to both 'normalized' knowledges and disciplinary powers" (*The Location* 86).

devises. She entreats him to seek out letters and notes in hiding places. Joanna occasionally prearranges some private rendezvous between them behind the bushes or underneath trees where she waits for him naked and exclaims, "Negro! Negro! Negro!" (260) in the wild throes. In those trysts, she even imagines herself a white virgin raped by a black rapist. Her construction of Joe as a "Negro" foreshadows the racial hysteria which the community whips up when Joanna is found dead. The townspeople of Jefferson, believing "that she ha[s] been ravished, too," weave a narrative that she is killed "not by a negro, but by Negro" (288). She is then aligned with white supremacy and Southern "rape complex" (Sundquist, *Faulkner* 82) just as her immersion in the sexual taboo manifests her racist view of black male sexuality.[54]

Joanna Burden becomes a "burden" to Joe by bearing down upon his consciousness to the extent that he finds he cannot dissociate himself from her no matter how much he tries to. She is a "burden" to whatever possibility Joe has of existing outside of racial classification.[55] In their relationship, she shows no sign of

---

54 In his discussion of Joe's death within the context of René Girard's conceptualization of scapegoating and ritualized sacrifice, Sundquist interprets Joanna's posthumous elevation from a "Yankee" and "nigger lover" to a victimized white southern woman as echoing the typical southern fear of miscegenation and race complex.

55 Duvall argues that "Joanna has come to represent every tormentor in Joe's life: she is McEachern praying over him [⋯] she is Doc Hines in her religious fanaticism; she is Mrs.

recognizing Joe as he wishes to be recognized, but only sees him "as if he were a stranger" (268), which in turn gives rise to Joe's sense of alienation:

> He saw her but once more within the next two months. He followed his daily routine, save that he did not approach the house at all now, taking his meals downtown again, as when he had first gone to work at the mill. But then, when he first went to work, he would not need to think of her during the day; he hardly ever thought about her. Now he could not help himself. She was in his mind so constantly that it was almost as if he were looking at her, there in the house, patient, waiting, inescapable, crazy. During the first phase it had been as though he were outside a house where snow was on the ground, trying to get into the house; during the second phase he was at the bottom of a pit in the hot wild darkness; now he was in the middle of a plain where there was no house, not even snow, not even wind. (269)

Those feelings of being driven out, being engulfed, and being

---

McEachern through the parallel food-throwing scenes; she is Bobbie Allen, only now the surprise is menopause instead of menstruation; she is the dietician because of her sexual desire, association with food, and perhaps even because when the gun fails to discharge she seems to deny an expected punishment" (*Faulkner's Marginal Couple* 24).

isolated are a variation of the "loneliness" which Joe thinks "he was trying to escape" (226) when he first reaches Jefferson after wandering around the country for fifteen years. Consequently, Joe never overcomes his self-alienation through his relationship with Joanna. Joanna attempts to impose on Joe, first, her desire to create him as a "Negro" and, second, her wish to "raise" him and lead him away from "wasting his life." When demanding that he attend a "nigger school" (276) and take over the finances of her philanthropic affairs, she is trying to make of him something he doesn't want to be. His immediate response to her demand that he accept his identity as a "Negro" shows to what extent Joe's consciousness still oscillates between the two racial identities in an insoluble ambiguity: "Tell niggers that I am a nigger too?" (277). Insisting that Joe act the "nigger" in order to save both of them from what she believes will be their eternal damnation, Joanna assumes that Joe's public act can serve to reestablish the proper boundaries of race relations. In other words, she seeks to absolve their transgressions of the color line by restoring conventional relations between a white female and a black male. When she entreats Joe to kneel and pray, Joanna ultimately refuses to accept his struggle for recognition. She hardly understands that Joe finds her attempts to save him through prayer condescending and even painful. In this sense, Joe's point-blank refusal of Joanna's solicitation to have a child takes on its full force: "No, if I give in now, I will deny all the thirty years that I have lived to make me what I choose to be" (265). Joe's determined opposition signals that he will resist Joanna's creation of him.

In her article, "Joe Christmas and 'Womanshenegro,'" Doreen Fowler suggests that Joe denies "a potential for qualities that, in his culture, are associated only with women and blacks" (153). In his turbulent relation to and often violent repudiation of nearly every woman he encounters in his lifetime from the dietician to the young black prostitute in the barn to Joanna Burden, Joe continually "perceives race and gender as uniting in the ultimate threat to his being" (Clarke 141). Race and gender are thus imbued with each other's resonance in Joe's tragedy of being both "doubleness" and "nothingness." Joe at the age of fourteen lures a young black woman to act out a ritual of puberty with other farm boys in a dark barn. When his turn comes, Joe, to one's surprise, begins to beat the woman. The other white boys appear to rarely feel any sense of guilt. In contrast, it incurs the risk of a social transgression for Joe to have a sex with a black girl. Whereas the other boys are empowered by acting out white male privilege, "taking" of a black woman embodies for Joe the threat of what it will incur if he were not white. When he makes an assault on the black girl, he is thus shattered by the threatening power of his *possible* blackness steeped in the sense of suffocation in the barn—the horror of sex superimposed upon the horror of race. This scene is pivotal because it looks back to that primal scene with the dietician and forward to a time when he believes that "[t]here is something that I am going to do" (271)—the murder of Joanna.

Likewise, Joe's relationship with Joanna becomes a power struggle constructed around gender as well as race, with Joe longing for Joanna's surrender as a female and Joanna waiting for his surrender as a "Negro." It should come as no surprise that the ambiguity of his racial identity is also played out in terms of the ambiguity of his gender roles in his sexual encounters with Joanna: "it was like I was the woman and she was the man" (235). To Joe, running from the threat of blackness is closely associated with escaping the threat of engaging with emasculation. When he does what he has decided to do to "show the bitch" (236), Joe acts not necessarily out of desire but out of a sense of acting out what is forbidden or fulfilling what he believes is expected of him as an embodiment of miscegenation. Paradoxically, then, in order for Joe to complete the drama of "masculinity regained," he must become "black," an identity that exposes him to the threat of racial hysteria and violence. When he is certain that he has "made a woman of her at last" (236) after proving himself the dominant male, Joe ironically reinforces the stereotype of the black male rapist attacking the white woman no matter what he has actually done to Joanna, which is suggestive of necrophilia. Townspeople readily believe that "she had been ravished too: at least once before her throat was cut and at least once afterward" (288). The very fact that Joe is castrated rather than lynched by Percy Grimm is certainly a compelling commentary on the emasculation that Joe associates with a black identity as well as the threat that his black sexuality poses to the white southern male. Accordingly, Percy Grimm exclaims over Joe's mutilated body, "Now you'll let white women alone, even in hell" (464).

History Entrapped in Circles

On the night before his murder of Joanna, Joe Christmas bursts forth naked into the headlights of an approaching car, watching "his body grow white out of the darkness like a Kodak print emerging from the liquid" (108). Attuned to this image, frequent references to the "parchmentcolored" skin color of Joe conjure the image of enigmatic racial identity that plagues Joe's psyche. The town itself creates an Other against whom it can establish an oppositional relation in order to fortify its sense of community. Not surprisingly, Joe Brown, who is called a "yellowbellied wop" (275), defines himself against Joe Christmas and frames Joe as what he is *not*—a "nigger"—to deny his complicity with Joe in crime and to claim his legitimate identity in the society: "I'm an American citizen" (426).[56] Faulkner portrays the degree to

---

56 James Snead suggests that "Lucas Burch (Joe Brown) is Christmas's darker double. He looks more like a 'foreigner' and 'nigger' and 'murderer' than Christmas does" (92).

which the white Jefferson society in general and Percy Grimm in particular depend on the fabrication of Joe as a "Negro." Joe Christmas' crime is not considered by the community that of murder *per se*.[57] It is rather a crime of crossing social boundaries and refusing to be defined as or made into one or the other. Joe becomes a menace to the South as long as his potentially miscegenated body remains as an undecipherable sign of race. Furthermore, Joanna is posthumously reconfigured as "white woman"—the status the townspeople have never granted the "nigger lover" in her life. Faulkner uncovers a contradiction within the white southerners who once cast out Joanna when alive but recall her when the scenario surrounding her death meets their racist expectation.[58] All of these illustrate how the southern

---

Snead even takes a step further from this suggestion by arguing that, given that "Joe and Lucas are really each other's dark doubles, sharing every duty and function, it must follow that the 'dark complected' Lucas, and not Joe Christmas is likely to have 'black blood'" (93).

57 Who killed Joanna Burden?—it is an intriguing mystery never cleared up throughout the novel even though the whole community (and probably the reader) readily declares Joe Christmas to be the culprit. Stephen E. Meats claims that Joe Brown may have killed Joanna after Joe left her alone and then tried to frame Christmas for the murder (271-77).

58 Faulkner's texts provide a variety of representations of southern women such as "the Confederate woman," "the mammy," "the tragic mulatta," "the new belle," "the night sister," and "the mother." For a comprehensive study of cultural images and stereotypes of southern women, see Diane Robert's *Faulkner and the Southern Womanhood* and Deborah Clarke's *Robbing the Mother: Women in Faulkner*.

society *enforces* its hegemonic power to come to terms with internal and external threats by creating "a simulated, or at least symbolically constituted, social reality" (Romine 3).[59]

Building upon Walter Benjamin's insight into the temporal paradox of modernity that the understanding of what is historically new is predicated on making up archaic time against which national progress can be captured, Bhabha identifies the "temporal anomaly" in the nationalist conception of historical continuity: "The problematic boundaries of modernity are enacted in these ambivalent temporalities of the nation-space. The language of culture and community is poised on the fissures of the present becoming the rhetorical figures of a national past" (*Location* 142). This contradictory temporality within nationalism, "veering between nostalgia for the past and the impatient, progressive sloughing off of the past," is managed by "figuring the contradiction in the representation of *time* as a natural division of *gender*" (McClintock 358-59). Women are

---

59 Romine asserts that the cohesiveness of communities lies less in agreement than in coercion. Romine takes aim at southern agrarian nativists' argument in a discussion of Faulkner that a true community is held together by manners and morals deriving from a commonly held view of reality. He instead argues that communities enforce rather than draw from foundational beliefs through practices of avoidance, deferral, and evasion. A community for Romine is "a social group that, lacking a commonly held view of reality, coheres by means of norms, codes, and manners that produce a simulated, or at least symbolically constituted, social reality" (3).

represented as authentic repositories of tradition and a guardian of national continuity. The language of nationalism, as Benedict Anderson observes, describes women using either the vocabulary of kinship or home, in order to denote something to which one is naturally tied (131). Viewed in this light, it is noteworthy that maintaining the *appearance* of coherence of the community as a microcosm of the US South goes hand in hand with masking the coercive reality of the community through the fabrication of Joanna's status—the way "an imagined community" is maneuvered into forging its own essentialist identity.

What is more problematic about the dramatic transformation of Joanna from a "Yankee," "foreigner," or even "enemy" (249) to a southern white woman is that she is positioned both within and without the South. Such an ambilateral position ironically opens up a space for fluid and ambivalent meanings of racial, communal, and national identities in line with the long, complex history of white imperialism on the part of the U.S. government in general and its southern region in particular. In the intricate lineage of the Burdens is inscribed "the story of Anglo-American expansion in the first half of the nineteenth century into what had been French and Spanish territories" (Ladd 160) that revolves around the turbulent and violent history of the Louisiana Purchase in 1803, the US-Mexico War (1846-1848), the anti-Catholic nativism of the 1840s, and so forth. The imperialists had their own plans for annexing some portions of Mexico, Cuba, and other points south, and these plans usually coincided with a nationalist desire to fulfill Manifest Destiny. It is of utmost importance to note the ways in which US imperial design worked to differentiate the US-Mexico War from the Spanish conquest of Mexico in its assertion of American Exceptionalism. It was a nervous attempt to transcend the contradiction of the ideological operation of US imperialism—a willed amnesia of "a nation divinely ordained for great deeds" with "a clear conscience":

> By the 1830s the Americans were eagerly grasping at reasons for their own success and for the failure of others. Although the white Americans of Jacksonian America wanted personal success and wealth, they also wanted a clear conscience. If the United States was to remain in the minds of its people a nation divinely ordained for great deeds, then the fault for the suffering inflicted in the rise to power and prosperity had to lie elsewhere. White Americans could rest easier if the sufferings of other races could be blamed on racial weakness rather than on the whites' relentless search for wealth and power. In the 1830s and 1840s, when it became obvious that American and Mexican interests were incompatible and that the Mexicans would suffer, innate weaknesses were found in the Mexicans. Americans, it was argued, were not to be blamed for forcibly taking the northern province of Mexico, for Mexicans, like Indians were unable to make proper use of the land. (Horsman 210)

The ideology of expansion was buttressed by emphasizing the Spanish Inquisition, Spanish atrocities in the New World, and, most importantly fostering the horrors of miscegenation. It is precisely at this juncture that the issue of color and ethnicity are intermingled, defining colonized Mexicans as Others, and embroiling the doomed lovers in the tragic history of the region and the nation. Ladd uses *Absalom* as a text for the discussion of how US nationalism changed into imperialism by identifying a connection between racial fears and desires for new territories and by marking the Caribbean as "the logical theater for dreams of U.S. expansion in the pre-Civil War era" (142).[60] However,

---

60 Ladd suggests that Faulkner makes indelible use of the imbrication of racial complexity, residual coloniality, and the U.S. imperial design in explaining why the young Sutpen should end up in the West Indies: "Despite the United States' refusal to recognize Jean Paul Boyer's mulatto government, Haiti, of all the West Indies Islands, was of the most economic importance to the United States during this time. The Caribbean was the logical theater for dreams of U.S. expansion in the pre-Civil War era (as it would be once again in Quentin's era), since the desire for expansion had certainly not been exhausted by the acquisition of the Louisiana Territory. What did happen between that time and the years preceding the Civil War was the development of a more articulate ideology of expansion in which the idea of the design as redemptive was more pronounced and more entangled with the ideology of race and slavery. Throughout the pre-Civil War era, dreams of worldly wealth for white Americans and dreams of a millennial civilization or terrestrial paradise, where even the enslavement of darker peoples could be seen as a step toward lifting them out of such darkness and into the light of God's righteous millennium, were united in that rhetoric. By extension, it was of great importance to preserve the United States from contamination by decadent Europe and its leveling influence, already visible in the

while the United States tried to displaces the remnants of colonial history and imperial expansion onto "darker" peoples, it could not choose but inherit the curses heaped upon what was once colonial territory—the curses that resurface through the tragedy of the doomed lovers. Not coincidentally, Joe's father is rumored to be either black or Mexican, and Joanna's father's first wife Juana is Mexican. In addition, Calvin, Joanna's grandfather, marries a woman of a family of Huguenot stock" (241). He seeks to recreate himself as a nationalist in this marriage by repudiating all of his connections with whatever is redolent of residual coloniality such as the "allegiance to the Catholic Church"—"a church full of frogeating slaveholders" (241)—and thus to act in concert with nationalist ideology in the mid-nineteenth century. His effort to get out of the nightmare of history and to redeem his family in accordance with the progressive nation, however, is treacherously bound in the recurrence of what is embodied in the dark mother, Evangeline.

As such, the Burdens are burdened by the history going around in "circles." The son Nathaniel goes to the south and south west once again as his father did and marries a Spanish Creole who resembles her mother he hardly remembers. When Calvin sees his grandson for the first time, he exclaims, "another damn

---

formation of Haiti as the first mulatto government in the New World" (142-43).

black burden," afraid that "[f]olks will think I bread to a damn slaver. And now he's got to breed to one, too" (247). It is a return of "bastard" sons and brothers, which mocks Thomas Sutpen's aspiration after absolute lineage that can be made possible only by preserving racial purity. It is a return of the repressed that can never be obliterated by willed amnesia of colonial history and expansion, too. Subsequently, Calvin regrets that "we done freed them now, both black and white alike. They'll bleach out now. In a hundred years they will be white folks again. Then maybe we'll let them come back into *America*" (247-48, emphasis mine). It is against the backdrop of all these historical subtexts when Percy Grimm, who longs to be a soldier in the war to redeem the United States, declares a personal but symbolic war, appoints himself commander-in-chief, and attempts to dramatically save the nation by not only murdering but also castrating a "white nigger." It then becomes clear why Joe Brown has to prove himself to be "an American citizen" to deny his connection with Joe in crime: he should be a member of the nation redeemed from the sin of slave holding and the curse of the dark impulse for other peoples' territories and markets. Therefore, Joe's crime is not merely a crime of murder. It is a crime of summoning a ghost of forgotten histories and bringing back the lingering sense of guilt.

Returning to the scene in which Joanna recounts the convoluted story of her family by the hidden gravesite of her grandfather and brother, one finds Joanna and Joe unwittingly touching upon the feeling of a land facing decline and fall. It is a land that not only retreats to a mythical past but also becomes imbricated in the forward-moving nation. When asked why her father Nathaniel did not avenge his own father and his son, Joanna answers:

> She in turn seemed to muse now, quiet, scarcebreathing, yet still with nothing of selfpity or retrospect: "I had thought of that. Why father didn't shoot Colonel Sartoris. I think that it was, because of his French blood."
> "French blood?" Christmas said. "Don't even Frenchmen get mad when a man kills his father and his son on the same day? I guess your father must have got religion. Turned preacher, maybe."
> She did not answer for a time. The fireflies drifted; somewhere a dog barked, mellow, sad, faraway. "I thought about that," she said. "It was all over then. The killing in uniform and with flags, and the killing without uniforms and flags. And none of it doing or did any good. None of it. And we were foreigners, strangers, that thought differently from the people whose country we had come into without being asked or wanted. And he was French, half of him. Enough French to respect anybody's love for the land where he and his people were born and to understand that a man would have to act as the land where he was born had trained him to act. I think that was it." (254-55)

As Ladd pointedly remarks, the fatality bound up with the French blood is suggestive of "the conceptual genealogy that ties the South to the slaveholding Creole cultures of the Deep South, which binds white slaveholders to the slave and to the French and Spanish colonialists who first brought slaves in the Louisiana territory, and, finally, that sets them all against Anglo-American nationalism" (163). Comprised not of a transparent, single narrative but of a network of conflicting (regional, post-regional, colonial, postcolonial) forces, the tortuous paths to the "conceptual genealogy" evoke multiple histories that cannot be flattened out into a coherent, single narrative. Those paths make visible the uniqueness of distinct mixture of wider and more complex relations that are sometimes incommensurable and yet can be evoked multiply at a single site—Faulkner's masterful craft of narrativizing the tragedy of the South by "hid[ing] everything while revealing it" (Glissant, *Faulkner* 15). The fabrication of Joanna's image from a Yankee to a white woman attests that while white southerners may have been annoyed at northern oppression, many of them surreptitiously fell in line with white imperialism, which was acceptable to them as long as it resulted in the domination of racial others. This complicity with the imperial expansion sheds light on the involvement of nineteenth- and early twentieth-century southerners in the nation's desire for other people's territories. The maneuvering—masking their imperial ambition while never completely abandoning their allegiance to white imperialism itself—works to help the South alleviate its own guilt of ostracizing racial others and avoid confrontation with its moral responsibilities. However, it ironically leads to the southern tragedy of self-hatred, resonating with the Shreve's question to Quentin in *Absalom, Absalom!*—"why do you hate the South?" (303).

As such, the family's hybrid genealogy belies the grandfather Calvin's desire to escape from the nightmare of history and to redeem himself and his children from any link to that history. By the same logic, Joanna is informed with not only the family legacy haunted by Negroes, Mexicans, and French Huguenots but also white supremacists' racial hysteria. What is brought to the fore here is the threatening difference of blackness symbolically inscribed in Joe and the creole metaphor embodied in Joanna. It is precisely at this point that the "memory," which "believes before knowing remembers" (119), is conjured up by a genealogy of the region, overdetermined not only by the internal divisions but also by its complicity with the nation and beyond. It is a kind of memory that "believes before knowing remembers" because it draws attention to what the region and the nation contrived to forget no less than what they remembered. In this light, Joe's sense of being entrapped in a series of circles is noteworthy because they serve as a compelling metaphor for the overdetermined genealogy of the South:

> Looking, he can see the smoke low on the sky, beyond an imperceptible corner; he is entering it again, the street which ran for thirty years. It had been a paved street, where going should be fast. It had made a circle and he is still inside of it. Though during the last seven days he has had no paved street, yet he has traveled further than in all the thirty years before. And yet he is still inside the circle. "And yet I have been further in these seven days than in all the thirty years," he thinks. "But I have never got outside that circle. I have never broken out of the ring of what I have already done and cannot ever undo," he thinks quietly, sitting on the seat, with planted on the dashboard before him the shoes, the black shoes smelling of negro: that mark on his ankles the gauge definite and ineradicable of the black tide creeping up his legs, moving from his feet upwards as death moves. (339)

The "circles" Joe can never break out of hark back to the "shadow" in which, as Nathaniel said to his young daughter, "we lived, all white people, all other people" (253). Ironically, Lena's baby is born in the cabin behind Joanna's house as Grimm slays Joe. When Mrs. Hines mistakes Lena's baby for her grandson, "Joey [⋯] My Milly's little baby" (398), Mrs. Hines brings the anguish of Joe into a heightened relief that is only surpassed by Lena's confusing of Joe Christmas with the child's father: "She keeps on talking about him like his pa was that—the one in jail, that Mr. Christmas. She keeps on, and then I get mixed up and it's like sometimes I cant—like I am mixed up too and I think that his pa is that Mr—Mr Christmas too" (409). Byron Bunch tells this story to Hightower: "In that cabin those thirty years did not exist—the child and its father whom she [Mrs. Hines] had never seen, and her grandson whom she had not seen since he was a baby like the other, and whose father likewise to her had never existed, all confused" (495). The merging of Joe and Lena in this scene both demonstrates that the desire to transcend history, an enormous mass of debris, is unobtainable and represents the "inextricable compositeness" (491) of the South in its acute "threat that an invisible menace will become all too visible" (Sundquist, *Faulkner* 75).[61]

"What is the South?" Confronted with such a pointed question, Glissant describes Faulkner's South as made by a "composite culture that suffers from wanting to become an atavistic one [one that venerates racial and cultural purity] and suffers in not being able to achieve that goal" (115). What we have reached by rethinking Faulkner's South through "geographical detours" is a counter-narrative that questions and critiques the

---

61 According to Snead who suggests that "the 'dark complected' Lucas, not Joe, is more likely to have 'black blood'" (93), Lena Grove's child can be another mulatto in a long string of uncertain progeny.

totalizing concepts of region deeply embedded in an insular southern sense of place and nation. In the Faulknerian world, the South is represented as a disruptive site riddled with the multiple connections with those outside the borders, in which the regional and national unity is rarely achieved. In contrast to the illusion of universalism of *e pluribus unum* (making one out of many), what constitutes Faulkner's South through geographical detours is a kind of "re-territorialization," the empowerment of place consistent with the sophisticated recognition of other places. This newly conceptualized southern sense of place does not merely mean an accidental coming together of many different flows in one location. Rather, it emphasizes a reconsideration of a place whose particularities can be recognized by its relations with others.

The Faulknerian world envisioned as such offers an antidote for the historical amnesia and social fabrication of memory. Faulkner unfolds to his reader an endless fascinating vista of the South sharing extensively with new-world memories, experiences, and histories. It refuses nostalgia for sacred filiation, forgoes the obsessive quest for pure origins, and throws doubt on the conceptual boundaries of center and periphery and the imaginative construct of nation/South. Glissant calls this working of Faulknerian vision "one of the thrilling moments in the modern poetics of Relation" (*Poetics of Relation* 22), which I would like to argue creates an *unruly* narrative that makes both historical continuity of the nation and cultural insularity of the region impossible. It is "unruly" not because it is unable to restore any authentic rootedness but because it ironically brings into sharp relief the as-yet-unexplored complexity and uncertainty with which new "relations" and "crossings" in a Glissantian sense are established in the Faulknerian world. For example, the creole metaphor and the threatening connotations of blackness mark the characters in *Light in August* as dangerous border figures. They claim to be or they are coerced into claiming to be "southern" or "American." But they always carry within themselves the traces of the displaced and thus act traitorously at some points, thereby deconstructing a single narrative of the region and the nation. In the world Faulkner creates, Glissantian relations and crossings are mapped not through the quest for a stabilizing center of a pure origin but through obscure pathways and traces. I have thus examined the meaning of the U.S. South through *geographical detours* and arrived at the regionally, intra-nationally, and transnationally inflected symbolic geography of the U.S. South in a wider sense across changing temporal and spatial axes. It is a South that is ultimately opened out to its multiple definitions well beyond the divide of nation and South as an imaginative construct.

Chapter 4

When Asian Americans Go the Suburbs

He's a real nowhere man,
sitting in his nowhere land,
making all his nowhere plans for nobody.

Doesn't have a point of view,
knows not where he's going to,
isn't he a bit like you and me?
Nowhere man, please listen,
you don't know what you're missing,
nowhere man, the world is at your command.

———

Beatles, "Nowhere Man"

Neither, neither
Who is mother tongue, who is father country?

———

Myung Mi Kim

When Immigrant Narratives Meet the U.S. Suburbs

"[I]n America [⋯] it's even hard to stay Korean"—the father of the protagonist of Chang-rae Lee's debut *Native Speaker* (1995) remarks as such (51). The first-generation Korean immigrant grocer in New York City, he has become the hero of a rags-to-riches story. With his American Dream limited to the purview of family loyalty and ethnic community membership, he is here blurting out his furtive nostalgic desire for belonging while seemingly splaying himself spectrally between the nation of origin and another of settlement. When now vexed relationship with one's origin becomes more and more prominent, it becomes even more difficult to define the parameters of Asian American identities with the national as an enabling locus of identification complicated. On the one hand, the sense of belonging may have become a kind of sentiment not necessarily associated with geographical location and statehood amidst the constant flows of capital, labor, cultures, languages, and translocal migrant communities. On the other, the imperative of nation-state still contests the way such transnational identities are constituted. It is then no less necessary to redefine the points, lines, and planes that build a map of the world than ever before. In other words, while one may emphasize salutary effects of nomadic and diasporic subjectivities, others find in those effects a desperate need for a strong sense of locality that dies hard as a foothold in the middle of the feelings of vulnerability. Therefore, one of the results of redrawing boundaries in our transnational age—such as a global sense of the local and transnationalizing the national—is that "as actual places and localities become ever more blurred and indeterminate, ideas of culturally and ethnically distinct places become perhaps even more salient" (Gupta and Ferguson 39). There is at least a desire not so much to pinpoint locations as to experience dislocation at work while orienting oneself becomes increasingly disorienting.

While the telos of immigration, settlement, assimilation, and citizenship has been an enduring narrative of American history, it has not always been aligned with the reality of immigrants' experiences and interactions with American society. Such is also the case with Asian American immigration given its history of exclusion. A logic of exclusion has existed in Asian American history even after the national origins quota system was abolished in 1965, not to mention the late nineteenth and early twentieth centuries' legal edifice of restriction such as the Chinese exclusion law of 1882, the Immigration Act of 1917, and the Johnson-Reed Immigration Act of 1924. The difficulty with which the two signifiers, "Asian" and "American," coexist in the formation of Asian American identity has engendered an in/out position among Asian Americans in the United States who live as both "official nationals" and "foreigners-within." Particularly, the opposing demands of capital and the US nation-state have been resolved through the racialization of Asian immigrants. As Lisa Lowe suggests, the racialization of Asian immigrant labor has served to cover the contradiction between the demands of capital that needs an influx of cheap labor and those of the US nation-state that must unify its members to constitute itself through a homogeneous citizenry (*Immigrant* Acts 5).

Accordingly, the liminal position of Asian Americans has not fit neatly into the U.S. nation-building prerogatives and, as a result, attests to the state's power to presuppose an outside within its domestic space while illustrating the contingent consolidation of the nation against itself—a kind of "[e]xceptionalism that defines and affirms a people by negating others, who form their opposition" (Okihiro 148). Put otherwise, the United States presents itself as an inclusive entity supposedly comprised of *all* American citizens with the rhetoric of *e pluribus unum*, yet its universality is contradicted by the very presence of its constitutive outside that is placed in opposition to the particular articulation of the nation. An irony here is that the excluded, who are presumed to be outside of the nation's universal norms and its coherence, become a kind of *anomaly* that is "internal to the state yet external to the national narrative" (Pease, "National Narratives" 549). It is precisely in this context that Lisa Lowe argues that Asian American culture is positioned to be pitted against the US national culture as "an alternative formation" as it is haunted by the memories of US nation-state based on Asian immigrant racialization and imperialist projects in Asia: "[t]his distance from the national culture constitutes Asian American culture as an alternative formation that produces cultural expressions materially and aesthetically at odds with the resolution of the citizen in the nation" (*Immigrant Acts* 6). The imperative of the nation has thus both defined and delimited the cultural identifications that make up Asian American identities. The most compelling of it is the internment of Japanese Americans during World War II, which, as Mae Ngai writes, still "stands as the most extreme case of the construction and consequences of alien citizenship in American history" (175).

Given such historical specificities of Asian American experience and significant transnational challenges, I seek in this chapter to reconsider how the nation's various articulation of nationhood can work against the backdrop of Asian America and "Asian" can be separated from "American" in the formation of Asian American identity with an eye toward the US suburb as a space of constantly shifting designations for redefining Asian

America—Asian America that is contingent upon what the nation is *not* as much as what it includes. In his discussion of how immigrants' move to suburban regions becomes a focal point of understanding of different types of assimilation narratives, David Palumbo-Liu maintains that "the move to the suburb by assimilated ethnics underscores the perpetuation of a particular narrative of ethnic mobility deeply linked to a closing off of space to any who have not passed through a specific space of becoming American" (281). This chapter explores how that "particular narrative" in Asian American literature is created by teasing out the US suburbs as "a specific space of becoming American" wherein immigrants supposedly achieve the American Dream translated into the hope of owning a single-family dwelling as a significant measure of the cultural enfranchisement. In addition, I will examine how the geographical shift from urban space to suburban one sheds light on the changing paradigms of topoi of location, identity, and agency through the lens of ever-shifting and yet distinctive boundaries of local/global and national/ transnational. I thus follow a double trajectory in this chapter: to assess how (sub)urban experiences both widen and diffuse the generic boundaries of Asian American narratives, and how the face of American suburbs can be read within and against the logic of transnationalism.

The protagonist of *Native Speaker* explains what changes his family's move to a respectable suburb has brought about as follows:

> I know over the years my father and his friends got together less and less. Certainly, after my mother died, he didn't seem to want go to the gathering anymore. But it wasn't just him. They all got busier and wealthier and lived farther and farther apart. Like us, their families moved to big houses with big yards to tend on weekends, they owned fancy cars that needed washing and waxing. They joined their own neighborhood pool and tennis clubs and were making drinking friends with Americans. (47)

A seamy side of suburban upward mobility for immigrants is that they may lose the residual traits of their own tradition and communal ties in moving up the social ladder. It may cause the deterioration of their ethnic group, and, as a result, persistent disenfranchisement from the core of social and cultural power. Thus emerge a new interface that challenges any simple notion of assimilation. Lee in his debut poses the questions of who belongs *here* and who rules *here* in the astringent atmospheres of contemporary New York City, a microcosm of multi-ethnic and polyglot America. As a follow-up, Lee's *A Gesture Life* (1999) continues to delve into the questions by placing a Korean-Japanese-American retiree in a suburban town in upstate New York. Of particular interest here is the shift of geopolitical setting from the American city fraught with racial and class anxieties to the suburb traditionally characterized by social conformity and complacency, from which arise the following questions: what happens in classic white-flight suburbs when immigrants become a growing presence there; how does immigrants' move transform social geographies of suburban spaces; and, can one conceive of any new form of integration across of a set of ethnic and racial differences or are new patterns of segregation likely to emerge?

To make one's unitary assumptions about suburban spaces more difficult, traditional suburban social geographies have been recently reshaped by a growing reliance upon transnational capital and labor in the service economy. Immigrants form their enclaves around suburban regions and immigrant workers perform substantial roles in middle- and upper-class homes during the day.[62] In this way, the traditional logic of suburban

---

62 Another interesting change in the suburban areas is that not a few immigrants have recently moved *directly* to the suburbs without living a certain a period of time in the inner city as earlier immigrants did to acquire sufficient financial resources for a suburban living: "In recent decades many suburban areas have transformed to multiracial and multicultural ones under the influence of international geopolitical and global economic restructuring, changing national immigration and trade policies and local demographic, economic, and political contexts. Many new immigrants with higher educational attainment, professional occupations, and financial resources settled directly into the suburbs without ever having experienced life in the inner city. This is different from prior generations of immigrants, who normally settled in inner-city neighborhoods first and moved out to the suburbs only after they moved up socio-economically. [⋯] Today, demographic characteristics, social and economic structures, and residential and commercial landscapes are undergoing drastic changes in the suburban areas of many large cosmopolitan areas across the globe"

regions used to secure suburban communities from urban ills has begun to erode. As the current labor market cannot operate within a core-periphery model of segregation, the boundaries between urban and suburban spaces blur. The suburban town where the protagonist of *A Gesture Life* settles is not free from the inflow of immigrants, either: the protagonist's best friend Renny who is an "East Asian" hospital purchasing manager; Renny's ex-girlfriend who is a Puerto Rican girl named Julia working in the hospital Food Services; the immigrant shop owners in the shopping mall of a neighboring town; a Russian doctor who performs an abortion operation on the Protagonist's teenage adoptee, Sunny. Parts of the suburban town may still feel suburban, but its social geography has been changed, if not considerably, by transnational labor. Such a new face of the suburb creates unexpected social tensions and thus opens up a national context to transnational frames of reference—"Third Worldization" of the American suburb as Palumbo-Liu terms it (266). The suburbs under discussion in this chapter bear the tortuous paths of the birth of Asian American space not only in a national context but also from a global, transnational perspective—the United States' (neo)colonial involvements in the Pacific Rim areas, their effects on U.S. domestic policies, and the projection of Asian American space onto the Pacific Rim areas.

(Wei Li 1-2).

The suburbs are gradually revealed to be conflicting and contested spaces informed by intersecting concerns about local, national, and transnational borders. Not the symbolic cultural signposts any more where apparent order and gentility supposedly prevail, they harbor the Asian American subjects' thwarted but everlasting desire for belonging.

Third Worldizing the U.S. Suburbs and Asian American Studies

The transnational implications in mapping a geography of the US suburb provide an entrée into a larger discussion of the transnational turn in Asian American studies. Preoccupied with the experiences of migration, immigration, displacement, and exile, and paralleling recent immigrant processes of the so-called "third wave" of immigration, Asian American literature has seen the emergence of many controversial debates on the effect of transnationalism on Asian American culture and history.[63] In its initial stage of institutionalization, Asian American literary

---

63 For an overview of the effects of the Immigration Act of 1965 and the different positions in the post-1965 immigration debates, see Nathan Glazer, *The Immigration: A Challenge to American Society* (1988); *Roger Daniels, Coming to America: A History of Immigration and Ethnicity in American Life* (1990); Aihwa Ong, *Flexible Citizenship: The Cultural Logics of Transnationality* (1999).

studies was generally discussed as articulating formations of Asian American identities as national ones with a focus on race, ethnicity, gender, and class. For example, the editorial interests of Roots: *An Asian American Reader* (1971) and *Aiiieeeee! An Anthology of Asian-American Writers* (1974) lie in the cultural potential of Asian American literature for promoting racial equality rarely coinciding with the American democratic ideals. One of the editorial endeavors is to distinguish Asian America from America through cultural negation of both ancestral Asia and white America.[64] In this logic, the "Asia" in Asian America merely indicates a region of diasporic descent and becomes a racial signifier for representing a particular kind of "American" who has been striving for national inclusion. This ethnic striving characterizes the boundaries of early Asian American culturalism with its institutional inception and growth rooted in the 1950s and

---

64 The editors of *Aiiieeeee!*, Frank Chin, Jefferey Paul Chan, and Lawson Fusao Inada, stressed their "Asian-American sensibilities and cultures that might be related to but are distinct from Asia and white America" as "American born and raised": "We have been encouraged to believe that we have no cultural integrity as Chinese- or Japanese-Americans, that we are either Asian (Chinese or Japanese) or American (white), or are measurably both. This myth of being either/or and the equally goofy concept of the dual personality haunted our lobes while our rejection by both Asian and white America proved we were neither one nor the other. Nor were we half and half or more one than the other. Neither Asian culture nor American culture was equipped to define us except in the most superficial terms" (viii).

1960s civil rights movement.[65] Smacking of Black nationalism in the 1960s, Asian American culturalism privileged race over gender and class and established a hierarchy based upon cultural authenticity by telling the "real" from the "fake."

Despite its exclusive bent, the preoccupation with the national in *Aiiieeeee!* is understandable in that the constantly shifting designation of Asian Americans' subject formation in America might be ineffective in political mobilization and community formation. So is the nation-based model that Elaine Kim's *Asian American Literature: An Introduction to the Writings and Their Social Context* (1982), the first comprehensive study of Asian American literature. For Kim, race serves as a major interpretative lens for examining writings by Asian Americans. Kim underscores her interest in "what Asians in America share" and in "how they can be compared within the context of their American experiences": "whatever its origins, the racial classification of Asian Americans does in fact have its advantages for us. Our racial

---

65 The first academic conference wholly dedicated to the issues of Asian American studies was held at the Oakland Museum in 1975, and national meetings of the Association for Asian American Studies have been annually held since 1985 (Sumida 151). The term, "Asian American studies," was coined by Yuji Ichioka, a Japanese American historian, who used it for the first time at a meeting in Berkeley in 1968 "out of analogy with other terms of ethnic identification, especially African American, which was at the source of much of the ethnic vocabulary of the time" (Dirlik, *What Is in a Rim?* 76).

unity has been contributing to our strength, to our efforts to build community, and to the maintenance and development of a vital Asian American culture" (xiii).[66]

The intractable tension between constructing Asian America fully part of America and disavowing the old racist stigma of foreignness and unassimilability—"*the transnational within the national*" (Chuh 69) and/or "the national within the transnational" reminds one of the ways in which African American studies has come to terms with such tensions. Paul Gilroy's *The Black Atlantic* (1995), for example, has encouraged a number of scholars to reimagine their disciplinary boundaries and their relations to local, regional, national, and global categories of racial and cultural difference, and to reconsider a modern space that can never neatly divided into African, Caribbean, or British. Instead, such a space is considered to be comprised of the entangled web of all those cultural identities. In accordance with the academic turn toward transnationalism, this shift of focus

---

66 "Sociohistorical and cultural contexts" of Asian American experience becomes very significant to Kim because they can highlight Asian Americans' striving for national inclusion: "I have deliberately chosen to emphasize how the literature elucidates the social history of Asians in the United States. The problem of understanding Asian American literature within its sociohistorical and cultural contexts is important to me because, when these contexts are unfamiliar, the literature is likely to be misunderstood and unappreciated" (xv).

calls into question the stress on a nationally bounded investigation into racialized language, literature, and cultural production by emphasizing African American studies' hemispheric identity as opposed to a North American boundedness, its relationship to Africa, and the transnational linkages of diasporic experience. The plight of African Americans is not inseparable from that of the oppressed and downtrodden throughout the world, connected not only by affinities of blood and culture but also by their shared experience of subjugation to the regimes of colonial and imperial design. When African American studies' shift toward transnationalism has been hailed for a very salutary purpose, it can help many scholars in related fields reterritorialize single-nation genealogies and mono-national narratives in the conceptualization of American and African American culture. It also enables them to develop a critical consciousness to situate themselves within a broader understanding of African American experience in a globally interconnected, racialized, and capitalist United States.

That said, I would like to argue that the transnational turn is not so much a "turn" as a renewed interest in the roots of African American studies. In line with the opposition to the war in Vietnam and mounting demand for an analysis of the racial dimensions of the US foreign policies, the first student strikes demanding the establishment of ethnic studies took place at San Francisco State University in 1968 under the banner of the

Third World Liberation Front. Examining roots and routes has been a central feature of recovery projects for Chicanos, African Americans, Native Americans, and Asian Americans as well as a means of interrogating United States' political interests in Latin America, Asia, Africa, and US-occupied tribal lands. As such, a transnational impetus was "there" from the start. As area studies paradigms frequently do not coincide with topographical and geographical distinctions, African American studies is not entirely African American in the same sense that African studies is not entirely African and African studies cannot be solely about the investigation of African-descended peoples and related cultural experience. African Americanists have successfully proved that literatures, cultures, languages, and ideologies rarely line up in the way that the taxonomical category, "African American," does since "African American" is not so much a self-evident category as an analytic one.

In addition, early templates of African American studies were informed with an African-diasporic or Pan-African perspective—black people and their histories, cultures, and struggles for freedom and equality exist within and across, between and beyond, nation-states. Indeed, the African slave trade, slavery in the Americas, and European colonization in the Americas and in Africa can be considered truly transnational enterprises. As W. E. B. Du Bois noted earlier, there are indisputable connections between lynching in the American

South and European colonization of Africa. Aime Cesaire, Leopold Senghor, and others also recognized cultural connections between African cultures and the diaspora, of which "negritude" is an early expression. Therefore, negritude serves not only as a counter-narrative to slavery and colonization but also as a usable past and diasporic consciousness against the chronic precariousness of many black folks confronting global forces of domination, thereby articulating a Pan-African or transnational approach to blackness that anticipates African diasporic studies.

In parallel fashion, while the "transnational turn" has been instrumental in honing new interpretative practices in Asian American literary studies that are not only expansive but also flexible enough to locate a literature in relation to other national traditions and within a global context, the very question—whether or not it is still premature to jump on the bandwagon called transnationalism—is a legitimate concern because the very prefix "trans" in transnationalism more often than not creates the illusion of a move beyond when there has been no such a move at all. A closer look at "the transnational within the national" and/or "the national within the transnational" would lay bare a discrepancy between what transnationalism claims to do and what it actually performs in redefining the boundaries of the national within a particular context of the transnational turn in Asian American literary studies. The role of Asian America in the construction of the United States as a national and transnational entity can be unfolded in a related register of the conflicting logic of US citizenship. As domestic policies against Asian Americans parallel US imperialistic involvements in Asian countries, the ideal of American citizenship is presented as a universal and inclusive category but translated historically as a practice of excluding Asians in America and the racialization of Asian immigrants. The very presence of the Japanese Americans held behind barbed wire during World War II illuminates the state's power to remap its interior by not only dictating its domestic policies but also reconfiguring its global influence—the interests of global ascendancy and militarization cannot be divorced from the continued neglect of ethnic communities *within* the United States.

The inextricable linkage between "the transnational within the national" and "the national within the transnational" is dramatically illustrated in the model minority myth as well. It was first rhetorically constructed to send other minorities such as African Americans the message that they collectively failed to take advantage of the American democratic promise the validity of which Japanese Americans had affirmed through their success stories.[67] What should be emphasize here is that the model

---

67 The model minority myth was first articulated in an article by social demographer William Petersen under the title of "Success Story, Japanese American Style" in the *New*

minority myth was also haunted by a sense of America's withering belief in its progressive historical change both domestically *and* globally: it was a desperate measure under pressure to contain the mounting demand for promoting equal civil rights and to redefine the Unites States' relation to the Pacific Rim as a response to the rise of Japan as a new economic power. The international remapping of America through the myth was still in progress in the 1970s alongside the Shanghai communiqué, the withdrawal of US troops from Vietnam, and the growing domestic economic crisis.[68] As such, the myth, which served both as an assimilationist narrative to neutralize activism and maintain US global ascendancy, is intra-nationally and globally inflected. An understanding of the racist figuration of Japanese Americans and Asian American experience as "living proof of America's expansionist history"

York Times Magazine on January 9, 1966. It should not go unnoticed that it was less than six months after the Watts Race Riots in Los Angeles.

68 The Joint Communiqué of the US and the PRC was an important diplomatic document issued on February 28, 1973 during the President Richard Nixon's visit to China. It announced the normalization of relation between the two countries. The murder of Vincent Chin in 1982 comes to one's mind here, too. Vincent Chin, a Chinese American, was beaten to death in June 1982 in Detroit, Michigan by two white autoworkers who misidentified Chin as Japanese at the height of anti-Japanese sentiments. The murder was undeniably a hate crime against Asian Americans as many autoworkers in Detroit, the heart of auto industry in the United States, were laid off because of the increasing market share of Japanese automakers.

(Bascara 8), not only within the borders of the United States but also within the context of a trans-Pacific extension of Japan in the United States, would unmask the contradictory incorporation of Japanese Americans, both marked as "minor" (even "interned" previously) and praised as "models."[69]

A transnational perspective has certainly contributed to recognizing border-crossing relations and a correspondingly wide variety of cultural practices. At the same time, it is necessary not to miss how the national is still providing the dominant forms of cultural production vis-à-vis the necessity of capturing a diverse and hybrid dynamics through the lens of transnationalism. The transnational reconfiguration of traditional patterns does not diminish the nation's role: it rather resituates the nation in relation to other forms of the former hegemony of nation-state. It may not be too much far-fetched to suggest that transnationalism not so much completely displaces as endorses the nation-state in a "new" way that ironically brings the reappearance of previously hidden

---

69 Bascara's *Model-Minority Imperialism* (2006) is a notable contribution to the scholarship on the model minority myth within the context of the American exceptionalism and the imperial aspects of US culture. It illustrates how the myth was articulated to de-emphasize the racist and imperial violence of the nation-state by examining "the main sites of convergence between Asian American cultural politics and the critical study of empire, two revisionist fields that have made previously unacknowledged histories undeniable" (xxii).

national identities or the appearance of new ones. In a nutshell, I would argue that claims about the global borderlessness and, as its logical corollary, the predicted demise of national sovereignties have been celebrated prematurely. When it comes to Asian American literary studies, adopting a diasporic perspective and espousing the expansiveness of the field may incur the suspicion that the transnational turn in practice creates new anxieties through its institutional shift away from its attention to racialized domestic subjects within in the United States.

The nation in the paradigms of ethnic studies for example continues to appear as a conglomerate of dissimilar and sometimes dissonant traditions, histories, and cultures, which intersect with the national but are not reducible to it in the last instance. Therefore, it may not be surprising that some of the most interesting transnational studies move well beyond the bounds of the national. The nation, however, has been sometimes (re)inscribed once again as a primordial—if ever fragmentary and multicultural—landscape of analytic intelligibility. Too much emphasis on the national may inadvertently reinscribe American exceptionalism against the logic of its own critical drive to disarticulate the official narrative of America as "big and generous" enough to embrace such heterogeneity. Nonetheless, Asian American studies in its most prevalent lines of inquiry has been a matter of US ethnic heterogeneity *within* its national boundaries no matter how much such boundaries can be extended historically and culturally by invoking transgeographical horizons and filiations. Such tricky nature of the transnational within the national and the national within the transnational always baffles us.

A demographic change in the Asian American community aided by the 1965 revision of the immigration law called for the acknowledgement of the predicament of "Asians located *not* 'in' Asia *nor* in the United States, but of shifting and often contradictory *predications* of 'Asia' onto and into the U.S. imaginary" (Palumbo-Liu 21). Post-1965 Asian immigrants are marked by Asian American immigrants' remarkable "hybridizing diversity." They are diverse in terms of national origin, ethnicity, language, social class, political situation, education backgrounds, and patterns of settlement. A different approach to Asian American identities and community formations emerged as transnational agenda brought with it a corresponding fluidity of the nature of the Asian American community and its location within national and transnational geographies.[70] The most important voice in the debates on the changing nature of Asian

---

70 In addition to the rapidly increasing number of Asian Americans from around 1, 357,000 in 1970 to approximately 3,700,000 in 1980, the immigration law of 1965 resulted in a profound change in the demography of Asian America in terms of the number of foreign-born Asian Americans: two-thirds of the population of Asian America were U.S.-born in 1970, but the foreign-born constituted more than two-thirds by 1980 (Dirlik, *What Is in a Rim?* 81).

American identity and its shifting location within national and transnational geographies is Lisa Lowe. In "Heterogeneity, Hybridity, Multiplicity: Making Asian American Differences" (1991), Lowe demonstrates how such a change opens up a space wherein one is enabled to re-envision Asian American culture as comprised of heterogeneous and conflicting positions, and to be thus aware of continued vigilance in highlighting Asian American differences that are so complex that they "refuse static or binary conceptions of ethnicity replacing notions of identity with multiplicity and shifting the emphasis from ethnic 'essence' to cultural hybridity" (33). Lowe concludes by arguing in a tone of reading a manifesto for a radical change of Asian American studies in the 1990s: "I want simply to remark that in the 1990s, we can afford to rethink the notion of ethnic identity in terms of cultural, class, and gender differences, rather than presuming similarities and making the erasure of particularity the basis of unity" (39). Lowe's call for re-envisioning Asian American culture as "heterogeneous," "hybrid," and "multiple" offers a critique of the unifying tendency of earlier Asian Americanists while her critical move is still dependent at some points upon the strength of those earlier essentialist strategies.[71]

---

71 An ongoing paradigm that binds Asian Americanists' critical works is their shared concerns over transnational implications in the field in the wake of Lowe's impact despite

Most notably, Palumbo-Liu, taking a step further than Lowe, problematizes the U.S. modernity itself by exploring America's rejection of, and yet attachment to Asian America in the imaging of Modern America. He delves into how the formation of "Asian" was divided from "America" especially in periods when the United States was involved in imperialist mission in East Asia. At such times, it was particularly threatening to mainstream America to have Asian America as a composite identity. Such a constantly shifting definition of Asian America leaves the question of Asian American identity open-ended and the growing emphasis on a transnational perspective presents other problems despite its emancipatory potentials: how can one conceive of ways in which internal heterogeneity is transformed into a collective unity without repeating the process in which heterogeneities and differences are necessarily subordinated

---

their different methodological approaches and focuses: see Palumbo-Liu's exhaustive analysis of the predicament of "Asians located *not* 'in' Asia *nor* in the United States, but of shifting and often contradictory *predications* of 'Asia' onto and into the U.S. imaginary" (21) in *Asian/American: Historical Crossings of a Racial Frontier* (1999); David Li's engagement of Asian American alienation and abjection as the contradiction of U.S. citizenship in *Imagining the Nation: Asian American Literature and Cultural Consent* (1998); Jinqui Ling's *Narrating Nationalism: Ideology and Form in Asian American Literature* (1998); Rachel Lee's *The Americas of Asian American Literature: Gendered Fictions of Nation and Transnation* (1999); and Kandice Chuh's *Imagine Otherwise: On Asian American Critique* (2003).

and another hierarchy is reproduced? How can Lowe's notion of "heterogeneity, hybridity, multiplicity" be deployed politically in organizing the consolidation of identity? How can one articulate the heterogeneous nature of Asian America and thoroughly problematize and displace in-/outside distinctions of Asian Americans, particularly given that recent versions of US culture can be perceived as an attempt to recreate official national culture out of its multiplicity and hybridity vis-à-vis transnational circumstance?

All these questions resurface in the debate between Sau-ling Wong and Susan Koshy over the implications of the transnational turn in Asian American studies. Wong, in her essay "Denationalization Reconsidered: Asian American Cultural Criticism at a Theoretical Crossroads" (1992), argues that the essentializing notion of cultural genealogy is still an integral part of Asian American racialization and thus seeks to locate the Asian American contradiction within the nation-state. Based upon her political appreciation of cultural nationalism and historicist critique of transnational rhetorics, Wong contends that it is in the national exclusion of Asian immigrants and in discriminatory policies against Asian immigrants as a minority population of the United States that the roots of Asian American studies lie. In contrast to Wong's concerns over the "denationalization" of Asian American studies, Susan Koshy endorses the transnationalization of the field's epistemology as a necessary step toward its articulation:

> While Wong acknowledges the significance of transnational influences on Asian American ethnicity, she cautions against a "trend" she sees as potentially depoliticizing: the loss of focus on "domestic" issues in a preoccupation with the "diasporic." However, the term "denationalization," which, according to the OED, means "to make (an institution, etc.) no longer national; to divest of its character as belonging to the whole nation, or to a particular nation" distorts the complexity, range and effects of transnational perspectives on the field. It is important to recognize that the *trans*national is not antithetical to the national; it both reconstitutes the national, and exceeds it in crucial ways. Hence, Wong's conceptualization of these phenomena through the term *de*nationalization is tendentious and fundamentally flawed. Moreover, the usage is vitiated by the associations of the term. The term "denationalized" is widely used in neoimperialist theory where it refers to the indigenous elites who collaborate with transnational corporate interests, setting them in an exploitative relationship to, and severed from the interests of, the people at large. Is Wong implying a parallel between transnational cultural critics and such elites? Since she does not indicate the source of her terminology, the prior associations of the term make her usage highly problematic. I would also argue that, in the politically

> contentious nineties, where the rhetoric against immigrants is so highly charged, a term like "denationalization" can be easily appropriated into right-wing arguments about the difficulty of incorporating Asians into American nationhood. (340)

As long as Asian American identity has been transformed by the continuous flow of people, capital, and products, its multiple and shifting definitions can be no longer of any use for its points of reference, places of origin, or destination. Koshy therefore places an emphasis on how diasporic concerns and transnational fluidity constitute American studies while skeptical of wholesale dismissal of cultural nationalism in the rhetoric of a celebratory transnationalism. Of particular importance here is to ask what the "crucial ways" are, in which Koshy argues the transnational "both reconstitutes the national and exceeds it." Does the prefix "trans" in transnationalism *always already* implicate what other prefixes such as "de" in "deterritorialization" and the "re" in "reterritorialization" imply? If the transnational renders any bounded sense of locality obsolete, contested, and unstable, can the transnational ever enable a creation of forms of solidarity and identity that do not rest on the boundaries of nation-states? If the national does not need to have boundaries in the form of division and simple enclosure, are boundaries still necessary in the sense that, as Palumbo-Liu points out, "there is no diaspora without borders and no borders without states" (344)? Kosh rarely confronts these questions and the recent Asian American studies seems to be straddling the divide between denationalization concerns and transnational challenges.

A Geography of Somewhere, a Geography of Nowhere

Thus far I have proposed that recent trends in Asian American (literary) studies has been concerned with the complex linkage between the national and the transnational alongside the ongoing national frames and the academic turn toward transnationalism. The vexing tug-of-war between Asian American studies' turn toward transnationalism and its misgivings about denationalizing tendencies of transnationalism can be brought to bear upon mapping suburban imaginaries in Asian American texts. Viewing with lingering hope tinged with skepticism about American transnational expansiveness and multicultural openness, I will read suburban imaginaries to discuss how Asian America can produce compelling narratives *not* in the manner of a "native informant" or a purveyor of outside perspectives for a case study. In order to make sense of transnationally framed Asian America's fluid and even contradictory claims rather than merely attribute a secure origin to the shared ethnic and cultural affinities, I will cast a critical eye on the ways in which transnational expansiveness and cultural openness can be used to undercut the theoretical purchase of resistance and to resuscitate the self-sufficient narrative that effectively internalizes and contains the heterogeneous elements within national boundaries. To this end, I will first situate my own reading of Asian American texts in material and historical grounding of the American suburb as a point of departure.

It is indisputable that one of the dramatic changes imprinted on the face of the American landscape after World War II is the suburban sprawl. The second half of the 20th century witnessed the massive development of the suburban landscape as a new type of terrain that problematized the urban/rural distinction. Such a change led Americans to a sudden doubt as to the distinctness of the urban and the rural, which had served as a mainstay of American topography up to that point. The expansion of the suburban environment as a significant historical phenomenon has eventually molded the United States into primarily a suburban nation with far more Americans living in the suburbs than in either urban or rural areas at the dawn of the twenty-first century.[72] The postwar expansion of the terrain marks not merely a revolution in demographics but a collective effect on American culture to the

---

72 As a result of all the supports for home ownership, a majority of the United States' white families lived in homes they owned for the first time in 1946. Between 1950 and 1970, the suburban population doubled, from 36 million to 74 million. 83 percent of the nation's population growth during those years took place in the suburbs. See Jackson, especially chapter 11 and 12.

extent that the suburban experience is vital for making sense of American way of life of today.[73]

Despite an extensive array of efforts to lay down a definition of its cultural identity, the suburb from the outset has never been a locatable location. Its uniform architectural styles and landscape designs may be instantly identifiable, but the suburb has instilled a contradictory sense of place and its explosion has drastically altered the ways in which Americans think about the environment surrounding them and their individual and collective relationship to it. Some of suburban cultural identifications may render the suburb tied to both the urban and rural spheres, yet not fully identifiable to be regarded as either—a kind of borderland that lacks a self-contained sense of place. In contrast to the traditional tableau of the suburb as an embodiment of a massive expansion

---

73 Given such a suburban tableau engraved in contemporary American psyche, it is no wonder that Hollywood has produced a set of movies, usually labeled "suburban films" with a strong anti-suburban sentiment particularly since the 1990s, such as Todd Solondz's debut, *Welcome to the Dollhouse* (1995), Ang Lee's screen adaptation of Rick Moody's *The Ice Storm* (1997), Peter *Weir's The Truman Show* (1998), Gary Ross' *Pleasantville* (1998), Sam Mendes' *American Beauty* (2004), the 2004 remake of *The Stepford Wives*, and recently *Revolutionary Road* (2008) among many others. While such cultural productions conflate the two standard images of suburbia in American culture, namely utopia and dystopia based upon the vignette of suburbia as white and middle class, the new patterns of movement, increasingly diversifying social stratum, and demographical changes have altered the shape of the suburbs.

of the middle class nuclear family gravitating toward social homogenization and conformity, the suburban landscape stands as a counterpart to specific drives and tendencies in American culture and lays bare a number of contradictory cultural elements—suburbia as both a source of material and emotional shelter and a place of alienation; a newly found matriarchal realm of female power and a place of suffocating male-dominated enclosure for women; and a welcoming place for *all* Americans and an exclusionary place with a racial overtone. In short, the suburban landscape developed in the decades following the end of World War II both reflects those intersecting tendencies, thereby looming up as a symbolic signpost of the values and contradictions of the U.S. culture.

In addition to its ever-changing nature, the U.S. suburb is not any longer "sub" to the urban areas in any commonsensical sense of the prefix. In fact, many American suburbs are now replete with a wide range of employment opportunities, shopping districts, and the systems of education, healthcare, and law enforcement.[74] Thus emerges a peculiar sense of place that distinguishes the suburbs from other parts of a larger metropolitan area and recreates them

---

74 By the mid-1990s, suburb-to-suburb commutes accounted for up to 40 percent of total communities in the United States while the once-traditional suburb-to-city commute accounted for only 20 percent of all such commuting patterns (Calthorpe xii).

self-sufficient economically, culturally, and politically as a rich site of population diversity in tune with those expanded services. With increasing decentralization of businesses and services, one can easily find in contemporary America a suburb lined with low-rent apartments beside gated developments and a neighborhood in which upwardly mobile minorities and working-class whites live together—variously called "centerless cities," "technoburb," "edge cities," and "ethnoburb."[75]

What this extensive change demonstrates is that the suburb exists in so shifting a way that it becomes more and more difficult to determine its parameters to the degree that it continues to metamorphose itself into an increasingly contested social terrain. As Dolores Hayden maintains, the suburb is not only a residential landscape but also a "site of promises, dreams, and fantasies" (3). It is this elusive nature of the suburb as both a physical and imaginary landscape that leads Americans to believe that the suburb continues to exist "somewhere" no matter how much complex it

---

75 "Centerless cities," "technoburb," "edge cities," and "ethnoburb" are terms respectively coined by Kenneth Jackson, Robert Fishman, Joel Garreau, and Li Wei. Their research varies in their range of scope and subjects of interest, but converge on two diverging views of the suburbs: an enduring metropolitan aspect of the suburbs still closely associated with distinct urban centers; and an autonomous suburban identity free of metropolitan associations. Most studies of the contemporary American suburbs in history, cultural studies, and social sciences revolve around such two different views.

becomes to define what the suburb is. While the suburban demise is trumpeted out, the suburb is not dismissed merely as a thing of the past, but repeatedly resurrects as an entity grounded in the present that can be felt tangibly and even as an embodiment of the deceptive temporality of the "hereafter" slipping into the future. Without recognizing this difficulty of locating the elusive location of the suburb, one can never fully understand why the suburb is still articulated as either a newly-found utopia or a contemporary version of Dante's inferno, and why contemporary Americans give it a look of scorn while reiterating an old-fashioned sense of community attached to it. Most Americans and many others well versed in American culture, at the mention of the word, suburb, would recall a set of familiar images such as the prefabricated identical houses on identical lots, backyard barbecues, station wagons, and the swimming pool. These images are densely fraught with a number of signifiers that, taken together, at once insinuate the middle-class American dream into popular culture in the postwar years and envision the inverse dream of the suburb as a place of soulless landscape of tepid conformity. A following question is then how the suburb, once lauded as the visible manifestation of the American way of life, came to acquire the image of a place of the spiritual death and emotional emptiness.

The suburb continuously changes—sprawling, evolving, becoming desolate, and even resurrecting in the face of its anticipated demise—as it is being reconfigured in light of *and* in opposition to its purported intent. It is therefore necessary for any analysis of the suburb to measure its representations alongside historical reality and to relate its discursive locus to its historical contexts since the suburb does not exist merely as the suburb itself: it is continuously recreated in and though various discourses. In order to reveal the tangled complexities, rich history, and gradual evolution of the suburb, it is of utmost importance not to reduce one's study of the suburb to an analytical gaze on a "real" suburb. Do suburbanites conceive of and thus shape their residential landscape or does the suburb influence the ways in which they think of it? The suburb is both subject to our perception and suggestive of things that resist such perception. It is precisely within this context that so much stress should be placed upon the discursive understanding of its cultural representation alongside historical approaches to the suburb.

Furthermore, the explosive growth of the suburbs carries in its blueprint a set of manifestations of symbolic values and mythologies of America as well as a set of practical possibilities. The suburban tableau reflects shared national experiences of space in American psyche from the westward movement, to the closing of the frontier in the late nineteenth century as announced by Frederick Jackson Turner, and then to the suburbanization and housing crises in mid-20th century. As an updated version of Henry Nash Smith's conception of the American west as "the garden of the world" and Leo Marx's "middle landscape" as "a new, distinctively American, post-romantic, industrial version of the pastoral design" (Marx 32), the suburb combines the city as a place of socio-political dynamism with the countryside where the pastoral ideal is supposed to survive.[76] As a result, the features of both the frontier and the pastoral are weaved into the suburb.

Although the postwar suburban culture has instilled dismissive attitudes toward its lack of individuality and mass-produced sameness, it is hard to deny that the suburbs did offer a modicum of comfort and convenience to growing families of modest means. Suburbanization was initially founded on the impulse to supply housing for all the Americans crowded in the inner cities. To meet pressing need for affordable housing in the late 1940s and to oppose further government participation in public housing programs, suburbs were advocated as a market-based alternative that flaunted the moral high ground of having

---

76 Smith holds that "Americans were unsentimental about unmodified nature" (141-42), which means they were eager to transform the wilderness into a "garden." While Smith laments at the conclusion of *Virgin Land* that the exclusively agricultural garden he describes "was powerless to confront issues arising from the advance of technology" (259), Marx in *Machine in the Garden* takes a step further by pointing out that the kind of garden Americans sought not only varied over time but gradually made room for "the machine." The suburban house was seen as creating a unity with nature to blend in with natural environment, but it was the unity that pictured nature as a tamed environment. The 1950s suburban architectural design conceived of the natural world in a simplified and controlled way that eliminated anything that was wild or irregular.

the general public's interest in mind. Later, merchant builders such as William J. Levitt, developer of Levittown, began to take a huge stride toward mass-produced suburban development by applying Fordist techniques of mass production to building suburban houses at a price within range for those not traditionally considered to be home owners. Like the 17,400 houses accommodating 82,000 residents in the first standardized suburban development built by Levitt, most postwar suburban houses had central heating, indoor plumbing, telephones, automatic stoves, refrigerators, and washing machines. The ideal of the freestanding single family dwelling furnished with conveniences that most middle-class families craved became possible for a larger range of families than ever before, facilitated by sustained economic growth, the GI Bill, cheap home mortgages, ingenious planning, energetic marketing, and federally subsidized interstate highways and new freeways.[77] Homes were affordable and available, and laborsaving devices and new appliances to fill those homes were multiplying at a staggering

---

77 The housing shortage of the 1940s, the postwar baby boom, the GI Bill Rights (the Servicemen's Readjustment Act of 1944) demanded increasing roles of the Federal Housing Administration (FHA) in earmarking guarantee money for new suburban housing projects, while affording federal insurance for loans to veterans in addition to the tax benefits for home owners. As a result, it became cheaper to buy than rent houses. For an expansive historical account of suburban sprawl in the United States, see Hayden, *Building Suburbia*, especially 3-16.

rate.

However, as opposed to its initial inception as a place for everybody where everyone supposedly can go to live the American dream, the all-inclusive suburban ideal coexisted with the excluding realities of specific suburban communities. Behind the new ideal of suburban living lurked the divisive desire for segregation that had been defining suburbs from the days when living there was still predominantly an upper-class privilege. For example, the suburban developments of the 1940s had to face opposition from nearby residents who feared that their privileged space would be threatened by the encroachment of people of a different class on their cherished upper-class values. Subsequently, the focus shifted to keeping out racial minorities. Robert Fishman thus raises the intriguing question, "how can a form based on the principle of exclusion include everyone?" (15). To be sure, the idea of a suburban utopia as a bulwark against the crowding, poverty, and industrialized urban life was historically predicated upon its ability to defend the white homestead with explicit racial overtones. The Federal Housing Administration's redlining policies gave rise to the creation of white suburban communities that systematically excluded people of color and gave an official stamp of approval to those exclusionary practices. Developers even used race-specific restrictions in order to market exclusion and actively promote suburbanization through segregation by insuring home loans for new single-family houses in homogeneous neighborhoods while multiracial communities were neglected. Levitt specified in contracts that "the residents must be of the Caucasian race" (Jackson 241; Hayden, *Building Suburbia* 135).[78] In spite of the 1968 Fair Housing Act to prohibit housing discrimination and residential segregation, the redlining practices resulted in a long-term social injustice coupled with the devastating effects of urban renewal. As such, white flight was inexplicably tied to the deterioration of the inner city and the suburban ideal was dependent upon exclusionary practices ensuring that homes were built for nuclear white families and that "undesirables" would be zoned out of the neighborhood. Such underlying racial anxieties were ready to threaten to disturb a sense of stability wedged into the suburb.

Claiming an ideological advantage of his mass-produced housing, William Levitt once said that "no man who has a house and lot can be a Communist" (Jackson 231). It is not a mere coincidence that Levitt was supported not only by generous home loan legislation for home builders but also by influential politicians like Senator Joseph McCarthy. This linkage of Levitt

---

78 William Levitt admitted ungrudgingly that "[w]e can solve a housing problem, or we can try to solve a racial problem. But we cannot combine the two" (Jackson 241). It is no wonder, as Kenneth Jackson notes, that Levittown did not have a single black resident in its early years. With 82,000 residents, it was the largest all-white community in the United States by 1960. Later, its 38 percent residents were African American around 1980.

as a prime facilitator of the suburban American dream and the McCarthy era of political hysteria is a very intriguing example of the suburban ideal in its cold war formulation.[79] Given that McCarthyism was directed against perceived internal danger by presupposing external enemies, it comes as no surprise that the Soviet Union loomed in the distance as an abstract symbol of what Americans might become if they became "soft." As a result, most Americans agreed that family stability modeled by white middle-class nuclear families in the suburbs should be the best bulwark against the threats of the Cold War. It did not take long for the consumer-oriented suburban dream house to land squarely in the center of Cold War politics. A showcase of the interwoven image of the suburb and the Cold War is the televised 1959 Nixon-Khrushchev "kitchen debate" at the American National Exhibition in Moscow.[80] At this exhibition, Vice-President Nixon

---

79 Persuading Congress into believing in the private industry's capability of providing home cheaply with the aid of Senator McCarthy, Levitt ingeniously made use of racism as a fear tactic with which Levitt and his powerful private housing lobby group propagandized public housing as a socialist policy (Baxandall and Ewen 94).

80 Marling captures "the causal relationship between the arms race and American prosperity" (277) embedded in the kitchen debate: "as Richard Nixon attempted to demonstrate in Moscow, the house wife's choice of a new appliance—pink, square, nonsensical, irrational: whatever—was a choice nonetheless and the habit of making them was a good working definition of the American way of life. The public virtues of democracy were woven into the fabric of private life, into the brand new, 1959-model textures and

landed a blow to his opponent by displaying the suburban homes as the visible manifestation of the American way of life and a proof of the superiority of American free enterprise over communism, well epitomized in a model house named "Splitnik." Nixon insisted that American superiority in the Cold War should hinge not on weapons but on the secure, abundant family life of modern suburban homes. In his rhetoric, consumerism and laborsaving appliances were symbolized as the backbone of a society where the opportunities for achieving individuality, leisure, and upward mobility are open to everyone. It should not go unnoticed here that Nixon, boasting to Khrushchev of the superiority of the American way of life, echoes in the background Levitt asserting that "no man who owns a house and lot can become a Communist." The direct link between the suburban American dream and the international dynamics of the Cold War is deeply embedded in this portrayal of the suburban family as a bastion of safety in an insecure world and a cornerstone of a unified nation blessed with widespread affluence. As such, if the fears over racial outsiders stirred up the sense of restlessness lurking beneath the thin veneer of suburban stability, the very connection between the culture of the Cold War

---

colors and shapes of the suburban kitchen. Pink porcelain, ersatz copper, or "the Platinum Look—the cool billion-dollar look" of brushed aluminum and everyday elegance: style meant leisure, pleasure, convenience, and the USA" (279).

and the domestic suburban culture worked as an inherent tension in the suburb.

Given the history of exclusion and the officially promoted family values in the context of the Cold War, one can identify a distinct way in which a peculiar sense of dislocation typifies the suburban experience of the American middle class while the suburb is always imbued with the moral force of stability and community that invokes the nostalgic vision of the sleepy rural town. It is noteworthy to remember here that the suburb is originally tied to the concept of physical and socio-economic mobility no matter how much suburbanites possess a long-term stake in their communities with an unwavering sense of belonging. The suburbs were essentially constructed for those who were able to move there and marketed to those who were willing to do so. Most notably, the rise of the suburb was aligned with the development of transportation-related infrastructure and the suburbanites were the main beneficiaries of enhanced mobility conditioned by the Interstate Highway Act in 1956, which provided commuter routes to the inner cities they had fled. The proliferation of the automobile, and the roads and the highways on which it travels gave rise to the twentieth-century suburban boom. Adventurousness and movement have always been in tandem with an impulse to find a private haven for belonging, boundedness, and immobility. The suburbs have thus functioned historically as a crucial gathering place for middle-class suburbanites, not in the passive sense that they end up there but in the active sense that the suburbs help them secure the belief in a fresh start and a new beginning. This strange blend of suburban stability and mobility is deeply inscribed in the suburban experience, and the fusion of motion and stillness reconfigures suburbanites as embarking on an adventure and pilgrimage rather than compliantly ensconced in a protected shelter to gain a sense of community. Put otherwise, suburban living from its inception has required continued access to mobility and mobility in return ensured that only those who were able and willing to get out could move to the suburb, which represented for many of its early residents the ability to leave behind the Depression, the war, and the crowded inner city. Furthermore, having once already to find their ideal community, the suburbanites understandably continue to move when more appealing residential options are available or when their own communities change in a way that requires a second escape.

For example, in Sloan Wilson's 1955 bestseller, *The Man in the Gray Flannel Suit*, the suburban discontent of the couple, Tom and Betsy Rath, translates aptly into a desire for mobility to move out and to move up the social ladder since "contentment was an object of contempt" (109) in their neighborhood.[81] Since its

---

81 While most professional critics found fault with *The Man in the Gray Flannel Suit* at the time of its publication in 1955 because they felt Sloan Wilson had played up

publication, the title of Sloan Wilson's novel has become a generic term that tersely characterizes the 1950s' culture—suburban conformity, a massive expansion of the middle class, a heightened valorization of the nuclear family, consequent reification of gender identities, the emergence of consumer society, and the reaffirmation of the American Dream in the form of upward social mobility.[82] As residents of Southport, Connecticut in early 1950s,

---

the universality of his characters too much, many a book merchant predicted that it would be an instant bestseller. The movie version of the novel, appearing so soon after the book's release, rejuvenated the public interest in the novel and helped keep the book's sales figures soaring in the year. Indeed, the novel became a symbol for the middle class, middle income, post-World War II working men. Undoubtedly, bestselling novels are defined by their success in finding audiences. They are defined by audience demand if distorted by some other influences such as large advertising budgets or a narrow choice of novels on the market. Bestsellers become bestsellers because they, in tune with popular demand, succeed in finding resonance with large segments of the reading public. They are an appropriate source for investigating widely held ideas, beliefs, cultural assumptions, and social order. In many respects, Sloan Wilson's *The Man in the Gray Flannel Suit* well meshes with the category of a bestselling popular fiction of the 1950s.

82 Wilson's bestselling novel was also an international bestseller, translated into 26 languages, and was immediately made into a movie in 1956, starring Gregory Peck and Jennifer Jones as Tom and Betsy Rath. The movie became hugely popular as much as the original novel, and was entered at the 1956 Cannes Film Festival. The silhouette of an executive of the publishing company, Simon and Shuster, dressed in a gray flannel suit with his hands clasped behind his back (later the image of Gregory Peck in the movie) became a recognizable symbol of this book that appeared everywhere the copies of the book were sold. The book brought out not only a literary and film hit, but also a fashion craze. A number of cardboard cutouts after the book's trademark silhouette hit department store

Tom and Betsy with three kids seem to enjoy a typical middle-class suburban life on the peaceful and leafy Greentree Avenue. Tom's life "can be summed up in numbers" that appear to indicate the stability of his typical suburban family life: Thomas R. Rath, thirty-three years old, making seven thousand dollars a year, owner of a 1939 ford, a six-room house, and ten thousand dollars' worth of G. I. life insurance [···] Six feet one and a half inches tall; weight, 198 pounds" (12). The expected suburban complacency and tranquility, however, are compromised by an undercurrent of their anxieties and discontentment: Betsy feels that Tom's job with a Manhattan charitable organization pays too little and urges him to interview for a job at a New York-based television network, UBC (United Broadcasting Company). The very first line of the novel begins with a kind of antisuburban manifesto

---

windows and major retailers across the United States saw the publishing of the book as an excellent opportunity for promotions to push gray flannel suit sales. As such, *The Man in the Gray Flannel Suit* took on a life outside its bookbinding and stirred the masses of an entire decade. This popularity of both the novel and the film stems from their resonance with many Americans in the 1950s. They did embody the fifties America so successfully that audiences could relate to the characters' concerns. Undeniably, Tom Rath is a post-war "everyman" to whom most Americans could relate, and Tom and Betsy are a typical newly-wed couple of World War II generation. Their contemporaries could easily identity with them with so much sympathy toward their war correspondence, their wartime sacrifices, and the necessity of having to grow up too quickly as parents of the baby-boomer generation.

of the couple, "they both detested it" (1). A notable symbol of their antisuburban sentiment is a crack near the floor "curving up from it almost to the ceiling in the shape of a question mark" that resurfaces throughout the text "as a perpetual reminder of Betsy's moment of extravagance, Tom's moment of violence, and their inability either to fix the walls properly or to pay to have them fixed" (1). They all begin to consider their suburban house not so much a cultural outpost of the American dream as "a trap" (3). Preoccupied with the idea of "getting out [their] house" (60). Betsy thinks that "it's not fair to the children to bring them up in a neighborhood like this!" and, when asked by Tom what is wrong with their neighborhood, she answers offhand, "it's dull" (61).[83] Interestingly, the postwar suburbs recombine mobility

---

83 This story of the suburbanites who live on the thin surface hiding anxieties and troubles brewing within is in tune with the sociological scrutiny of the period that consistently linked the uniformity of the suburban landscape to detrimental effects on the resident. Lewis Mumford, urban historian, suggests in his seminal *The City in History* (1961) suggested that the U. S. suburb was fast becoming a "low-grade uniform environment from which escape was impossible" (486). Seeing suburbia through the lens of postwar critics like Mumford, many observers painted a monochrome picture of the suburban world as white, affluent, and conformist. David Riesman in *The Lonely Crowd* (1950) argued that similarity of environmental and social experience was fostering the emergence of the conformist mindset. William H. Whyte in his 1956 *The Organization Man* expressed concern over the corporatized nature of home life, seeing in the prefabricated, socially homogeneous suburbs a mirror image of the "gray flannel" corporate world.

and stability in its reconfiguration of frontier principle and stasis of family life.[84] If the suburbs consolidate both the frontierism

---

84 While it may be a truism among cultural historians that the postwar suburban sprawl was part of a general return to family values, less attention has been devoted to the question of another, at times contradictory, ideal in postwar ideology—that of neighborhood bonding and community participation. Suburbia emerged as a place where belonging to the neighborhood network was just as important as the return to family life. Indeed, the new domesticity was not merely experienced as a retreat from the public sphere, but it gave people a sense of belonging to the community. By purchasing their detached suburban homes, the young couples of the middle class participated in the construction of a new community of values; in magazines, in films, and on the airwaves they became the cultural representatives of the "good life." In this sense, in the new suburban culture was the construction of a particular discursive space through which the family could mediate the contradictory impulses for a private haven on the one hand, and community participation on the other. By lining up individual housing units on connecting plots of land, the suburban tract was itself the ideal articulation of this discursive space—the dual goals of separation from and integration into the larger community was the basis of tract design. Moreover, the domestic architecture of the period mediated the tension between the inside and outside world. Benefiting from modernist architecture, the modernized suburban homes blurred distinction between inside and outside spaces even in uniformly prefabricated suburbs like the 17000-house suburb of Levittown.
Historically, the suburban white middle-class angst about sedentary family life was counteracted by the notion of movement. Most notably, the suburbanites were the beneficiaries of enhanced mobility conditioned by the Interstate Highway Act in 1956, which provided commuter routes to the inner cities that they had fled. In addition, the promotional rhetorical on portable television in the 1960s demonstrated the ways in which the new technology was designed for and predicated on broader technological transition in American family life, bridging the Eisenhower era's emphasis on nuclear-family consumer life style and the Kennedy-era ideal of "New Frontierism." As such, adventurousness and movements always goes hand in hand with an impulse to find a private haven for belonging,

and pastoral idealism in its precarious blending of motion and stillness, Westport is exactly a place where a frontier principle encodes stasis of family life at its very heart and a stalled motion is in need of reactivation. It is within this context that most townspeople including the Raths are preoccupied with the idea of moving out and up. This suburban white middle-class angst about sedentary family life is thus reinforced by their desire for movement.[85]

Catherine Jurca in her comprehensive study of US suburban novel begins to analyze suburban pathology by framing an intriguing question of why suburbanites feel a sense of entrapment at home as if they are "spiritually and culturally impoverished by prosperity" (*White Diaspora* 7). She argues that "the suburb is the exemplary location, not only of middle-class advantages, but

---

boundedness, and immobility.

85 "Almost all the houses were occupied by couples with young children, and few people considered Greentree Avenue a permanent stop—the place was just a crossroads where families waited until they could afford to move on to something better. The finances of almost every household were an open book. Budgets were frankly discussed, and the public celebration of increases in salary was common. The biggest parties of all were moving-out parties, given by those who finally were able to buy a bigger house. Of course, there were few men in the area who had given up hope of rising in the world, and a few who had moved from worse surroundings and considered Greentree Avenue a desirable end of the road, but they and their families suffered a kind of social ostracism. On Greentree Avenue, contentment was an object of contempt" (109).

of middle-class abasement; moreover, its abasement is a function of its advantages" since "material benefits" may serve for the suburbanites as "cultural and spiritual handicaps" (*white Diaspora* 4). Viewed in this light, it is understandable that Jurca in her pathological view of the suburban life suggests that "thinking of oneself as a victim may be necessary condition for becoming one" ("The Sanctimonious Suburbanite" 87). It is precisely within this context that Tom and Betsy feel homeless at home and dream the "dreams of escaping to an entirely different sort of life" (109) while safely ensconced in the prestigious homeownership and the ideal of a freestanding single family dwelling. Not coincidentally, Tom, who is always pushed to make more money for a better settlement, is plunged into a fantasy of flight whenever he sees a huge billboard with a sign of "Fly to Miami" (45) on his way to New York City on a commuter train. If the image of Dr. T. J. Eckleburg's gigantic eyes on a billboard in *The Great Gatsby*, overlooking the valley of ashes, is an incisive commentary on faulty vision of the characters, the "Fly to Miami" billboard becomes a compelling metaphor for the myopia of the suburbanites including Tom Rath who can never see beyond the immediate and the superficial aspects of his dream vision.

Tom is constantly warned by his wife Betsy that life's prizes go to the optimists, the forward-looking go-getters, and this spur for mobility is emphasized by the frequent use of the prepositions such as "on," "toward," and "out" throughout the novel. In actuality,

The Man in the Gray Flannel Suit is fraught with such mobile images, which is also the case with its cinematic adaptation: the movie begins by showing an image of a commuter train; western movies appear on almost every TV screen; Tom's war memories are shot through with the typical masculine mobility on the battle field such as parachute jumping and rushing the enemy's position. However, all of this mobility is always undercut by its counterpart—a kind of suburban immobility. The commuter train is mobile only to the extent that it guarantees "back home" in the endless cycle of departure and return. The frontierism echoed in the western movies is oddly opposed to the claustrophobic atmosphere of the living room of Tom's suburban house and his office at UBC. Even wartime extremes are juxtaposed with suburban ordinariness. For example, when Tom's mind drifts back to his Italian girlfriend, his recollections are immediately are set alongside his postwar suburban life, bringing such wartime mobility into the center of suburban stasis that cannot allow such movement any more. Tom's parachute jumping carries over into his anxieties he feels over the abyss of total uncertainty whenever taking a step in his postwar life. In that sense, the suburbanites' disillusion with their dwelling place and fascination with just going are never held together firmly by a shared sense of having to keep going. Their desire for mobility is limited and fragile one because their preoccupation with mobility not infrequently takes the form of immobility. Such a kind of mobility is strenuous and chronic, and yet, simultaneously, directionless. They seem to have little control over it. As the call of the open road never serves as an answer to the complexities of social and moral experience in the suburb, it is no surprise that Tom's furtive desire for moving out and up lapses into a bundle of clichés about a brighter future and being at peace with the present life. As such, the yearning for movement fused with suburban stability brings into sharp relief the elusive location of the suburb that seems to exist in and for motion. The suburban ideal is not only what already existed in the suburbs when the family arrived. Rather, it is the journey home for leaving home again—a cycle of "living for leaving" and "leaving for living"—that matters in the American experience of suburban life. Viewed in this light, suburban stability is nothing but a flip side of the same coin of suburban mobility—a stalled motion waiting to be reactivated. It is precisely due to this double-edged nature of suburban stability that the fleeting presence of the suburb is felt only by continuously conjuring up the original migration in American cultural imagination.

Michel Foucault argues that "heterotopia" is an "effectively enacted utopia in which the real sites, all the other sites that can be found within the culture, are simultaneously represented, contested, and inverted" since it is "absolutely different from all the sites that they reflect and speak about" (24). Serving as a mirror to the very society that has produced it, "heterotopia" becomes "a space that is other, another real space, as perfect, as meticulous, as well arranged as ours is messy, ill constructed, and jumbled" (26). Building upon and extending Foucault's notion of heterotopia, I suggest that the American suburb can act out a kind of "heterotopic mirror" to mainstream American culture: the suburb is nothing if not a heterotopic mirror in which a utopian dream of middle-class complacency is invocated and, at the same time, the social realities offsetting such a fantasy vision are incessantly evoked. If the suburb, straddling a precarious line between a vision reality, exists in a spatial uncertainty as a heterotopic mirror to the traditional suburban tableau, this spatial disparity between "somewhereness" and "nowhereness" is not inseparable from suburban temporal dissonance—the heterochronic nature of suburbia that brings into being the uncanny temporal dimensions of heterotopia. Interestingly, the contemporary images of a suburban future are laden with nostalgia, not for the 1950s *per se* but for the 1950s vision of the future, consistent with media's and popular culture's representations of the 1950s suburbs through the recreation of an old-fashioned sense of community. This collective nostalgia not for real families but rather the image of white, middle-class, suburban families comes to us not infrequently through popular culture such as sitcoms set in the 1950s and films, and it is directly wedded to the vision of family values promoted in contemporary political life in the United States. This uncanny parallel between "what was once" and "what is now" poses a problematic temporality of the suburb, perpetuating the notion that the suburb is elsewhere and causing the difficulty of conceiving of a suburban future.

The most striking examples of this suburban temporal dissonance, both reaching back into the past and slipping into the future, can be seen in fully preplanned Disney's Celebration, founded in 1995 as a commuter suburb for workers at Disney World and other attractions nearby Orlando, and Seaside, Florida, a "new urban" community. These two towns demonstrate the latest manifestation of a US suburb such as the gated and neotraditional communities favored by the movement known as "New Urbanism" that aims at striking a balance between individualism and community spirit.[86] The visions of New Urbanism trace back to the Chicago School of urban sociology in the 1920s, which studied the demographics, urban planning, and social relations in the classic industrial cities of the East and Midwest with a rigorous analysis of the experience of urbanism. The methodology of the School depended on traditional thinking about "centers" and "peripheries," and about circulation and service zones. In the 1950s and 1960s, Jane Jacobs, partly grounded on legacy of the Chicago School, set out to defend urban neighborhoods by valuing the diversity of street life in ways that resonate today

---

86 For a discussion of Seaside and Celebration alongside the rise of New Urbanism, see Hayden, *Building Suburbia* 203-15.

throughout the debates about New Urbanism. Later, even the division between city and suburb, let alone between either of them and country, has been questioned since the publication of Joel Garreau's 1991 *Edge City*. More recently, there is an ongoing debate about the nature of new urban or posturban potentials and alternatives that reconceptualize the notions of social space and urbanism. For example, Edward Soja in *Postmodern Geographies* regards Los Angeles and, more generally, Southern California not as a centered city but as a virtually archaeological site wherein *multiple* urbanisms coexist.

One of the problems arising from the development of modern suburban divisions like Seaside and Celebration is that these communities are envisioned outside of history while invoking historicity itself. The historicity invoked in the "new urban" are so distant that nobody cares if such a thing as a suburban community did really exist. The historicity itself is merely conjured up unsubstantially only to the extent that the imagined past of a community is never questioned. Contemporary suburbanites' dream to live *there* once again can never be realized. Likewise, modern suburban developments, following the New Urbanist movement after the decline of the original suburban ideal, ingeniously use the desire to recapture historical illusions by making allusions to insubstantial distant histories. As such, the suburb evolves as the procession of simulacrum in a Baudrilliardian sense.[87] What emerges here is an irony that the suburb has erased its origins through its continuous repetition as an imaginary construct and shaken the belief that there is anything real underneath its development while reinforcing the idea that a real suburb still exists *elsewhere.*[88]

The suburban growth explosion was fueled partially, if not completely, by postwar white flight from urban communities. In addition, the peak of suburbanization corresponds to the period of the emergence and outburst of the civil rights and women's movement. Therefore, the suburb has inevitably been a major site of contention for social reform. Pitted against these historical contexts, the New Urbanists' belief that managing such elements as architectural design, street orientation, and visual perspective

---

87 Baudrillard suggests that "Disneyland is presented as imaginary in order to make us believe that the rest is real" (40).

88 Peter Weir's 1998 film, *The Truman Show*, is an interesting case in point here. It was shot on Seaside, Florida while announcing itself as a biting critique of mass-produced suburbs. As noted earlier, Seaside, embraced as an antidote to suburban sprawl, is a most notable embodiment of the contemporary New Urbanism architectural movement and a post-urban, neo-traditional urban design philosophy. The location in the film looks like a classic suburb in the 1950s. What this intentional melding of contemporary and postwar visions of the suburb entails is an irony: Weir's choice of the master-planned, post-urban Seaside as the physical setting to represent his make-believe suburban sitcom set mirroring old-fashioned American suburbia becomes a kind of meta-commentary on neo-traditionalism, nostalgia, and contemporary planned community.

can instill a sense of community poses a serious problem at the end of American's suburban century. Such a naïve belief harbors a desire for "what was once" that resists historical change and the convergence of contemporary and postwar visions of the suburb betrays the anxiety over an implausible future caught between an unlocatble present and a frozen past.

Fredric Jameson in his study of postwar science fiction contends that the genre is no longer able to imagine utopia but rather can only serve to defamiliarize the present (279-96). If the hopelessness or impossibility of envisioning utopia brings for Jameson "nostalgia for the present," a nostalgic longing of the contemporary US suburb for the "real" that ends up simulating the Cold War past ironically gives rise to "nostalgia for the future." Put otherwise, as long as temporal dissonance of the contemporary suburb, fractured between "what was once" and "what is now," is not able to articulate what the suburb is and, in turn, where it is going, *hereafter* it is not possible to conceptualize the ways to get "there," either. This implausible geography of the "hereafter" might be called a heterochronic dimension of the suburb—an uncanny temporal nature of heterotopia. Although the suburb itself has continued to evolve, the geography of the "hereafter" remains out of reach as long as the suburb continuously returns to the nostalgic past, reminding us of what is not yet found. This is the "nostalgia for the future" that ironically propels the suburb on to the past, not with a forward-looking gaze but with the impulse to find its own future in the past. If one can conceive of any suburban future only in terms of the past, such a future is unavoidably foreclosed from its inception and a suburban future will come not with the liberating time of the "hereafter" but only in the form of "back to the future" as long as the suburb continues to perpetuate itself through its retrospectively invoked nostalgic historicity. "Back to the future" is then the only way to inhabit the unfulfilled time of a suburban future.

Place of Gesture, Gesture of Place

"Everybody knows me here"—it is the first line of *A Gesture Life*, but the narrator's unwavering sense of belonging immediately becomes ironic when it is located within the temporal and spatial matrix of the complex suburban sense of belonging. The narrator is a Japanese immigrant, Franklin Kurohata, who is enjoying his well-earned retirement in the respectable suburban town of Bedley Run in upstate New York. An upstanding citizen who enjoys "an almost Oriental veneration as an elder" (1) and former long-time owner of a successful medical supply store on the main street in town, Hata is hailed as "Doc" by townspeople who have benefited from his over-the-counter advice. His well-organized routines—daily rounds of exercise in his beloved pool, afternoon walks, evening readings, and even fending off never-ending inquiries of local realtors—consolidate his reiterated confidence that "everyone here knows perfectly who I am" (1). This suburban complacency and tranquility seem to fit in with what should be an uneventful life of a retiree.

> People know me here. It wasn't always so. But living thirty-odd years in the same place beings to show on a man. In the course of such time, without even realizing it, one takes on the characteristics of the locality, the color and stamp of the prevailing dress and gait and even speech—those gentle bells of the sidewalk passerby, their *How are yous and Good days and Hellos*. And in a gradual and accruing recognition of one's face, of being, as far as anyone can recall, from around here. There's no longer a linger or vacant stare, and you can taste the small but unequaled pleasure that comes with being a familiar sight to the eyes. In my case, everyone here knows perfectly who I am. It's a simple determination. Whenever I step into a shop in the main part of the village, invariably someone will say, "Hey, it's good Doc *Hata*." (1)

What follows the protagonist's assertion, however, foreshadows an undercurrent of emptiness in Hata's life. After an accidental fire in his living room that lands him in the hospital with smoke inhalation, Hata's period of recuperation both in the hospital and later at home is interrupted by disturbing memories that impinge on his routines and forces an Updike-style self-examination. In the course of passing through traces of Hata's bygone years, one is invited into his innermost memories just as he or she experiences defamiliarization in reading the "Dick-and-Jane Primer" in Toni Morrison's *The Bluest Eye* (1970): "Here is the house. It is green and white. It has a red door. It is very pretty. Here is the family. Mother, Father, Dick, and Jane live in the green-and-white house. They are very happy …" (7). The elementary primer passage is twice repeated in the Morrison's novel—the first time without punctuation, capitalization, and the second without even spaces between words. The final run-on version makes readers skeptical about the ideal image of Dick-and-Jane's perfect American family by breaking up conventional syntactic structures with decreasing decipherability. Just as Morrison prefaces subsequent chapters with the formal practices with portions of the text of the primer, Lee ingeniously leads readers to reevaluate the cultural signposts which give the measure and meaning to what constitutes Hata's seemingly successful immigrant life. What follows is my own version of "Doc Hata Primer": "Here is Doc Hata. People know him here. He lives in a respectable suburb. Here is the two-story Tudor House. It is very pretty. He is enjoying his retirement life. Everyone here perfectly knows who he is."

As one is compelled to reconfigure the familiar image of Dick-and-Jane primer behind the progressive elimination of markers and the running-together of words in Morrison's novel, we need to defamiliarize and refamiliarize the suburban mold of Hata's life to unearth the meanings of his life in Bedley Run. At first out of place in the respectable New York suburb where he has settled, Hata works hard to achieve acceptance there and takes pains to fit in, creating no disturbances and never complaining even when provoked by thoughtless schoolchildren or narrow-minded adults—a life of "gesture" as his rebellious teenage adoptee calls it: "all I've ever seen is how careful you are with everything. With our fancy big house and this store and all the customers. How you sweep the sidewalk and nice-talk to other shopkeepers. You make a whole life out of gesture and politeness. You're always having to be the ideal partner and colleague" (95). Dipping into memories, Hata himself defines his presence in the community as "an unexpected condition of transparence" and "a walking case of others' certitude" (21-22).

The conflict that lies beneath his comfortable suburban life is the ongoing state of suspension in which he has lived as an outsider and the heartbreaking bargains an outsider has to make to adapt to his surroundings. In addition, his sense of belonging goes beyond the confines of "here" and "now": as a native-born Korean adoptee in Japan, he tried to fit into Japanese culture and fell in love with a Korean "comfort woman" while serving as a paramedic during World War II in the imperial Japanese army. He, then, adopting a child himself from Korea, attempted a similar bit of incorporation into his community as an immigrant in postwar

America. Navigating the tangled memories through the Pacific Rim and the US suburb during and after the Second World War, *A Gesture Life* continually calls into question the manifold meanings of belonging—the life as a cultural, racial, emotional exile and outsider, "molding to whatever is at hand" (290) and doing "what is necessary in being complimentary, as a citizen, colleague, and partner" (135).

As such, the narrative of *A Gesture Life* consists of two plotlines—one in the Pacific Rim during the 1940s when "lieutenant Kurohata" served in the Japanese imperial army, the other in the American suburb where "Franklin Hata" adopts, raises, and finally forms an uneasy rapport with his daughter, Sunny. Oddly enough, Lee scarcely gives an account of what motivated Hata to move the United States after the war, which would make a link between the protagonist's suburban experiences and the gradual disclosure of ambiguities and feelings secretly created from a past time. That missing link, however, can be found in the following description of how Hata ended up in Bedley Run in 1963:

> I'd read about the town in the paper, a brief-slice-of-life article with a picture of a meadow that had been completely cleared for new suburban style homes, just white stakes in the frozen ground to mark where the streets would be. It looked sterile and desolate like fresh blast ground, not in the least hopeful,

and yet I felt strangely drawn to the town, in part because of the peaceful pace of life that the article noted, the simple tranquility of the order, village section that made me think of the small city where I lived my youth, on the western coast of Japan. [···] I'd ask for directions at a garage, or buy some gum at a candy store, and an awkward quiet would arise, that certain clippedness, and though I never heard any comments, I could tell I wasn't being welcomed to remain too long. [···]
Fundamentally, it seems to me, the people in a particular area are given to a common set of conditions and influences, like the growth in a part of a forest. There may be many types of flora, but only the resident soil and climate provide for them, either richly or poorly or with indifference. I suppose it was because Bedleyville was still Bedleyville then, not yet Bedley Run (though desperately wanting to be), and pretty much anybody new to town was seen as a positive addition to the census and tax base. It was 1963, and from what I'd seen during my brief travels in this country, everyone for the most part lived together, except, I suppose, for certain groups, such as the blacks, or the Chinese in the cities, who for one reason or another seemed to live apart. Still, I had assumed that once I settled someplace, I would be treated as those people were treated, and in fact I was fully prepared for it. But wherever I went—and in particular, here in Bedley Run—it seemed people took an odd interest in telling me that I wasn't *un*welcome. (2-3)

The story of Hata settling down in Bedley Run, which used to be sleepy place with a railroad station, here runs parallel to the dramatic transition America has gone through in the twentieth century—the exodus from cities to suburbs. However, Hata never escaped from the city nearby, but he is a sort of refugee who left behind another country and his whole life. Just as Bedley Run began to take on the appearance of cohesion and affluence, Hata took full advantage of the American Dream that seemed to promise that he could have the old feeling of making a new start in life once again like many other Americans in the suburbs. After changing his name from Kurohata, which means "a black flag" to the more mellifluous and innocuous-sounding Hata (a flag), he has always done his best avoid conflict and to be passively friendly—a fresh start seemingly guaranteed by a new suburban life, but actually a "gesture life." Hata's second life in Bedley Run can be then viewed as a way of erasing his past rather than confront it. However, the US suburb as a defining icon of middle-class complacency has very ironic meanings when juxtaposed with the history of Asian America, particularly the internment of Japanese Americans during World War II, which. For a discussion of the presence of the Japanese Americans held behind barbed wire as a compelling metaphor for the state power to remap its interiority by refusing to acknowledge the legal rights of Japanese Americans, it is worth reconsidering John Okada's *No-No Boy* (1957) with an eye toward the protagonist, Ichiro Yamada's plight of inhabiting postinternment America as a space of contradiction and Okada's strategy of articulating postinternment anxieties through lens of suburban imaginaries.

The title of Okada's novel derives from the history of the internment of Japanese Americans during World War II. On February 19, President Franklin D. Roosevelt issued "Executive Order 9066" under which about 12,000 Japanese and Japanese Americans were "relocated" throughout the Pacific coast region to desolate internment camps.[89] In 1943, the War Department planned to recruit young Nisei (second-generation Japanese American) internees and they were administered a Selective Service questionnaire. As a security-clearance measure, internees were asked about their willingness to serve in the American forces and were compelled to forswear allegiance to Japan. Ichiro Yamada is among those who answered "no" to both questions and, like other "no-no boys," was jailed for disloyalty.[90] Having experienced displacement and disruption, and having been

---

89 See Takaki, 379-405.

90 The two questions to which no-no boys answered "no" are as follows: "Are you willing to serve in the armed forces of the United States in combat duty wherever ordered?"; "Will you swear unqualified allegiance to the United States of America and faithfully defend the United States from any or all attacks of foreign or domestic forces, and forswear any form of allegiance or obedience to the Japanese Emperor, to any other foreign government, power or organization?" (Takaki 397).

"denied a place as citizens" (*No-No Boy* 52) due to their Japanese origins and ties, returned internees were in urgent need of an act of *re*-membering against *dis*-membering by reconfiguring their lives in old places, and they were faced also with the growing pressure to blend into a postwar America steeped in consensus politics and conformist sentiment. Returned internees' desire to reclaim a place of their own is thus at the heart of *No-No Boy*, which I suggest deals with the aftermath of the internment no less than the internment per se.[91] Confronted with such urgency to propose an alternative reconstruction by inhabiting the nation as a space of contradiction, *No-No Boy* becomes a story of competing spatial logics and desires. The no-no boy's surreptitious desire for belonging led by his suburban fantasies entails a set of questions. What happens when the idea of postwar suburb meets up with returned internees' and no-no boys' compulsory struggle for national belonging? What is gained and lost if they shift their allegiances from the old ethnic ties to a new suburban ideal in postwar America? Is the move to postwar suburbia likely to lead to a pluralistic integration in tune with the postwar pressures to conform across racial boundaries or to reinforcing racial identities by resorting to a defensive ethnic mobilization to preserve a sense

---

91 Concurring with Jinqui Ling and Viet Nguyen, Kim positions *No-No Boy* as a text of the 1950s (65-66).

of cultural distinctiveness? All these questions are inseparable from the postwar suburban culture deeply embedded in the values of homeownership, marriage, childbearing, conformity, and the middle-class, consumer-oriented way of life.

No-No Boy opens with Ichiro returning home after four years' absence, "two in camp and two in prison" (1). As soon as he steps off the bus, Ichiro runs into an old Japanese American friend named Eto. Eto, however, turns hostile and spits in Ichiro's face as soon as he learns that his friend is a no-no boy who did not serve in the US army but instead chose to go to prison. The "despising hatred" (3), repeatedly surfacing in Ichiro's encounters with other returned Nisei soldiers, has a deep resonance throughout the text. Still preoccupied with polarized definitions of "American" and "Japanese," postwar Nisei nationalism regards no-no boys who wear a "scarlet letter" of disloyalty as a stain on their community. What actually makes Nisei youths hostile toward no-no boys, however, is that no-no boys stir up what they truly wish to forget: they are also "Japs" despite their "badges of courage." The insulting epithet "Japs" that Japanese American veterans use to despise no-no boys returns to them the very moment they seek to separate themselves from "disloyal" no-no boys as sharply as possible. With the crushing weight of assimilation and conformity on their shoulders, Nisei veterans turn their faces away from the root causes of their alienation from the mainstream society. As a result, they can never fully understand that no-no boys have attempted to live out the "American promise" on their own terms by squarely confronting the contradiction of American citizenship.

The festering opposition between "Japanese" and "American" awaits Ichiro at home as well. Mrs. Yamada takes pride in Ichiro's "choice," which she sees as his complete identification with her Japanese nationalism, and the "Japanese" mother welcomes the nation's "prodigal son" warm-heartedly: "I am proud to call you my son" (11). As a fanatic Japanese nationalist, she never accepts the Japanese defeat and waits for the ships from Japan that she hopes will be sent by the Japanese government to take home the "loyal" Japanese, including her family. In contrast, Ichiro's younger brother, Taro, feels so compelled to prove his Americanness and atone for his brother's "sin" that he cannot wait for the day he turns eighteen to enlist in the army. Caught in the American/Japanese split, Taro even lures Ichiro out of the Club Oriental so that his Nisei friends can assault his brother.

Ichiro's postwar Japanese American community has thus become an arena of competing strategies of assimilation/ resistance, conformity/ dissent, and accommodation/ confrontation. Ichiro is seeking to get away from his community's restrictive definitions of who he is, but it is hard for him to completely dissociate himself from his past. What is more painful to Ichiro than a matter of whether or not to leave his hometown is his realization that there are very few geographical alternatives for him, in both physical and psychological senses. His dilemma is not so much whether he should stay or go but that he has nowhere to go. He feels mounting pressure to reconfigure the world which he must share with the returned veterans and internees. The fear of finding himself always "out of place" trails Ichiro no matter where he goes. As the two questions of "who he is" and "where he belongs" are imbued with each other's resonance, Ichiro's surreptitious desire to carve out a niche for himself is merged with his fear of never being able to find it. The preface of *No-No Boy* addresses this issue with an account of a Japanese American soldier, presumably Okada's persona, who is on the reconnaissance mission to Japan.[92] When asked by his lieutenant, a "blond giant from Nebraska," where he is from, all the Nisei soldier comes up with is equivocation, "No place in particular" (x). Aligned with Ichiro's plight of having no clear destination, the Nisei soldier's evasive answer implies that neither returning to an old place nor leaving it will ever be a redemptive experience for Ichiro.

Since "being American is a terribly incomplete thing" (54), Ichiro never shrugs off the fear that he will never be able to belong to either of the two worlds that interpellate him respectively as a nation's prodigal son and a mother's Japanese son. Meandering

---

92 Unlike his fictional protagonist, Okada served as an officer in the US Air Force in World War II, "hanging out of an airplane over Japanese-held islands asking their occupants in their own language to give up" (Chin 256).

through "the ugly street with ugly buildings among the ugly people which was a part of America and, at the same time, would never be wholly America" (71), Ichiro comes to fantasize about a geographical and social anonymity from the two worlds as "his heart mercifully stacked the blocks of hope into the pattern of an America which would someday hold an unquestionable place for him" (52). He continues:

> Was there no hope of redemption? Surely there must be. He was still a citizen. He could still vote. He was free to travel and work and study and marry and drink and gamble. People forgot and, in forgetting, forgave. Time would erase the rupture which now separated him from the young Japanese who were Americans because they had fought for America and believed in it. And time would destroy the old Japanese who, living in America and being denied a place as citizens, nevertheless had become inextricably a part of the country which by its vastness and goodness and fairness and plenitude drew them into its fold, or else they would not have understood why it was that their sons, who looked as Japanese as they themselves, were not Japanese at all but Americans of the country America. In time, he thought, in time there will be again a place for me. I will buy a home and love my family and I will walk down the street holding my son's hand and people will stop and talk with us about the weather and the ball games and the elections. (51-52)

Interestingly, Ichiro's longing to "start anew" is fleshed out in the form of "an unquestionable place," where forgetting and forgiveness are recalled as an adequate, if not outright permanent, solution to Ichiro's plight. While this new sense of place sometimes borders on despair, it is not a fleeting vision for Ichiro. It rather recurs like a leitmotif throughout the novel, demonstrating how Ichiro seeks to displace his trauma onto space to gain a safe, reassuring distance from the past and to map out a future. Furthermore, such a new sense of place keyed to the country's "vastness," "goodness," "fairness," and "plenitude" is predicated upon the clichés of suburban domesticity of the 1950s and middle-class lifestyle in the mass-produced suburbs—the period's reigning ideals that came to dominate America's cultural landscape after World War II. As the novel unfolds, Ichiro's desire for a new, fresh start in the US postwar suburb takes on a more distinctive form with the visible indices of middle-class suburban family life accreted.

While Ichiro's ties to Jackson Street and the Japanese American community are never moored to a specific site such as a house, a bar, an apartment, and a farm, an ardent desire for taking root in "un unquestionable place" begins to elaborate Ichiro's aspirations for a suburban life. For instance, Ichiro is envious of Kumasaka family's decision for settlement. When his mother pays a visit with him to the Kumasakas bereft of their son in the war, she flaunts her "Japanese" son to them who she believes have sacrificed their son on the altar of loyalty. The Kumasakas, who once ran a dry-cleaning shop before the war, have arrived at a decision of "finally sinking roots into the land" (26) and bought "a freshly painted frame house" with "a neatly kept lawn" (25). Sitting down on the sofa in a room furnished with "rugs and soft furniture and lamps and end tables and pictures on recently papered walls" (26), Ichiro cannot choose but covet the house that is "like the millions of other homes in America and could never be his own" (26).

Kenji's father is another character who has opted for rooting. He has been "fixed for a long time," which he takes positively as "a good feeling" (118). His house is laden with "the new rugs and furniture and lamps and the big television set with the radio and phonograph all built into one impressive blond console" (118). In a family gathering at the house with Kenji's siblings, in-laws, and their children the night before Kenji heads for a hospital in Portland for his second operation, it is revealed that "the family has thoroughly adopted the behavior and values of the American middle class of that era" (Yogi 70). They are talking about "baseball on television" (128), how "to keep two cars in the double garage behind a large brick house in a pretty good neighborhood" (129-30), and so on, most of which epitomize the expansive, consumer-oriented, and conformist suburban lifestyle in the postwar US society. Although the festive atmosphere of the occasion is clouded by an undercurrent of fear of Kenji's impending fate, the gathering bears an imprint of the cultural milieu of the 1950s deeply embedded in the suburban culture.[93]

It is Emi who significantly affects Ichiro by planting herself firmly in his quest for a spatial alternative inextricably tied to the postwar American suburb. Separated from (or abandoned by) her husband who refuses to return home after war, Emi serves as both a lover and mother to Ichiro and provides for him the maternal nurturing that he no longer receives from his own mother. Emi exhorts Ichiro to "start anew" by telling him to "[a]dmit your mistake and do something about it" (95). Her rhetoric echoes the familiar American sense of place that enables Ichiro to "start clean" while admitting that "[t]o forget completely would be impossible" (112): "This is a big country with a big heart. There's room here for all kinds of people. Maybe what you've done doesn't make you one of the better ones but you're not among the worst either" (95).

---

93 Asian Americans' move to the suburbs from their ethnic neighborhoods clearly reflects their sense of vulnerability and unrelenting pressure to conform in the Cold War era: "Asian-Americans also had good reason to celebrate home and family life. With the end of the exclusion of Chinese immigrants during World War II, wives and war brides began to enter the country, transforming communities like New York's Chinatown from small societies of bachelors into thriving family oriented communities. Japanese-Americans, after the humiliations, disruptions, and anguish of internment, were eager to put their families and lives back together. [⋯] Children of immigrants moved from ethnic neighborhoods with extended kin and community ties to homogeneous suburbs, where they formed nuclear families and invested them with high hopes. Suburban homes offered freedom from kinship obligations, along with material comforts that had not been available on the farm or in the ethnic urban ghetto" (May 18-19).

Emi's rhetoric of the bigness of the country is conditioned here by her belief in its capability to forgive. While it is questionable if Emi's narrative of forgetting and forgiveness can be soothing to Ichiro's wounded self, she, at least, seems to pave the way for Ichiro's relentless quest for a place of belonging.

In addition, it is noteworthy that Emi is described as a Caucasian-like woman rather than a typical Asian woman: "Emi was several inches taller than Kenji. She was slender, with heavy breasts … and her long legs were strong and shapely like a white woman's" (83). This description of Emi's features stands in stark contrast to that of Ichiro's "Japanese" mother who is portrayed as "a small, flat-chested shapeless woman" who has a "skinny body of a thirteen-year-old" (10). It is in this context that Kenji's advice to Ichiro echoes: "Go someplace where there isn't another Jap within a thousand miles. Marry a white girl or a Negro or an Italian or even a Chinese" (164). Attuned to Kenji's desire for a new life in a color-blind society, Emi's racial identity is ingeniously equivocated. As Ichiro becomes more and more involved in his love affair with Emi, she figures as an eligible woman with whom he wishes to have a family in a suburban neighborhood, as he once imagines, "holding his son's hand" and talking about "the weather and the ball games and the elections" with his neighbors on the street:

> Where is that place they talk of and paint nice pictures of and describe in all the homey magazines? Where is that place

> with the clean, white cottages surrounding the new, red-brick church with the clean, white steeple, where the families all have two children, one boy and one girl, and a shiny new car in the garage and a dog and a cat and life is like living in the land of the happily ever-after? Sure it must be around here someplace, some place in America. (159)

Keyed to Emi's preaching of forgetting and forgiveness, Ichiro fantasizes about a suburban life that he hopes will allow his trauma to be healed. Not accidentally, Ichiro suddenly realizes that he has turned twenty-five years old—a scintillating recognition that he is old enough to have his own family.[94]

Ichiro's fantasy about a suburban life is deeply wedged into the dramatic transition the United States had gone through in the twentieth century, thereby posing the following questions: do Ichiro's suburban fantasies mean a retreat into a nostalgic longing for an abstract, generalized sense of place rooted in community and racial homogeneity; can the no-no boy's move to the suburbs really serve as a conduit for having a clean, fresh start? As *No-*

---

94 See May for birth rate, marriage age, and American families in the Cold War era in general. The median marriage age ranged between twenty and twenty one in the early 1950s, and most families had three to four children. This generation is also "the most marrying generation on record: 96.4 percent of the women and 94.1 percent of the men" (14).

No Boy comes close to its ending, the reader can feel a sense of redemption more and more with Ichiro's experiences taking a favorable turn. When he accompanies Kenji to the hospital in Portland, Ichiro has a job interview with a man called Mr. Carrick who regards the internment as a "black mark in the annals of American history" (150) and sympathizes with Ichiro's no-no boy position. Ichiro decides not to accept his job offer after due consideration, but Mr. Carrick's apologist gesture allows Ichiro to see himself without relying on the split of "Japanese" and "American." Ichiro's internal reconciliation seems to be achieved when he goes dancing with Emi after the funeral of his mother. He is seen eventually unleashing himself from the fetters of his mother's obstinate pro-Japanese standpoint: "I feel a little bit freer, a bit more hopeful" (196). Apparently, the dance floor, on which Ichiro and Emi dance together in each other's arms, harks back to Emi's rhetoric of forgetting and forgiveness:

> This is the way it ought to be, he thought to himself, to be able to dance with a girl you like and really get a kick out of it because everything is on an even keel and one's worries are only the usual ones of unpaid bills and sickness in the family and being late to work too often. Why can't it be that way for me? Nobody's looking twice at us. Nobody's asking me where I was during the war or what the hell I am doing back on the Coast. [···] I've got to love the world the way I used to. I've got

> to love it and the people so I'll feel good, and feeling good will make life worthwhile. There's no point in crying about what's done. There's a place for me and Emi and Freddie here on the dance floor and out there in the hustle of things if we'll let it be that way. I've been fighting it and hating it and letting my bitterness against myself and Ma and Pa and even Taro throw the whole universe out of perspective. I want only to go on living and be happy. I've only to let myself do so." (209)

When a slightly drunken white man buys Ichiro and Emi a drink, Ichiro prefers to think that the man "saw a young couple and liked their looks and felt he wanted to buy them a drink and did" (211) regardless of what they are and what they were. Well beyond the constraints and confines of his burdening dilemma, Ichiro is "feeling immensely full" (211) by embracing the country's "bigness," "vastness," and "forgiveness" once lauded by Emi. With Ichiro's suburban fantasies and Emi's preaching of forgiveness symbolically projected onto the dance floor as such, an image of a suburbanite couple begins to take shape.

Apparently, Ichiro's groping for a sense of wholeness never loses its momentum as it accretes with phrases fraught with Ichiro's growing confidence, such as "He was young still, but a little wiser" (232), "After the rain, the sunshine" (232), "A glimmer of hope" (250), and an "insinuation of promise" (251). However, it still remains to be seen if Ichiro's suburban American dream will fully live up to its promise and if the postwar suburb is presented as a means of solution to Ichiro's plight. As noted earlier, Ichiro's implied assimilation into the postwar suburb, attuned to Emi's advice of amnesia and forgiveness, is problematic because it is not so much a cultural counter-practice as a compliance with an amnesic reaction to the "evacuated" history of the internment of Japanese Americans and racial overtones implicit in the postwar suburb. The following quote deserves a closer look in this regard:

> They're on the outside looking in, just like that kind and just like me and just like everybody else I've ever seen or known. Even Mr. Carrick. Why isn't he in? Why is he on the outside squandering his goodness on outcasts like me? Maybe the answer is that there is no in. Maybe the whole damned country is pushing and shoving and screaming to get into some place that doesn't exist, because they don't know that the outside could be the inside if only they could stop all this pushing and shoving and screaming, and they haven't got enough sense to realize that. That makes sense. I've got the answer all figured out, simple and neat and sensible." (159-60)

Struggling with his no-no boy plight alongside a dream of a suburban family life, Ichiro asks himself what it means to be "on the outside looking in." Apposite here would be a critique of the governmental narrative of internment enacted by the ingenious remapping of the nation's interior and defining its identity against others who are excluded from a particular vision of the nation's interior enacted. What should be revealed is how such expression of national interior space ironically contains within itself a constitutive outside opposed to the particular articulation—the presence of "an American in an American concentration camp," which is "enclosed by wire fencing" and sentineled by "guards who were American soldiers like himself" (121). Then, Ichiro's suburban vision could disclose the fact that the nation's interiority is actually established by its interaction with the outside that is therefore itself a part of what constitutes national interior, and that the interior is apt to be turned *out* insofar as it depends on an outside that provides its conditions of possibility. While Ichiro's sudden doubt as to the distinctness of inside and outside evokes the nation's remapping of its space by holding internees behind barbed wire that corresponds to a revisionist act of making an outside within the nation's interior, it never lasts long enough for Ichiro to work it tenaciously through to the point where it threatens to dismantle what lies under the veneer of a suburban way of life for Japanese Americans.

That problem is not without its implication for the ambiguous ending of the novel. Okada never ends the novel with Ichiro's assimilation into his suburban dream, and the very place Ichiro craves throughout the novel is not conclusively presented as reducible to an actual geographical location. Accordingly, one may quibble with the future Ichiro maps out for himself at the end of the novel, who is still "thinking, searching, thinking and probing [···] in the darkness of the alley of the community that was a tiny bit of America" and chasing "that faint and elusive insinuation of promise as it continues to take shape in mind and in heart" (251). Will Ichiro and Emi enter marriage in a model suburban home adorned with laborsaving appliances and furnishings, and play their roles respectively as a successful breadwinner and a supporting attractive homemaker? Will Ichiro ever recognize that his suburban fantasy is likely to be caught up in the suburban conformity rather than envision an alternative interpretation of place? What is at issue here is to assess whether the author resolves those questions or merely glosses over them as articulated by the traditional scholarship on *No-No Boy*, which has read the novel as a postinternment Asian American text that, resignedly, if not outright eagerly, embraces postwar US ideologies gravitating toward a unified American culture.

It is at this juncture that Emi's rhetoric of forgetting and forgiveness, aligned with the powerful political consensus of the era, strikes quite a different chord. Issuing from a character whose rhetoric of forgetting and forgiveness is straightforwardly articulated throughout the text as much as the obstinate Japanese nationalist attitudes of Ichiro's mother, Emi's naïve belief in the country's capability to forgive readily calls itself into question and thus, as Ling suggests, should be read as a parody of "the mainstream culture's portrayals of the United States as a happy melting pot" (*Narrating* 48). As a parallel, one should take with a grain of salt Kenji's exhortation to Ichiro to live a life in a place of social anonymity where he is no more afflicted by his split identity. That place evokes the dance floor represented earlier as a compelling metaphor for a utopian society where the no-no boy's anxieties becomes a matter of attitudes—dancing with a girl you love and buying a drink at your pleasure to whomever you run into and instantly like. Kenji sounds quite ironic here, particularly given his sardonic manner, corroded bit by bit by the premonition of death and renunciation of all the hopes for life.

Ling's exploration of Ichiro's plight by locating *No-No Boy* in a larger context of cultural production in the late 1950s serves here as a case in point. Given the Japanese American community's reluctance to revisit the years just past and given the postwar consensus, the most tricky question Okada was confronting, according to Ling, is "how to convey the severity of the World War II rupture in Japanese American life within the limited cultural space allowed for Asian American literary expression" ("Race" 362). Ling continues to argue that Okada was well aware of "the era's conditional receptivity to Asian American literary writings" and that "an autobiographical—hence documentary—account of Japanese Americans' wartime sufferings would be either too shocking for postwar readers or too vulnerable to ideological censorship" ("Race" 362).

Building upon and extending Ling's insightful investigation of such a discursive terrain within which *No-No Boy* was produced, I would like to put forth an argument that Ichiro's suburban fantasies are effectively utilized as an "elusive insinuation of promise" (251) as Okada insinuates himself into the text by projecting his authorial concerns onto his protagonist's suburban fantasies. Okada represents a suburb fantasized by his character not as a "lived" place but as an "imagined" place that can never be reached. Such elusiveness is both symptomatic and determining of the extent to which Okada's textual intervention works through postinternment anxieties. In other words, if an urgent task confronting Okada is not merely a matter of resisting the dominant culture or advocating postwar American ideologies, the "limited cultural space" allowed for him becomes rather a space wherein a contingent formation of Japanese American identity appears in relation to multiple contingencies—caring for postinternment Japanese American community, a sense of control over one's recent historical trauma, a renewed sense of self-respect, public recognition, and reclaiming American identity.

Okada's textual intervention here meets up with Ichiro's plight and Okada stands in for Ichiro as another kind of "no-no boy" in the postwar US society by opting for neither conformity nor dissent. Okada transforms his protagonist into a would-be postwar suburbanite who links concerns about Japanese American authorship and Americanness with concerns about survival on both the material and cultural levels. It is precisely in this context that one is able to understand why Okada has presented what Ichiro is eager to belong to as a "place that doesn't exist" (160). It is a vexed but counter-hegemonic space where readers are enabled to recognize what cultural consent or confrontation entails for both the author and the no-no boy. As such, Okada insinuates himself into Ichiro's plight, postinternment anxieties, and cultural contingencies of the 1950s in America. It is because the author does not bypasses such postinternment anxieties through the lens of a suburban way of life with which one is supposed to start anew that he does not point to a moment beyond a specific point as the prefix, "post" in "postinternment," may signal. He resists an ending rooted in a utopian moment by neither privileging the "post" nor accepting that a status for Japanese Americans of social exclusion internal to the nation is over. Such an elusive nature of Okada's rendition of Ichiro's suburban fantasies—both desirous of a specific moment "beyond" and skeptical of it—is at the heart of *No-No Boy*.

As a parallel to Ichiro's suburban fantasy in the wake of post-internment anxieties, Hata also seeks social anonymity and a safe, reassuring distance from his past. In this light, the story of the chronic outsider who has made "a whole life out of gesture and politeness" harks back to the various modes in which America has situated Asian Americans as a "potential enemy within" (the internment) or positively as "models" (the myth of model minority since the 1960s), articulating its variable nationhood against the backdrop of Asian America. Hata's spacious and well-maintained mock Tudor house serves as a major trope through *A Gesture Life*. Corresponding to the minutiae of the town, Hata's almost obsessive attention to his house is no less than an attempt to sanitize and wholly appropriate his space of privacy: history is bracketed out and atemporality takes over in the house. The fire in his house and its renovation induce Hata's speculation on his past in his periods of recuperation. Interestingly, when that space is violated, time resumes: Hata's adopted daughter Sunny runs away, chooses escape and promiscuity for rebellion, and eventually brings him back a long-stored memory. It is no coincidence that Hata first introduces Sunny in this way: "Sunny, I'm afraid, always hated the house" (26).

Layering history upon history, Hata's failure as father is revealed to be related to his wartime trauma and his memories of the comfort women named "Khutaeh" that means the lastborn of the family in Korean or K. Through his emotional involvement with the Korean comfort woman in the Burmese jungle during World War II, Hata is so overwhelmed by his passion for her that he brushes aside all notions of duty and respect for his authority. The tragedy of the situation is that he is ultimately unable to prevent her from suffering a hideous and violent death despite his acts of surprising courage. Hata's view of his daughter is shaped by his recollection of K and both women are defined in equal measure by their vulnerability. The strained relationship between father and daughter and his desire to protect her from the horrors of the world can be read in terms of his residual love for K. The two roads intersect at the point of Hata's responsibilities to these women and shed light on how much his lifelong efforts to be accepted cost due to his inability to love the people closest to him beyond "gesture."

Hata's affair with Mary Burns in their middle age is another instance that initiates the surfacing of Hata's conflicts that underlie his apparent life of tranquility. Mary Burns, a widow in his neighborhood, not only helping Hata with Sunny but being his lover, trespasses into his private realm and yet amicably leaves him after finding him unable to return her affection. As he has fled all the relationships with his beloved people, this time he never allows his romance with the widow to get too passionate beyond his prescribed gestures that ultimately limit his connection with others. Lee complicates and mixes up threads of Hata's life so that they seem not be easily sutured together by suburban fantasies or illusions of complacency. The discontinuous moments in the histories of the annexation of the Korean Peninsula by Japan, Japanese imperial expansion in the Pacific Rim, and its clash with another imperial power in that area lurk under the veneer of suburban social decorum and yet continue to impinge on Hata's present life. The life of the exemplary suburbanite who is "the living, breathing expression of what people here wanted—privacy and decorum and the quietude of hard-earned privilege" (275) is thus revealed to be quietly as devastating as the American suburb, where he has hidden away his past by freezing time and fixing space.

Can the Spy/Suburbanite Speak?

In order to disentangle the threads that render complicated Hata's sense of belonging, we need to first understand how Lee in *Native Speaker* gives very negative spins to both celebrations of heterogeneous ethnic identity and immigrant cosmopolitanism in the United States. His debut explores a basic question latent beneath the formation of Asian American identity in terms of Du Boisian double-consciousness: what is it like to be an Asian American in contemporary America—how to live in the betweenness that mediates the two identities? The protagonist, Henry Park, is employed in a detective agency with multicultural staff which specializes in gathering useful information on non-white subjects for shadowy clients. Working as a spy, Henry feels an ironic conflation of his marginal position as an Asian American and his professional interests as a spy because it is ironically his (in)visibility that his spymaster prizes as Tina Chen suggests:

> Henry Park is an invisible man. Like the nameless protagonist of Ralph Ellison's Invisible Man, he suffers from the refusal

of others to see him. However, unlike Ellison's character, his invisibility is both a matter of the refusal of others to see him and the logical effect of his occupation. In Chang-rae Lee's *Native Speaker*, Henry Park is a spook, haunting those against whom is paid to spy. That Lee' s protagonist is a spy is no coincidence. Henry's vanishing acts, a professional opportunity to enact the spy's "multiple roles," are a logical extension of his personal history as a Korean American struggling to negotiate the divide that separates how others perceive him and how he sees himself. [⋯]

A good father, a dutiful son, a loving husband, a trustworthy friend, and an accomplished spy: he is, at times, all of these things as well as none of them. Lost behind the masks and impostures he effects as part of his job, he discovers that his consummate ability to cast for others "the perfect picture of a face" (12) carries with it a heavy price: the dissolution of self-coherence. Working as an undercover "ethnic operative" for Glimmer and Co., an intelligence firm specializing in the accumulation and exchange of information, Henry eventually confronts "the magnificent and horrifying level of [his own] virtuosity" (150) in all areas of his life. That confrontation, provoked by the death of his son, his wife's subsequent decision to leave him, and his interactions with councilman John Kwang, forces Henry to deal with the extent to which his identity is the result both of his own performative choices and

> of his American education that leads him to enact a particular role. (638-39)

Henry is assigned to infiltrate the campaign of John Kwang, a rising Korean American New York City councilperson and a potential Democratic frontrunner for the next mayoral race. Compared to Henry's father, who is a successful first-generation Korean immigrant, Kwang is described as an ambitious politician whose political goals expand the purview of family loyalty honored by Henry's father and encompass all immigrants, all nationalities. Kwang refuses to remain merely "a minority politician" or "an underdog champion." Lee illustrates how Henry and Kwang as Asian Americans can never belong to the strident and aggressive city of New York, a microcosm of multiethnic America. On the one hand, a dilemma for a person caught between two worlds like Henry is to live within the hyphen that defines his or her identity and yet to be able to articulate the hyphenation. Can one transgress or transcend the hyphen itself without obviating any possibility of articulation and representation? On the other hand, John Kwang's political enterprise is more than double: it is not simply a matter of establishing oneself and resisting the dominant culture that seeks to marginalize him or her. It becomes rather a space wherein a contingent formation of Asian American identity appears in relation to multiple identifications which are themselves driven by specific contingencies. It should implicate a double process of the formulation of a political identity and the critical task of situating heterogeneity within. Henry's dilemma is merged with and expanded into John Kwang's project of political affiliation based on crossing differences by emphasizing similar antagonistic relationships to the dominant culture. What is at issue here is that the very process of peeling-off of Kwang's "last mask" (131) through which his perdition is delineated is suggestive of the fact that his political collapse results not only from a social power structure marked by hierarchically arranged differences in which "they always win the game" but from hybrid positionalities interacting one another within Kwang's constituency—thus "in every betrayal dwells a self-betrayal" (292).

The stories of John Kwang's immigration, his emerging as a political figure, and his marriage to May cast additional sinister shadows on his political ambition. Kwang's wife, May, "born Kwon So-Jung, in Seoul [⋯] Ewha Women's University, degree in English literature," is a daughter of "a founder of one of the industrial conglomerates" (34). How did an immigrant of a very obscure background who was once a Korean War orphan and a houseboy of an American retiring two-star general get married to a women perfectly eligible by any standard in Korean society? The question takes on its full force when juxtaposed with the parallel story of immigration of Henry's father. Wondering why his father, who is a graduate of the most prestigious university in Korea and has a Master's degree in engineering, chose to come to America,

Henry recollects his father's answer: "something about the 'big network' in Korean business, how someone from the rural regions of the country could only get so far in Seoul" (52). It is strongly hinted here that the marriage of John, a successful businessperson with a political ambition, and May, a daughter of a business tycoon in Korea, may be a marriage of convenience—literally a marriage of interests of business and politics. This suspicion evokes the collusion of business and political elites in the high-growth era in Korea. Under the Park Chung-Hee's dictatorial leadership between 1961 and 1979, business and political elites exchanged bribes for political favors. Politicians used these political funds to buy votes and to serve basic greed. Businessmen used the rents from cheap capital granted to them through the political ties to expand as rapidly as possible, thus ensuring their continued political and economic importance. The agenda of state development and money politics proceeded hand in hand.[95] Given this clue to the secret story of Kwang's success in the United States, the legitimacy of Kwang's politics of affiliation becomes open to question as it is subtly intimated that what has conditioned Kwang's success also made Henry's father leave his home country.

Symbolically, Henry becomes conscious of the ever-lasting smell of Korean foodstuff at the basement of Kwang's house—the

---

95 See Cumings, 359-79.

"Korean-ness" that can never be completely sealed up. Influential politician as he is, being Korean makes Kwang subject to the possibility of a conflation that is more likely to occur outside of Korea—a conflation ensuring that he can be anyone, but only as long as that anyone is also Korean just like Henry. As a result, John Kwang's politics of crossing differences is caught in that treacherous bind. The fundamental issue confronting the conceptualization of Asian American identity echoes the question Spivak poses in "Can the Subaltern Speak?": can the subaltern speak for him/herself, or is the subaltern inevitably condemned to be spoken *for* in a necessarily interested fashion; if the subaltern could speak, that is, speak in a way that really matters to us, then, would not it be subaltern? To this problem of articulation is related that of representation—representation not merely as "re-presentation" but as "speaking for" (Spivak 70). In the face of the dilemma of "how there must be a way to speak truthfully and not be demonized or made a traitor" (*Native Speaker* 183), Lee leaves it unresolved by ending his debut with the description of the protagonist caught in a subaltern bind, as foreshadowed by the epigraph from Walt Whitman—"I turn but do not extricate myself, Confused, a past-reading, another, but with darkness yet."

An ensuing question in Lee's second novel is then if the suburbanite can speak. As noted earlier, Hata's suburban life is revealed as plural and fragmented, and memories from his remote past collide with highly charged emotional and cultural antithesis of his present life. What is telling about the suburbanite's life is that the bounded security of the suburb meets the changing conditions and relations. A realtor's words of praise for Hata, "Doc Hata is Bedley Run. He is what his place is about" (136) begin to have a quite different ring: Hata is also an embodiment of overwhelming, intersecting histories of Korean, Japan, and the United States in the twentieth century—the histories that are not easily flattened out into suburban stability and homogeneity. This recognition leads to the remapping of Hata's whole life. First, in the Burmese jungle during the war, Hata and the Korean comfort woman named "K" are basically positioned as colonizer and colonized despite his love for her. However, as they have more conversations in his "childhood language," the "Korean-ness" in his identity Hata has refused to acknowledge begins to calls into question his identification with Japanese nationality. To put it otherwise, "K seems to have successfully unhinged Hata's loyalty toward his [adopted] country" and, subsequently, Hata "ceases to identify himself with the moral and cultural apparatuses of his nation" (Y. Lee 150). Thus emerges a contradictory pattern of psychic affect in colonial relations that undermines the assumption that the identities and positionings of colonizer and colonized exist in stable and unitary terms. As far as Hata is attracted to a Korean woman and simultaneously repulsed from his Korean-ness, he always finds himself suspended between and among the worlds—his life-long dilemma that constitutes his gesture life.

Secondly, Hata's troubled relationship with his adopted daughter Sunny problematizes his suburban life that he desires to start anew in the postwar American suburb *as* an American. Sunny, a Korean orphan, comes to stand in for K whose death Hata takes responsibility for, as his lover Mary Burns unknowingly touches the core of the bizarre father-daughter relationship: "it's as if she's a woman to whom you're beholden [⋯] as if she's someone you hurt once, or betrayed, and now you're obliged to do whatever she wishes, which is never good for anyone much less a child" (60). If K makes visible "colonial mimicry" inscribed in Hata's Japanese identity, Sunny figures as a character who put Hata's American identity in question because it is intimated that Sunny, who has "thick, way black hair and dark-hued skin," is probably "the product of a much less dignified circumstance, a night's wanton encounter between a GI and a local bar girl" (204). What emerges from Sunny's "enfiguration of U.S. military intervention in Korea" and Hata's failure in building a family through adoption "suggests the inadequacy of the U.S. hegemonic narrative that explains Korean freedom from Japanese occupation as gifted by U.S. force" (Chuh 15). Furthermore, it is also a nuanced commentary of the United States' responsibility for partitioning of the Korean Peninsula after the independence from Japan and consolidation of the divide in a larger dynamics of the Cold War. Hata's relations with K and Sunny, therefore, contain a set of spatio-temporal references of how "this" place is connected to other places.

The subaltern predicament, à la Spivak once again, is how one can retrieve the silenced and erased voices of the subaltern from a subject position *not* recognized as authoritative when the very act of retrieving necessarily involves speaking *for* the subaltern. My understanding of a Spivakian way of dealing with this paradox is to benefit from that paradox by recognizing that it is ironically what the subaltern *cannot* speak that makes the subaltern consciousness epistemologically and politically meaningful: she leaves the subaltern experience as a kind of "strategic blankness" so that it lays bare the horizon and limits of the dominant discourse.[96] Having established a link between the subaltern question and the suburbanite's dilemma of articulation, I would like to argue that the tortuous paths of Hata's life could become an empowering discursive space in which multiple histories are evoked, not any more under the disguise of simultaneity and homogeneity. As Radhakrishnan suggests, living on the hyphen is never "a matter of neutrality or of benign participation in the conjuncturality of 'equal' histories." If the hyphen can speak, it is only by addressing "the existing imbalance between the two histories" rather than being "registered as a free-floating hybridity devoid of historical baggage" ("Conjunctural Identities" 253). Multiply evoked

---

96 Spivak arrives at this argument via Pierre Marcherey's famous formula for the interpretation of ideology: what is important in a work is what it does not say.

asymmetries between and among histories, and the uniqueness of distinct mixture of wide and complex relations inscribed in Hata's life, therefore, become a space for articulation by making visible those incommensarabilities and unequal relations of histories.

"Come Almost Home"

As the novel comes to an end, Hata finds Sunny quite by chance in the deteriorating neighboring town of Ebbington and discovers that he is a grandfather to six-year-old Thomas. After negotiating a shaky truce with his fiercely independent daughter, he devotes as much time as he is allowed to looking after the boy and slowly reawakens to the joy of living in the moment and a renewed vigor for life. Finally, Sunny's emotional distance erodes until she forgives, if not completely, Hata. A possibility of reconciliation appears in the shape of his grandson, who is also a person of mixed-blood. One may quibble with the future Hata maps out for himself at the end of the novel:

> Perhaps I'll travel to where Sunny wouldn't go, to the south and west and maybe father still, across the oceans to land on former shores. But I think it won't be any kind of pilgrimage. I won't be seeking out my destiny or fate. I won't attempt to find comfort in the visage of a creator or the forgiving dead. Let me simply

> bear my flesh, and blood, and bones. I will fly a flag. Tomorrow, when this house is alive and full, I will be outside looking in. I will be already on a walk someplace, in this town or the next or the five thousand miles away. I will circle round and arrive again. Come almost home. (355-56)

What does Hata's sense of "coming home" mean in these concluding paragraphs? Is he going to move to a retirement town in the South or on the West Coast, or maybe farther still across the oceans to land on former shores? What will happen to this man who has lived in constant suspension and empty gestures all his life, "molding to whatever is at hand"? Several decades ago, Ichiro, no-no boy, recognized in postwar America that everybody was "on the outside looking in": "there is no in. Maybe the whole damn country is pushing and shoving and screaming to get into some place that doesn't exist, because they don't know that the outside could be the inside if only they would stop all this pushing and shoving and realize that. That makes sense. I've got the answer all figured out, simple and neat and sensible" (159). A sudden doubt as to the certainty of inside and the distinctness of outside echoes the various modes that have placed Asian Americans in a liminal space in America. Despite this scintillating insight, Ichiro, however, envisions a color-blind ideal American suburb as a means of escape from his problems—a place that actually "doesn't exist." One is not sure where he would live and where he would do elsewhere. At least, Ichiro cannot be said to have gone the full distance to shift the perspective from the outside looking in and to demand that the outsider's view should look inward and then outward, not to mention problematizing the outsidedness of his own view. The effect of the unresolved ending is to leave intact the question of "move on to where"—where will be the ultimate destination for Ichiro? It is quite doubtful if he can really escape from the very place that reminds him of what he has left behind. He may feel at home anywhere, but it also means that the seemingly mobile young Nisei internee are in fact to feel at home nowhere and to find himself still adrift. Therefore, Ichiro may be still subject to an unappeasable restlessness because "home" for him is always a kind of simulacrum of a thing he has not found and he will not reach. He seems to have freedom to move where and when he pleases. It remains to be seen where he wants to be or how he wants to get there. The ending replicates his homelessness at the very moment it is supposed to alleviate it. *No-No Boy* certainly has succeeded in making itself as the quintessential embodiment of the post-internment anxieties in chronicling the returning internee's struggle for a new life against the backdrop of the suburban culture in the 1950s. Nonetheless, it has never reached a point where a yet unrealized possibility of utopian energy is more fully invested in a suburban dream rather than diluted.[97]

---

97 In comparison with the elusive nature of *No-No Boy's* ending, *The Man in the Gray Flannel Suit* by its end becomes a story of taking responsibility for one's own life, being true to one's own life, and living the life one wants to lead, not the life one is expected to lead. Tom at first pretends to be the right man for a great executive position. However, he is actually a basic nine-to-five of a good ability and modest ambition. In contrast, the head of the UBC, Ralph Hopkins represents the single-minded drive towards achievement. He is shown as an overdriven man whose addiction to work has ruined his family, but may be necessary for a leader of corporate enterprise. When Tom turns down a high-pressure position to work normal hours and spend more time with his family, his decision does not indicate a rupture in the connection between individual success, personal happiness, and social progress. It rather expresses a new recognition of the costs of success, a new conceptualization of work and personal happiness forming a mutually reinforcing totality. Such a twist to the old story of success through the deployment of virtues established by the old ideology of success in the service of something new may make *The Man in the Gray Flannel Suit* more accurate than most melodramatic cultural products as it situates Tom not boldly climbing the corporate ladder, but matter-of-factly standing midway in a very ordinary career.

However, all the problems that have plagued him have been solved all of a sudden by his keeping the old wisdom of "honesty is the best policy," being true to himself instead of sacrificing his family life for social success, and deciding to live the life he wants to live. By the end of the novel, Tom recalls the inscription on a stone bench at his grandmother's mansion—Robert Browning's lines, "God's in his heaven, all's right with the world." Tom has reassured himself that "thing are going to be better" and he has "become almost an optimist" (273). This forced, if not outright melodramatic, ending clearly elides the undercurrent of anxieties and contingencies at the heart of his suburban life such as the bad war memories, stalled careers, and small destinies awaiting for him as well as his contemporaries. As a result, a possibility of renewal in his decision to "live his own life" is set alongside doubts and questionings about the reality of such a decision. Pitted against Updike and Yates, Sloan Wilson's formulation of the shift to a new definition of success

In contrast, the ending of *A Gesture Life* shows why Chang-Rae Lee is located in the tradition of the suburban novels by John Updike, John Cheever, Richard Yeats—the way of seeing

---

may on the one hand express a sharp social transition, but, on the other, it also masks the quality of accommodation in Tom's choice. The decision to give up the entrepreneurial ideal of unlimited aspiration in favor of a balance between work and privatized familial happiness is not merely a revolt against the old, but also accommodation to the confines and constraints of the new.

In the last chapter, Tom and Betsy are seen coming into Judge Bernstein's office. They ask him to handle the trust fund for his son in Italy, and the judge replies without any hesitation that he would be happy to do it without charge. The novel ends with Tom joining Betsy in the parking, seen from the perspective of the judge at his office window. Particularly in the film version of the novel, the judge's point of view watching over Tom and Betsy who are heading up to Vermont for vacation in a new car is clearly presented as shared by the audience. We are all now "on the outside looking in." The effect of looking at the Raths through the eyes of the indulgent judge who have already shown deep respect for their decision is to make us feel that the problems surrounding the couple have not really been resolved but rather diluted under the guise of the ending's melodramatic tone. The melodramatic ending of *The Man in the Gray Flannel Suit* has been a target for criticism as a clear indication of a popular novel and a melodramatic movie. More importantly, what is at issue here is that the ending leaves intact the question of where will be the ultimate destination for Tom and Betsy? The crack in the form of a question mark is here echoed as a haunting trope of the unanswerability of that question. Their one-week escape in Vermont is *temporary* as long as it is spelled out as a travel only in terms of return. They can never escape from the very place that reminds them of what they have left behind and thus of what they have not yet found. They may now feel at home anywhere, but it also means that the seemingly mobile young nuclear family are in fact to feel at home nowhere and to find themselves adrift. The Raths' journey home is reinscribed at just the point it is supposed to end, without developing a new kind of roots to replace what they have left behind.

themselves as simultaneously within, yet implicitly critical of the place they inevitably crave to fit in. Hata's whole life of gesture once set him on the path toward reconciling within himself the two competing notions of being at "home" and never being in a place that feels like home, and of connecting with the people in his life without conflict and of being more engaged with life. Such a strenuous effort for reconciliation has been at the heart of Hata's peculiar sense of "being in a place and not being there" (290)—simultaneously accepted on the one hand and left to feel out of place on the other. His neither-here-nor-there attitude is what may ironically enables him fit in, but it also disables him from putting down true roots and forging connection to the world. Lee earlier anticipates the novel's ambiguous last line, "almost home," by portraying Hata who wonders, "if I would ever in my life call such a house my home" (22) and feels as if "I have not lived there for the last thirty years of my life" (119). He finally has to work out the meaning of his own house as a home after realizing that he has lived the kind of life that is always *arriving* but never *arrived*.

Hata's life of gesture may be defined, in Geertz's words, as that of a man who "lives in the world in general" (262), as Hata himself summarizes in a confessional tone: "I feel I have not really been living anywhere or anytime, not for the future and not in the past and not at all of-the-moment, but rather in the lonely dream of an oblivion, the nothing-of-nothing drift from one pulse beat to the next, which is really the most bloodless marking-out, automatic and involuntary" (320-21). It is because we all live in some limited stretch of the place even in a world where all appears as flux and movement with corresponding lack of stable territories that none of us live in the world in general. While our own lives are built by a general set of wider relations, the encompassing spatio-temporal reference is meaningless unless we are *always already* situated in a place. That irony is at the heart of Hata's peculiar sense of "being in a place and not being there." Hata, however, opts for moving on in life and paying off symbolic debts after selling his house, realizing that revisions and repressions through a series of gestures will not change his life. Just a more simplistic life awaits him—a life that spurs him into action and responsibility, into making amends and facing up to his failings, and ultimately into assessing the prospect for full engagement and understanding. He has learned what it means to arrive home and how to turn that lifelong yearning for keep floating into the expectation for running aground and moving forward. A journey Hata is about to take thus reveals that he is not as lost as he once was as long as he is ready to move and to act. An idealized home may be topographically nowhere for Hata, but he now knows that home should be always lived as a relationship and a tension and that the concepts of home as "ideal" and home as "reality" are integral to the sense of "coming almost home." The home Hata envisions eventually is less about where he is from and where he wants to go but more about a way of understanding home that holds the real and imagined in tension rather than in opposition. The "where" is not important for Hata's journey. What is more important is that his "home" *does* exist no matter how elusive it may be and that he will arrive there.

Bibliography

Agnew, John. "Space: Place." *Spaces of Geographical Thought*. Eds. Paul Cloke and R. J. Johnston. London: Sage, 2005. 142-74.

——, "Space and Place." *The Sage Handbook of Geographical Knowledge*. Eds. John Agnew and David Livingstone. London: Sage, 2011. 316-30.

Aiken, Charles S. "Faulkner's Yoknapatawpha County: Geographical Fact into Fiction." *Geographical Review* 67 (1977): 1-21.

——, "Faulkner's Yoknapatawpha County: A Place in the American South." *Geographical Review* 69 (1979): 331-348.

——, *William Faulkner and the Southern Landscape*. GA, Athens: U of Georgia Press, 2009.

Aiken, Susan Hardy, et al., eds, *Making Worlds: Gender, Metaphor, Materiality*. Tucson: U of Arizona P, 1998.

Althusser, Louis. *Lenin and Philosophy and Other Essays*. Trans. Ben Brewster. New York: Monthly Review Press, 1971.

Anderson, Benedict. *Imagined Communities: Reflections on the Origin and Spread of Nationalism*. London: Verso, 1991.

Anzaldúa, Gloria. *Borderlands/La Frontera*. San Francisco: Aunt Lute, 1999.

Appadurai, Arjun. *Modernity at Large: Cultural Dimensions of Globalization*. Minneapolis: U of Minnesota P, 1996.

Appiah, Anthony. "Is the Post- in Postmodernims the Post- in Postcolonialism?" *Critical Inquiry* 17.2 (1991): 336-57.

Augé, Marc. *Non-Places: Introduction to an Anthology of Supermodernity*. London: Verso, 1995.

Awkward, Michael. *Negotiating Difference: Race, Gender, and the Politics of Positionality*. Chicago: U of Chicago P. 1995.

Bachelard, Gaston. *The Poetics of Space*. Tr. Maria Jolas. New York: Orion Press, 1964.

Baker Jr., Houston A. *Afro-American Poetics: Revision of Harlem and the Black Aesthetics*. Madison: U of Wisconsin P, 1988.

_____, *Blues, Ideology, and Afro-American Literature: A Vernacular Theory*. Chicago: U of Chicago P, 1984.

_____, "In Dubious Battle." *New Literary History* 18.2 (1987): 363-69.

_____, *The Journey Back: Issues in Black Literature and Criticism*. Chicago: U of Chicago P, 1980.

_____, *Workings of the Spirit: The Poetics of Afro-American Women's Writing*. Chicago and London: U of Chicago P, 1991.

Baker, Jr., Houston, and Dana D. Nelson. "Violence, the Body, and 'the South.'" Preface. *American Literature* 73.2 (2001): 231-44.

Baker Jr., Houston, and Patricia Redmond. *Afro-American Study in the 1990s*. Chicago: U of Chicago P, 1989.

Bakhtin, Mikhail M. *The Dialogic Imagination: Four Essays*. Trans. Caryl Emerson and Michael Holquist. Austin: U of Texas P, 1981.

Baldwin, James. *The Fire Next Time*. 1963. New York: Vintage Books, 1993.

Balibar, Etienne and Immanuel Wallerstein. *Race, Nation, Class: Ambiguous Identities*. Trans. Chris Turner. New York: Verso, 1991.

Bascara, Victor. *Model-Minority Imperialism*. Minneapolis: U of Minnesota P, 2006.

Baudrillard, Jean. *Simulacra and Simulation*. Trans. Sheila Faria Glaser. Michigan: The U of Michigan P, 1994.

Baxandall, Rosalyn, and Elizabeth Ewen. *Picture Windows: How the Suburbs Happened*. New York: Basic Books, 2000.

Benjamin, Walter. *Illuminations*: Essays and Reflections. Trans. Harry Zohn. New York: Schocken Books, 1968.

Bercovitch, Sacvan. *The American Jeremiad*. Madison: U of Wisconsin P, 1978.

Berman, Marshall. *All That Is Solid Melts into Air: The Experience of Modernity*. New York: Penguin, 1988.

Bhabha, Homi. "Location, Intervention, Incommensurability: A Conversation with Homi Bhabha." *Emergences* 1.1: 63-88.

——, *The Location of Culture*. London & New York: Routledge, 1994.

——, ed. *Nation and Narration*. London: Routledge, 1990.

——, "The Third Space: Interview with Homi Bhabha." *Identity, Community, Culture, Difference*. Ed. J. Rutherford. London: Lawrence and Wishart, 1990. 207-21.

——, "The World and the Home." *Social Text. Social Text*. 0.31-32 (1992): 141-53.

Beauvoir, S. de. *The Second Sex*. Tr. H. M. Parshley. London: Picador, 1988.

Benjamin, Walter. *Illuminations: Essays and Reflections*. Trans. Harry Zohn. New York: Schocken Books, 1968.

Bouson, J. Brooks. *Quiet As It's kept: Shame, Trauma, and Race in the Novels of Toni Morrison*. Albany: State U of New York P, 2000.

Brennan, Timothy. "The National Longing for Form." *Nation and Narration*. Ed.

Homi Bhabha. New York: Routledge, 1990. 44-70.

Brooks, Cleanth, *William Faulkner: The Yoknapatawpha Country*. New Haven & London: Yale UP, 1963.

Brown, Calvin S. "Faulkner's Geography and Topography." *PMLA* 77.5 (1962): 652-59.

_____, *A Glossary of Faulkner's South*. New Haven: Yale UP, 1976.

Buell, Lawrence. "The timeliness of Place: Response to the Presidential Address." *American Quarterly* 58.1 (2006): 17-22.

Butler-Evans, Elliot. *Race, Gender, and Desire: Narrative Strategies in the Fiction of Toni Cade Bambara, Toni Morrison, and Alice Walker*. Philadelphia: Temple UP, 1989.

Butler, Judith. *Gender Trouble: Feminism and the Subversion of Identity*. New York: Routledge, 1999.

Calthorpe, Peter. "Region." The New Urbanism: Toward an Architecture of Community. Ed. Peter Katz. New York: McGraw-Hill, 1993. xi-xvi.

Casey, Edward S. *The Fate of Place: A Philosophical History*. Berkeley: U of California P, 1998.

Certeau, Michel de. *The Practice of Everyday Life*. Trans. Steven Rendall. Berkley: U of California P, 1984.

Cha, Theresa Hak Kyung. *Dictee*. Berkeley: U of California P, 2001

Chambers, Lain. *Migrancy, Culture, Identity*. London: Routledge, 1994.

Chen, Tina. "Impersonation and Other Disappearing Acts in *Native Speaker* by Chang-Rae Lee." *MFS: Modern Fiction Studies* 48.3 (2002): 637-67.

Cheng, Anne Anlin. *The Melancholy of Race: Psychoanalysis, Assimilation, and Hidden Grief*. New York: Oxford UP, 2000.

Cheung, King-Kok, ed. *An Interethnic Companion to Asian American*

Literature. Cambridge: Cambridge UP: 1997.

Chin, Frank. Afterword. *No-No Boy*. By John Okada. 1957. Seattle: U of Washington P, 1992. 253-60.

Chow, Rey. *Writing Diaspora: Tactics of Intervention in Contemporary culture*. Bloomington: Indiana UP, 1993.

Christian, Barbara. *Black Feminist Criticism: Perspectives on Black Women Writers*. New York: Pergamon Press, 1985.

Chuh, Kandice. "Discomforting Knowledge: Or, Korean 'Comfort Women' and Asian Americanist Critical Practice." *Journal of Asian American Studies* 6.1 (2003): 5-23.

____, *Imagine Otherwise: On Asian Americanist Critique*. Durham: Duke UP, 2003.

Chu, Patricia P. *Assimilating Asians: Gendered Strategies of Authorship in Asian America*. Durham: Duke UP, 2000.

Clarke, Deborah. "Gender, Race, and Language in Light in August." American Literature 61:3 (1989): 398-413.

____, *Robbing the Mother: Women in Faulkner*. Jackson: UP of Mississippi, 1994.

Cleaver, Eldridge. *Soul on Ice*. New York: Dell, 1968.

Cohn, Deborah. *History and Memory in the Two Souths: Recent Southern and Spanish American Fiction*. Nashville, Vanderbilt UP, 1999.

Cosgrove, Denis. "Towards a Radical Cultural Geography: Problems of Theory." Antipode 15 (1983): 1-11.

Cowley, Malcolm. *The Portable Faulkner*. New York: Penguin Books, 1967.

Cromarte, John and Carol Stack. "Reinterpreting Black Return and Nonreturn Migration 1975-1980." *Geographical Review* 79 (1989): 297-370.

Culler, Jonathan. *Literary Theory: A Very Short Introduction*. Oxford: Oxford UP, 1997.

Cuming, Bruce. *Korea's Place in the Sun: A Modern History*. New York: Norton, 1997.

Daemmrich, Ingrid. "*Paradise* and Storytelling: Interconnecting Gender, Motif, and Narrative Structure." *Narrative* 11.2 (2003): 213-233.

Dalsgard, Katrine. "The One All-Black Town Worth the Pain: (African) American Exceptionalism, Historical Narration, and the Critique of Nationhood in Toni Morrison's *Paradise*." *African American Review* 35.2 (2001): 233-48.

Daniels, Roger. *Coming to America: A History of Immigration and Ethnicity in American Life*. New York: HarperCollins, 1990.

Davis, Kimberly Chabot. "'Postmodern Blackness': Toni Morrison's *Beloved* and the End of History." *Twentieth Century Literature* 44.2 (1998): 242-260.

Davis, Thadious M. *Faulkner's "Negro": Art and the Southern Context*. Baton Rouge: Louisiana State UP, 1983.

Deleuze, Gilles and Felix Guattari. *Anti-Oedipus: Capitalism and Schizophrenia*. Trans, Robert Hurley, Mark Seem, and Helen R. Lane. New York: Viking Press, 1977.

———, *Thousand Plateau: Capitalism and Schizophrenia*. Trans. Brian Massumi. Minnesota: U of Minnesota P, 1987.

Derrida, Jacques. *Margins of Philosophy*. Trans. Alan Bass. Chicago: Chicago UP, 1982.

———, *Writing and Difference*. Tr. Alan Bass. Chicago: University of Chicago Press, 1978.

Dirlik, Arif. "Asians on the Rim: Transnational Capital and Local Community in the Making of Contemporary Asian America." *Armesia Journal* 22.3 (1996): 1-24.

——, *What Is in a Rim?: Critical Perspectives on the Pacific Region Idea.* Lanham MD: Rowman & Littlefield, 1998.

Dixon, Melvine. *Ride Out the Wilderness: Geography and Identity in Afro-American Literature.* Chicago: U of Illinois P, 1987.

Dubey, Madhu. *Black Women Novelists and the Nationalist Aesthetic.* Bloomington and Indianapolis: Indiana UP, 1994.

Du Bois, W. E. B. *The Souls of Black Folk.* 1903. New York: Alfred Knopf, 1993.

DuCille, Ann. *The Coupling Convention: Sex, Text, and Tradition in Black Women's Fiction.* New York: Oxford UP, 1993.

Duvall, John N. *Faulkner's Marginal Couple: Invisible, Outlaw, and Unspeakable Communities.* Austin: U of Texas P, 1990.

——, *The Identifying Fictions of Toni Morrison: Modernist Authenticity and Postmodern Blackness.* New York: Palgrave, 2000.

Duvall, John N, and Ann J. Abadie, eds. *Faulkner and Postmodernism: Faulkner and Yoknapatawpha,* 1999. Jackson: U of Mississippi P, 2002.

Eagleton, Terry. *Literary Theory: An Introduction.* Oxford: Basil Blackwell, 1983.

Elden, Stuart. *Understanding Henri Lefebvre: Theory and the Possible.* London: Contiuum, 2004.

Ellison, Ralph. "Going to the Territory." *Going to the Territory.* New York: Vintage, 1986. 104-12.

——, *Invisible Man.* 1952. New York: Vintage, 1995.

——, *Shadow and Act.* New York: Random House, 1964.

——, "What America Would Be Like Without Blacks?" *Going to the Territory.* New York: Vintage, 1986. 120-44.

Emerson, Ralph Waldo. "The American Scholar." 1837. *Nature; Addresses and Lectures*, 49–70. Boston: J. Munroe, 1849.

Eperjesi, John R. *The Imperialist Imarginary: Visions of Asia and The Pacific in American Culture*. Hanober: Dartmouth College P, 2005.

Evans, Sara. *Personal Politics: The Roots of Women's Liberation in the Civil Rights Movement and the New Left*. New York: Vintage, 1980.

Fanon, Frantz. *Black Skin, White Masks*. Trans. Constance Farrington. New York: Grove Press, 1967.

_____, *The Wretched of the Earth*. Trans. Constance Farrington. New York: Grove Press, 1963.

Faulkner, William. *Absalom, Absalom!* 1936. New York: Vintage, 1990.

_____, *As I Lay Dying*. 1930. New York: Vintage, 1990.

_____, *Go Down, Moses*. 1942. New York: Vintage, 1990.

_____, *Light in August*. 1932. New York: Vintage, 1990.

_____, *The Sound and Fury*. 1929. New York: Vintage, 1990.

Feld, Steven and Keith H. Basso, eds. *Senses of Place*. Santa Fe: School of American Research P, 1996.

Fisher, Philip. "American Literary and Cultural Studies Since the Civil War." *Redrawing the Boundaries: The Transformation of English and American Literary Studies*. Eds. Stephen Greenblatt and Giles Gunn. New York: MLA, 1992. 232-50.

Fishman, Robert. *Bourgeois Utopias: The Rise and Fall of Suburbia*. New York: Basic Book, 1989.

Fitzgerald, F. Scott. *The Great Gatsby*. 1925. New York: Scribner, 2003.

Foote, Stephanie. "The Cultural Work of American Regionalism." *A Companion to the Regional Literatures of America*. Ed. Charles L. Crow. Malden MA:

Blackwell, 2003. 25-41.

Foucault, Michel. *The Archaeology of Knowledge*. Trans. A.M. Sheridan Smith. London, Tavistock Publications, 1972.

——, *Discipline and Punish: The Birth of the Prison*. Trans. Alan Sheridan. New York: Pantheon Books, 1975.

——, "Of Other Spaces." Tr. Jay Miskowiec. *Diacritics* 16 (1986): 22-27.

——, "Questions on Geography." *Power/Knowledge*. Tr. C. Gordon. New York: Pantheon: 63-77.

——, "Space, Power, and Knowledge." *The Foucault Reader*. Ed. Paul Rabinow. New York: Pantheon, 1984. 239-56.

Fowler, Doreen. "Joe Christmas and 'Womanshenegro.'" *Faulkner and Women*. Eds. Doreen Fowler and Ann J. Abadie. Jackson: UP of Mississippi, 1986. 144-61.

——, *Faulkner: The Return of the Repressed*. Charlotville: UP of Virginia, 1997.

Fraile-Marcos, Anna Maria. "Hybridizing the 'City upon a Hill' in Toni Morrison's *Paradise*." *MELUS* 25.4 (2003): 3-33.

Frank, Joseph. *The Idea of Spatial Form*. New Brunswick: Rutgers UP, 1991.

Franklin, Wayne and Michael Steiner. "Taking Place: Toward the Regrounding of American Studies." *Mapping American Culture*. Ed. Wayne Franklin and Michael Steiner. Iowa City: U of Iowa P, 1992. 3-23.

Fromm, Harold. "Real Life, Literary Criticism, and the Perils of Bourgeoisification." *New Literary History* 20.1 (1988): 49-64.

Frye, Northrop. *Anatomy of Criticism*. 1957. Princeton: Princeton UP, 1990.

Fryer, Judith. Felicitous Space: *The Imaginative Structures of Edith Wharton and Willa Cather*. Chapel Hill: U of North Carolina P, 1986.

Fuller, Hoyt W. "Towards a Black Aesthetic." Gayle 3-12.

Fultz, Lucille P. *Toni Morrison: Playing with Difference*. Urbana: U of Illinois P, 2003.

Garreau, Joel. *Edge City: Life on the New Frontier*. New York: Doubleday, 1991.

Gates Jr., Henry Louis, ed. *Black Literature and Literary Theory*. London: Methuen, 1984.

_____, "Canon Formation, Literary History, and the Afro-American Tradition: From the Seen to the Told." *Falling into Theory: Conflicting Views on Reading Literature*. Ed. David H. Richter. Boston: Bedford, 1994. 172-80.

_____, "Introduction: Criticism in De Jungle." *Black American Literature Forum* 15.4 (1981): 123-27.

_____, Editor's Introduction: Writing 'Race' and the Difference It Makes. *"Race," Writing, and Difference*. Ed. Henry Louis Gates, Jr. Chicago: U of Chicago Press, 1986. 1-20.

_____, *Figures in Black: Words, Signs, and the "Racial" Self*. New York: Oxford UP, 1987.

_____, ed. "Race," *Writing, Difference. Chicago*: U of Chicago P, 1986.

_____, *The Signifying Monkey: A Theory of Afro-American Literary Criticism*. New York: Oxford UP, 1988.

_____, "'What's Love Got to Do with It': Critical Theory, Integrity, and the Black Idiom." *New Literary History* 18.2 (1987): 345-62.

Gates Jr., Henry Louis and K. A. Appiah, ed. *Toni Morrison: Critical Perspectives Past and Present*. New York: Amistad, 1993.

Gauthier, Marni. "The Other Side of *Paradise*: Toni Morrison's (Un)Making of Mythic History." *African American Review* 39.3 (2005): 395-413.

Gayle, Addison Jr. Introduction. *The Black Aesthetic*. xv-xxiv.

_____, ed. *The Black Aesthetic*. Garden City: Doubleday, 1971.

Geertz, Clifford. Afterword. *Senses of Place*. Ed. Steven Feld and Keith H. Basso. Santa Fe: School of American Research Press, 1996. 259-62.

Gilroy, Paul. *Against Race: Imagining the Political Culture Beyond the Color Line*. Cambridge: Harvard UP, 2000.

——, *The Black Atlantic: Modernity and Double Consciousness*. Cambridge: Harvard UP, 1993.

Glazer, Nathan. *The New Immigration: A Challenge to American Society*. San Diego: San Diego State UP, 1988.

Glissant, Édouard. "Creolization in the Making of the Americas." *Race, Discourse, and the Origin of the Americas*. Eds. Vera Lawrence Hyatt and Rexnettle Ford. Washington DC: Smithsonian Institution Press, 1995. 268-275.

——, *Faulkner, Mississippi*. Trans. Barbara Lewis and Thomas C. Spear. Chicago: U of Chicago P, 1996.

——, *Poetics of Relation*. Trans. Betsy Wing. Ann Arbor: U of Michigan P, 1997.

Godden, Richard. "Absalom, Absalom!, Haiti and Labor History: Reading Unreadable Revolutions." *ELH* 61.3 (1994): 685-720.

Grant, Robert. "Absence into Presence: The Thematics of Memory and 'Missing' Subject in Toni Morrison's *Sula*." *Critical Essays on Toni Morrison*. Ed. Nellie Y. McKay. Boston: Hall, 1988.

Gray, Richard. *Southern Aberrations: Writers of the American South and the Problems of Regionalism*. Baton Rouge: Louisiana State UP, 2000.

Greeson, Jennifer Rae. "The Figure of the South and the Nationalizing Imperatives of Early United States Literature." *The Yale Journal of Criticism* 12.2 (1999): 209-248.

Gregory, Drek, Ron Martin and Graham Smith, eds. *Human Geography: Society,*

Space, and Social Science. Minneapolis: U of Minnesota P, 1994.

Griffin, Farah Jasmine. *"Who Sets You Flowin'?": The African American Migration Narrative*. New York: Oxford UP, 1995.

Gupta, Akhil, and James Ferguson. "Beyond 'Culture': Space, Identity, and the Politics of Difference." *Cultural Anthropology* 7.2 (1992): 6-23.

_____, *Culture Power Place: Explorations in Critical Anthropology*. Durham and London: Duke UP, 1997.

Gwynn, Frederick L. *Faulkner in the University*. Charlottesville: U of Virginia P, 1959.

Hall, Stuart. "The Local and the Global: Globalization and Ethnicity." *Culture, Globalization and the World System: Contemporary Conditions for the Representation of Identity*. Ed. Anthony D. King. Binghamton: Department of Art and Art History, State U of New York at Binghamton, 1991. 19-39.

_____, "New Ethnicity." *Black Film/British Cinema*. London: ICA Documents 7, 1988. 27-30.

Halttunen, Karen. "Groundwork: American Studies in Place." *American Quarterly* 58.1 (2006): 1-15.

Handley, George. *Postslavery Literatures in the Americas: Family Portrait in Black and White*. Charlottesville: UP of Virginia, 2000.

Harding, Wendy and Jacky Martin. *A World of Difference: An Inter-Cultural Study of Toni Morrison's Novels*. Westport: Greenwood Press, 1994.

Hardt, Michael and Antonio Negri. *Empire*. Cambridge: Harvard UP, 2000.

Harris, Norman. *Connecting Times: The Sixties in Afro-American Fiction*. Jackson: Mississippi UP, 1988.

Harvey, David. The *Condition of Postmodernity: An Enquiry into the Origins of Cultural Change*. Oxford: Blackwell, 1989.

———, *Consciousness and the Urban Experience: Studies in the History and Theory Capitalist Urbanization*. Baltimore: Johns Hopkins UP, 1985.

———, *Justice, Nature, and the Geography of Difference*. Cambridge: Blackwell, 1996.

Hayden, Dolores. *Building Suburbia: Green Fields and Urban Growth, 1820-2000*. New York: Pantheon Books, 2003.

———, *The Power of Place: Urban Landscapes as Public History*. Cambridge: MIT P, 1995.

———, *Redesigning the American Dream: The Future of Housing, Work, and Family Life*. New York: Norton, 1984.

Heidegger, Martin. "Building Dwelling Thinking" *Poetry, Language, Thought*. Trans. Albert Hofstadter. New York: Harper, 1971.

Heinze, Denise. *The Dilemma of Double Consciousness: Toni Morrison's Novels*. Athens: The U of Georgia P, 1993.

Henderson, Stephen E. "Saturation: Progress Report on a Theory of Black Literature." 1975. *Africa American Theory: A Reader*. Ed. Winston Napier. N.Y. & London: New York UP, 2000. 102-12.

Herod, Andrew and Melissa W. Wright, eds. *Geographies of Power: Placing Scale*. Malden MA: Blackwell, 2002.

Hollinger, David A. *Postethnic America: Beyond Multiculturalism*. New York: BasicBooks, 1995.

Irwin, John. *Doubling and Incent/Repetition and Revenge: A Speculative Reading of Faulkner*. Baltimore: Johns Hopkins UP, 1975.

hooks, bell. *Yearning: Race, Gender, and Cultural Politics*. Boston: South End, 1990.

Jackson, Kenneth T. *Crabgrass Frontier: The Suburbanization of the United*

States. New York: Oxford UP, 1985.

Jacob, Jane. *The Death and Life of Great American Cities*. New York: Vintage Books, 1961.

Jameson, Fredric. *Postmodernism, or The Cultural Logic of Late Capitalism*. Durham: Duke UP, 1991.

_____, "Third-World Literature in the Era of Multinational Capitalism." *Social Text* 15 (1986): 65–88.

JanMohamed, Abdul R. and David Lloyd. """Introduction: Toward a Theory of Minority Discourse: What is to be done? *The Nature and Context of Minority Discourse*. Ed. Abdul R. JanMohamed and David Lloyd. New York: Oxford UP. 1990. 5-12.

Jehlen, Myra. *American Incarnation: The individual, The Nation, and the Continent*. Cambridge: Harvard UP, 1986.

Jenkin, McKay. *The South in Black and White: Race, Sex, and Literature in the 1940s*. Chapel Hill: U of North Carolina P, 1999.

Joyce, Joyce A. "The Black Canon: Reconstructing Black American Criticism." *New Literary History* 18.2 (1987): 335-44.

_____, "'Who the Cap Fit': Unconsciousness and Unconscionableness in the Criticism of Houston A. Baker Jr., and Henry Louis Gates Jr." *New Literary History* 18.2 (1987): 371-84.

Jurca, Catherine. *White Diaspora: The Suburb and the Twentieth-Century American Novel*. Princeton: Princeton UP, 2001.

Kang, Laura Hyun Yi. *Compositional Subjects: Enfiguring Asian/American Women*. Durham: Duke UP, 2002.

Kaplan, Amy. "Manifest Domesticity." *American Literature* 70 (1998): 581-606.

Kaplan, Amy and Donald Pease, eds. *Cultures of United States Imperialism*.

Durham: Duke UP, 1996.

Keith, Michael and Steve Pile, eds. *Place and Politics of Identity*. London: Routledge, 1993.

Kerr, Elizabeth M. *Yoknapatawpha: Faulkner's "Little Postage Stamp of Native Soil."* New York: Fordham UP, 1969.

Kim, Elaine H. *Asian American Literature: An Introduction to the Writings and Their Social Context*. Philadelphia: Philadelphia UP, 1982.

——, ed. *Writing Self Writing Nation: A Collection of Essays on* Dictee *by Theresa Hak Kyung cha*. Berkeley: Third Woman Press, 1994.

——, Preface. *Charlie Chan Is Dead: An Anthology of Contemporary Asian American Fiction*. Ed. Jessica Hegadorn. New York: Penguin, 1993. xii-xiv.

Kim, Elaine H., and Lisa Lowe. Guest Editors' Introduction. *postitions* 5.2 (1997): v-xiv.

Kling, Rob, Spencer Olin, and Mark Poster, eds. *Postsuburban California: The Transformation of Orange Since World War Two*. Berkeley: U of California P, 1991.

Kolodny, Annette. *The Lay of the Land: Metaphor as Experience and History in American Life and Letters*. Chapel Hill: U of North Carolina P, 1975.

Koshy, Susan. "The Fiction of Asian American Literature." *The Yale Journal of Criticism* 9.2 (1996): 315-46.

Kreyling, Michael. I*nventing Southern Literature*. Jackson: UP of Mississippi, 1998.

Krumholtz, Linda J. "Reading and Insight in Toni Morrison's *Paradise*." *African American Review* 36.1 (2002): 21-34.

Kunstler, James Howard. *The Geography of Nowhere: The Rise and Decline of America's Man-Made Landscape*. New York: Simon and Schuster, 1993.

Kutzinsky, Vera M. "Borders and Bodies: The United States, America, and the Caribbean." *The New Centennial Review* 1.2 (2001): 55-88.

Ladd, Barbara. *Nationalism and the color line in George W. Cable, Mark Twain, and William Faulkner*. Baton Rouge: Louisiana State University Press, 1996.

_____, "William Faulkner, Edouard Glissant, and a Creole Poetics of History and Body in *Absalom, Absalom!* and *A Fable*." *Faulkner in the Twenty-First Century: Faulkner and Yoknapatawpha*, 2000. Eds. Robert W. Hamblin and Ann J. Abadie. UP of Mississippi, 2003.

Lawrence, D.H. *Studies in Classic American Literature*. 1923. New York: Viking Press, 1964.

Lee, Chang-Rae. *A Gesture Life*. New York: Riverhead, 1999.

_____, *Native Speaker*. New York: Riverhead, 1995.

Lee, Rachel C. *The Americas of Asian American Literature: Gendered Fictions of Nation and Transnation*. Princeton, New Jersey: Princeton UP, 1999.

Lefebvre, Henri. *The Production of Space*. Trans. Donald Nicholson-Smith. Malden MA: Blackwell, 1991.

Lehan, Richard. *The City in Literature: An Intellectual and Cultural History*. Berkeley: U of California P, 1998.

Lemann, Nicholas. *The Promised Land: The Great Black Migration and How It Changed America*. New York: A. A. Knopf, 1991.

Lewis, R.W.B. *The American Adam: Innocence, Tragedy, and Tradition in the Nineteenth Century*. 1955. Chicago: U of Chicago P. 1995.

Li, David Leiwei. *Imagining the Nation: Asian American Literature and Cultural Consent*. Stanford: Stanford UP, 1998.

Li, Wei. "Introduction: Asian American Community in the Pacific Rim." *From*

Urban Enclave to Ethic Suburb. Ed. Wei Li. Honolulu: U of Hawaii P, 2006.

Light, Andrew and Jonathan M. Smith, eds. *Philosophy and Geography II: The Production of Public Space*. Lanham MD: Rowman & Littlefield, 1998.

Ling, Jinqi. *Narrating Nationalism: Ideology and Form in Asian American Literature*. New York: Oxford UP, 1998.

Lowe, John. "Reconstruction Revisited: Plantation School Writers, Postcolonial Theory, and Confederates in Brazil." *Mississippi Quarterly* 57.1 (2003-04): 5-26.

Lowe, Lisa. "Heterogeneity, Hybridity, Multiplicity: Making Asian American Differences." *Diaspora* 1.1 (1991): 24-44.

____, *Immigrant Acts*. Durham: Duke UP, 1996.

Lubiano, Wahneema, ed. *The House That Race Built*. New York: Vintage Book, 1998.

Marks, Barry. "The Concept of Myth in *Virgin Land*." *American Quarterly* 5.1 (1953): 71-76.

Marling, Karal A. *As Seen on TV: The Visual Culture of Everyday Life in the 1950s*. Cambridge: Harvard UP, 1994.

Marx, Leo. *The Machine in the Garden: Technology and the Pastoral Ideal in America*. New York: Oxford UP, 1964.

Massey, Doreen. *For Space*. London: Sage, 2005.

____, *Space, Place, and Gender*. Minneapolis: U of Minnesota P, 1994.

Matthews, John T. "Recalling the West Indies: From Yoknapatawpha to Haiti and Back." *American Literary History* 16.2 (2004): 238-262.

May, Elaine Tyler. *Homeward Bound: American Families in the Cold War Era*. New York: Basic Books, 1988.

McDonald, Dorothy Ritsuko. "After the Imprisonment: Ichiro's Search for

Redemption in *No-No Boy*." *MELUS* 6.3 (1979): 19-26.

McDowell, Deborah, "Boundaries: Or Distant Relations and Close Kin." *Afro-American Literary Study in the 1990s*. Ed. Houston A. Baker Jr. & Patricia Redmond. Chicago: University of Chicago Press, 1989. 51-70.

McDowell, Linda. *Gender, Identity and Place: Understanding Feminist Geographies*. Minneapolis: U of Minnesota P, 1999.

____, ed. *Undoing Place?: A Geographical Reader*. London: Arnold, 1998.

McClintock, Anne. *Imperial Leather: Race, Gender, and Sexuality in the Colonial Conquest*. New York: Routledge, 1995.

McKay, Nellie. Y, ed. *Critical Essays on Toni Morrison*. Boston: Hall, 1988.

McKee, Patricia. "Geographies of Paradise." *The New Centennial Review* 3.1 (2003): 197-223.

____, *Producing American Races: Henry James, William Faulkner, Toni Morrison*. Durham: Duke UP, 1999.

McNamara, Kevin R. *Urban Verbs: Arts and Discourse of American Cities*. Stanford: Stanford UP, 1996.

Meats, Stephen E. "Who Killed Joanna Burden?" *Mississippi Quarterly* 24 (1971): 271-77.

Miller, James Hillis. *Topographies*. Stanford: Stanford UP, 1995

Minder, Ward L. *The World of William Faulkner*. New York: Cooper Square Publisher, 1952.

Minh-ha, Trinh T. *Woman, Native, Other: Writing Postcoloniality and Feminism*. Bloomington: Indiana UP, 1989.

More, Thomas. *Utopia*. New York: Norton, 1992.

Morrison, Toni. *Beloved*. New York: Knopf, 1987.

____, *The Bluest Eye*. New York: Washington Square, 1970.

———, "City Limits, Village Values: Concepts of the Neighborhood in Black Fiction." *Literature and the Urban Experience*. Eds. Michael C. Jaye and Ann Chalmers Watts. New Brunswick: Rutgers UP, 1981. 35-43.

———, "Home." *The House That Race Built*. Ed. Wahneema Lubiano. New York: Pantheon, 1997. 3-12.

———, *Jazz*. New York: Knopf, 1992.

———, "Life in His Language." *James Baldwin: The Legacy*. Ed. Quincy Troupe. New York: Simon & Schuster, 1989.

———, *Paradise*. New York: Knopf, 1998.

———, *Playing in the Dark: Whiteness and the Literary Imagination*. Cambridge: Harvard UP, 1992.

———, "Rootedness: Ancestor as Foundation." *Black Woman Writers (1950-1980): A Critical Evaluation*. Ed. Mari Evans. Garden City, New York: Doubleday Anchor, 1984. 339-45.

———, "The Site of Memory." *Inventing the Truth: The Art and Craft of Memoir*. Ed. William Zinsser. Boston: Houghton, 1987. 103-24.

———, *Song of Solomon*. New York: Knopf, 1977.

———, *Sula*. New York: Knopf, 1974.

———, *Tar Baby*. New York: Knopf, 1981.

———, "Unspeakable Things Unspoken: The Afro-American Presence in American Literature." *Michigan Quarterly Review* 28.1 (1989): 1-34.

Moynihan, Daniel Patrick. *The Negro Family: The Case for National action*. 1965. *The Moynihan Report and the Politics of Controversy*. Eds. Lee Rainwater and William L. Yancy. Cmabridge: MIT P, 1967: 39-124.

Mumford, Lewis. *The city in History: Iits Origins, Its Transformations, and Its Prospects*. New York: Harcourt, 1961.

Ngai, Mae M. *Impossible Subjects: Illegal Aliens and the Making of Modern America*. Princeton: Princeton UP, 2004.

Nguyen Viet T. *Race and Resistance: Literature and Politics in Asian America*. New York: Oxford UP, 2002.

Ogborn, Miles. "Mapping Words." *New Formation* 57 (2005): 145-49.

Okada, John. *No-No Boy*. Seattle: U of Washington P, 1957.

Okihiro, Gary Y. *Margins and Mainstreams: Asians in American History and Culture*. Seattle: U of Washington P, 1994.

Olaniyan, Tejumola. "African-American Critical Discourse and the Invention of Cultural Identities." *African American Review* 26.4 (1992): 533-45.

Ong, Aihwa. *Flexible Citizenship: The Cultural Logics of Transnationality*. Durham: Duke UP, 1999.

Page, Philip. *Dangerous Freedom: Fusion and Fragmentation in Toni Morrison's Novels*. Jackson: UP of Mississippi, 1995.

____, "Furrowing All the Furrows: Interpretation and the Transcendent in Toni Morrison's *Paradise*." *African American Review* 35.4 (2001): 637-649.

Palumbo-Liu, David. *Asian/American: Historical Crossings of a Racial Frontier*. Stanford: Stanford UP, 1999.

Pease, Donald, ed. *National Identities and Post-Americanist Narratives*. Durham: Duke UP, 1994.

____, "National Narratives, Postnational Narration." *Reviews in American History* 24.3 (1996): 542-53.

Peterson, Nancy J. *Against Amnesia: Contemporary Women Writers and the Crises of Historical Memory*. Philadelphia: University of Pennsylvania Press, 2001.

____, ed. *Toni Morrison: Critical and Theoretical Approaches*. Baltimore and

London: The Johns Hopkins UP, 1997.

Peyer, Thomas. *Utopia and Cosmopolis: Globalization in the Era of American Literary Realism*. Durham: Duke UP, 1998.

Poirier, Richard. *A World Elsewhere: The Place of Style in American Literature*. New York: Oxford UP, 1966.

Radhakrishnan, R. "Conjunctural Identities, Academic Adjacencies." *Orientations: Mapping Studies in the Asian Diaspora*. Eds. Kandice Chuh and Karen Shimakawa. Durham, NC: Duke UP, 2001. 249-263.

____, *Diasporic Mediations: Between Home and Location*. Minneapolis: U of Minnesota P, 1996.

____, *Theory in an Uneven World*. Malden MA: Blackwell, 2003.

Rainwater, Lee, and William L. Yancey. *The Moynihan Report and the Politics of Controversy*. Cambridge: MIT P, 1967.

Riesman, David, Nathan Glazer, and Ruel Denney. *The Lonely Crowd: A Study of the Changing American Character*. 1950. New Haven: Yale UP, 2001.

Relph, E. *Place and Placelessness*. London: Pion, 1976.

Roberts, Diane. *Faulkner and the Southern Womanhood*. Athens: U of Georgia P, 1994.

Rodgers, Lawrence R. *Canaan Bound: The African-American Great Migration Novel*. Chicago:U of Illinois P, 1997.

Romine, Scott. *The Narrative Forms of Southern Community*. Baton Rouge: Louisiana State UP, 1999.

Rose, Gillian. F*eminism and Geography: The Limits of Geographical Knowledge*. Minneapolis: U of Minnesota P, 1993.

Rubenstein, Roberta. *Home Matters: Longing and Belonging, Nostalgia and Mourning in Women's Fiction*. New York: Palgrave, 2001.

Rutherford, Jonathan, ed. *Identity: Community, Culture, Difference*. London: Lawrence and Wishart, 1990.

Saldívar, José David. *Border Matters: Remapping American Cultural Studies*. Berkeley: U of California P, 1997.

Sauer, Carl. "The Morphology of Landscape." 1925. *Land and Life*. Ed. Leighly J. U of California P, 1963. 315-50.

Schur, Richard L. "Locating Paradise in the Post-Civil Rights Era: Toni Morrison and Critical Race Theory." *Contemporary Literature* 45.2 (2004): 276-99.

Schwartz, Lawrence. *Creating Faulkner's Reputation: The Politiccs of Modern Literary Criticism*. Knoxville: U of Tennessee P, 1988.

Scruggs, Charles. *Sweet Home: Invisible Cities in the Afro-American Novel*. Baltimore: Johns Hopkins UP, 1993.

Sibley, David. *Geographies of Exclusion*. London: Routledge, 1995.

Singh, Amritjit and Peter Smith, eds. *Postcolonial Theory and the United States: Race, Ethnicity, and Literature*. Jackson: UP of Mississippi, 2000.

Smethurst, James. *The Black Arts Movement: Literary Nationalism in the 1960s and 1970s*. Chapel Hill: U of North Carolina P, 2005.

——, The New Red Negro: *The Literary Left and African American Poetry, 1930-1946*. New York: Oxford UP, 1999.

Smethurst, James and Bill Mullen, eds. *Left of the Color Line: Race, Radicalism, and Twentieth-Century Literature of the United States*. Chapel Hill: U of North Carolina P, 2003.

Smith, Barbara. "Toward a Black Feminist Criticism." *Within the Circle: An Anthology of African American Criticism from the Harlem Renaissance to the Present*. Ed. Angelyn Mitchell. Durham: Duke UP, 1994. 410-27.

Smith, Henry Nash. *Virgin Land: The American West as Symbol and Myth*. New

York: Vintage Books, 1950.

Smith, John and Deborah Cohn, ed. *Look Away! The U.S. South in New World Studies*. Durham: Duke UP, 2004.

Smith, Neil. "Geography, Difference and Politics of Scale." *Postmodernism and the Social Sciences*. Ed. Joe Doherty et al. N.Y.: St. Martin's Press, 1992.

Smith, Neil and Cindi Katz. "Grounding Metaphor: Towards a Sptialized Politics." *Place and Politics of Identity*. Eds. Michael Keith and Steve Pile. London: Routledge, 1993. 67-83.

Snead, James A. *Figures of Division: William Faulkner's Major Novels*. New York: Methuen, 1986.

Soja, Edward W. *Postmodern Geographies: The Reassertion of Space in Critical Social Theory*. London: Verso, 1989.

____, *Thirdspace: Journeys to Los Angeles and Other Real and Imagined Places*. Malden MA: Blackwell, 1996.

Sollors, Werner. *Beyond Ethnicity: Consent and Descent in American Culture*. New York: Oxford UP: 1986.

Spigel, Lynn. *Welcome to the Dreamhouse: Popolar Media and Postwar Suburbs*. Durham: Duke UP, 2001.

Spivak, Gayatri Chakravorty. "Bonding in Difference: Interview with Alfred Arteaga." *The Spivak Reader: Selected Works of Gayatri Chakravorty Spivak*. Ed. Donna Lardy & Gerald MacLean. New York & London: Routledge, 1996. 15-28.

____, "Can the Subaltern Speak?" *Colonial Discourse and Post-Colonial Theory. A Reader*. Ed. Patrick Williams and Laura Chrisman. New York: Columbia UP, 1994. 66-111.

____, *In Other Worlds: Essays in Cultural Politics*. New York: Routledge, 1988.

_____, "A Literary Representation of the Subaltern: A Woman's Text from The Third World." *In Other Worlds: Essays in Cultural Politics*. New York: Routledge, 1988. 241-68.

_____, "Subaltern Studies: Deconstructing Historiography." *In Other Worlds*. New York: Routledge, 1987. 197-221.

Stepto, Robert. *From Behind the Veil: A Study of Afro-American Narrative*. Urbana: U of Illinois P, 1979.

_____, "Intimate Things in Place: A Conversation with Toni Morrison." *Conversation with Toni Morison*. Ed. Daniel Taylor Guthrie. Jackson: UP of Mississippi, 1994. 10-29.

Slotkin, Richard. *The Fatal Environment: The Myth of the Frontier in the Age of Industrialization, 1800-1890*. New York: Atheneum, 1985.

_____, *Gunfighter Nation: The Myth of the Frontier in the Twentieth-Century America*. New York: Atheneum, 1992.

_____, *Regeneration Through Violence: The Mythology of the Frontier, 1600-1860*. Middletown CT: Wesleyan UP, 1973.

Sumida, Stephen. "Asian American Literature in the 1980s." *Frontiers of Asian American Studies: Writing, Research, and Commentary*. Ed. Gail Nomura et al. Pullman: Washington State UP, 1989. 151-58.

Sundquist, Eric J. *Faulkner: House Divided*. Baltimore: Johns Hopkins UP, 1983.

_____, *To Wake the Nation: Race in the Making of American Literature*. Cambridge: Harvard UP, 1993.

Sweeney, Megan. "Racial House, Big House, Home: Contemporary Abolitionism in Toni Morrison's Paradise." *Meridians: Feminism, Race, Transnationalism* 4.2 (2004): 40-67.

Takaki, Ronald. *Strangers from a Different Shore: A History of Asian Americans*.

New York: Penguin, 1989.

Tate, Allen. "The New Provincialism." *Collected Essays*. Denver: Allan Swallow, 1956.

Tate, Claudia. "Toni Morrison." *Conversation with Toni Morrison*. Ed. Daniel Taylor Guthrie. Jackson: UP of Mississippi, 1994. 156-70.

Taylor, Walter. *Faulkner's Search for a South*. Urbana: U of Illinois P, 1983.

Trefzer, Annette. "Introduction." *Global Faulkner*. Eds. Annette Trefzer and Ann J. Abadie. Jackson: UP of Mississippi, 2009. ix-xiv.

Tuan, Yi-Fu. *Space and Place: The Perspective of Experience*. Minneapolis: U of Minnesota P, 1977.

——, *Topophilia: A Study of Environmental Perception, Attitudes, and Values*, New York: Columbia UP, 1990.

Turner, Frederick Jackson. "The Significance of the Frontier in American History." *History, Frontier, and Section: Three Essays by Frederick Jackson Turner*. Albuquerque, NM: U of New Mexico P, 1993, 59-91.

Twain, Mark. *Pudd'nhead Wilson and Those Extraordinary Twins*. 1884. New York: Penguin, 1969.

Waggoner, Hyatt. *William Faulkner: From Jefferson to the World*. Lexington: U of Kentucky P, 1959.

Wald, Priscilla. *Constituting Americans: Cultural Anxiety and Narrative Form*. Durham: Duke UP, 1995.

Warf, Barney and Santa Arias. "Introduction: The Reassertion of Space into the Social Sciences and Humanities." *The Spatial Turn: Interdisciplinary Perspectives*. Eds. Barney Warf and Santa Arias. London: Routledge, 2009. 1-10.

Wei, Li. Ed. *From Urban Enclave to Ethnic Suburb: New Asian Communities in*

Pacific Rim Countries. Honolulu: U of Hawaii P, 2006.

Weinstein, Philip. *What Else But Love?: The Ordeal of Race in Faulkner and Morrison*. New York: Columbia UP, 1996.

Welty, Eudora. "Place in Fiction." *The Eye of the Story: Selected Essays and Reviews*. New York: Random House, 1978: 116–22.

West, Cornel. *Race Matters*. Boston: Beacon, 1993.

White, Hayden. *The Content of the Form: Narrative Discourse and Historical Representation*. Baltimore: Johns Hopkins UP, 1987.

Whyte, William H., Jr. *The Organization Man*. 1956. New York: Anchor, 2002.

Wilson, Rob and Wimal Dissanayake, eds. *Global/Local: Cultural Production and the Transnational Imaginary*. Durham: Duke UP, 1996.

Wilson, Sloan. *The Man in the Gray Flannel Suit*. 1955. Cambridge, MA: Da Capo Press, 2002.

Wong, Sau-ling Cynthia. "Denationalization Reconsidered: Asian American Cultural Criticism at a Theoretical Crossroads." *Armesia Journal* 21.1-2 (1992): 1-27.

____, *Reading Asian American Literature: From Necessity to Extravagance*. Princeton: Princeton UP, 1993.

Woodward, C. Vann. *American Counterpoint: Slavery and Racism in the North-South Dialogue*. Boston: Little Brown, 1971.

____, *The Burden of Southern History*. Baton Rouge: Louisiana State UP, 1968.

____, *Origins of the New South, 1877-1913*. Baton Rouge: Louisiana State UP, 1971.

____, *The Strange Career of Jim Crow*. New York: Oxford UP, 1957.

Yaeger, Patricia. *Dirt and Desire: Reconstituting Southern Women's Writing, 1930-1990*. Chicago: Chicago UP, 2000.

———, ed. *The Geography of Identity*. Ann Arbor: U of Michigan P, 1996.

Yogi, Stan. "'You had to be one or the other': Oppositions and Reconciliation in John Okada's *No-No Boy*." *MELUS* 21.2 (1996): 63-77.

Young, Robert. *Colonial Desire: Hybridity in Theory, Culture and Race*. London: Routledge, 1995.

Zukin, Sharon. *Landscapes of Power: From Detroit to Disney World*. Berkeley: U of California P, 1991.

Index

윤성호 서울대학교 영문과에서 학사와 석사를, 미국 매사추세츠대학 영문과에서 박사학위를 받았다. 현재 한양대학교 영문과 교수이다. 첫 저서 『언더독의 글쓰기: 아시아계 미국문학의 지형학』으로 2012년 한국영어영문학회 학술상을 수상했다. '미국'이라는 복잡다단한 기호의 의미를 이해하고 미국 문화의 핵심에 다가서려는 노력을 하고 있다.

SEONGHO YOON is Professor of English at Hanyang University in Seoul, Korea. He received his B.A. and M.A. in English from Seoul National University and his Ph.D. in English from the University of Massachusetts Amherst. He is the author of Writing as an *Underdog: A Geography of Asian American Literature* (Seoul National University), which won the distinguished scholarship prize of The English and Literature Association of Korea. His primary research areas are 20th-century American literature and culture, with a particular emphasis on multiethnic literature and cultural geography.

TRANSGRESSIVE SPATIAL IMAGINATION
IN THE 20TH-CENTURY AMERICAN NOVEL

20세기 미국 소설에 나타난 위반의 공간적 상상력

펴낸날 2018년 4월 20일 초판 1쇄

지은이 윤성호 · **펴낸이** 이영무

펴낸곳 한양대학교출판부 · **출판등록** 제4-7호(1972.2.29)

주소 서울 성동구 왕십리로 222 · **전화** 02.2220.1432-4 · **팩스** 02.2220.1435

홈페이지 press.hanyang.ac.kr · **이메일** presshy@hanyang.ac.kr

디자인 안광일 · **편집** 오은애 · **인쇄** 현문

정가는 뒤표지에 있습니다. 잘못된 책은 구입하신 곳에서 교환해드립니다.

ISBN 978.89.7218.576.5 (93840)